Journey through the Inferno

by ADAM BOREN

with an introduction by MENACHEM Z. ROSENSAFT

THE UNITED STATES HOLOCAUST MEMORIAL MUSEUM AND
THE HOLOCAUST SURVIVORS' MEMOIRS PROJECT

This book is published by the United States Holocaust Memorial Museum, 100 Raoul Wallenberg Place, SW, Washington, DC 20024-2126.

The Holocaust Survivors' Memoirs Project is an initiative of Nobel Peace Prize laureate Elie Wiesel, under the auspices of the United States Holocaust Memorial Museum and the World Jewish Congress. The Holocaust Survivors' Memoirs Project was launched through a generous grant from Random House Inc., New York, and is under the editorial direction of Menachem Z. Rosensaft.

Cover photo: Adam Boren, Hamburg, Germany, November 1945

ISBN: 0-89604-161-1

Printed in the United States of America.

CONTENTS

INTRODUCTION

Since the end of World War II, historians have tended to focus on the twisted personalities who implemented the German government's "Final Solution of the Jewish question" at the expense of their victims. Psychological studies of Hitler, the diaries of Joseph Goebbels, and autobiographies of Albert Speer and other Nazi leaders are prominently featured in most bibliographies of the Holocaust. At the same time, many Holocaust historians routinely ignore the memoirs and diaries of Holocaust survivors. Elie Wiesel's powerful *Night* and Alexander Donat's *The Holocaust Kingdom* are among the exceptions. For numerous reasons, most of which require an understanding more of psychology than of history, uninformed contemporary society frequently prefers to think of European Jewry during the Shoah as faceless, nameless victims, as anonymous corpses.

In a similar vein, the survivors have generally been depicted as two-dimensional skeletal figures staring blankly into the camera in their concentration camp uniforms. Most studies of the Holocaust portray and analyze the event almost exclusively from the perspective of the perpetrators. It is apparently far easier to deal with sterile German documents ordering the annihilation of thousands than to make an effort to come to terms with the personal testimonies of Jews who tried to live as best they could in the shadow of imminent death, and who demonstrated superhuman strength in reclaiming control of their destiny as soon as the yoke of oppression was lifted from their shoulders.

Both the dead and the survivors deserve the dignity of a permanent historical presence, not as impersonal objects but as individual protagonists with names, voices, and emotions. That is why each memoir written by a survivor is so critically important. Individually, each volume is a memorial as well as a personal testimony. Collectively, these books provide a sense of both the diversity of European Jewry and the commonality of their fate.

In a classic lecture entitled "Against Despair," Elie Wiesel recalled a Hasidic tale: "Somewhere," said Rebbe Nahman of Bratzlav, "there lives a man who asks a question to which there is no answer; a generation later, in another place, there lives a man who asks another question to which there is no answer either—and he doesn't know, he cannot know, that his question is actually an answer to the first."

Adam Boren's *Journey through the Inferno* raises the most fundamental questions about the human condition, and in so doing provides the answers that can come only from deep inside the survivors of the Shoah. They and the dead alone felt their pain, their anguish, their despair, and only the survivors can tell the story of the cataclysm in an authentic voice.

Journey through the Inferno describes one life and those touched by that life, before, during, and after the Holocaust. But it also forces the reader to remember that although the Germans were able to persecute, oppress, torture, and murder their victims, they were unable to dehumanize them. Adam Boren's odyssey takes us from the outbreak of World War II in Warsaw through the Soviet occupation of Białystok, his capture by and escape from the Germans, his return to the Warsaw ghetto, his exploits as a courier during the Uprising, deportation to Majdanek and then Auschwitz, and, ultimately, liberation and a return to life. We feel his anguish as his father is humiliated, tortured, and ultimately killed. We share his helplessness as he discovers that his beloved sister has died of typhoid fever during his absence from Warsaw. We read the names of his family members and friends, and we understand that this book is both an important addition to the historiography of the Shoah and a memorial to a destroyed world, for *Journey through the Inferno* is the only place anywhere that these names are perpetuated.

Among the most powerful scenes is Boren's description of how he learned that his mother had been killed during the Uprising. Adam and Kazik, a fellow courier, were on a rooftop observing the German destruction of the ghetto. Kazik left to tell the others in their bunker what was happening.

A couple of hours later Kazik returned. His face was chalky white and he was sobbing. When I asked him what was wrong, what had happened, he could not look at me. Finally, in a shaking whisper he stammered out the truth. "Our bunker was discovered by the Germans," he sobbed. "They blew it up with everybody in it and set it on fire. No one in the bunker survived; they are all dead."

I wanted to scream, *"My Mother!"* But Kazik clamped his hand over my mouth. I fell to my knees, sobbing. "I am going to the bunker!" I cried. "I want to see for myself if my mother is among the dead."

"You can't go there," he said. "The bunker is totally covered in rubble from the explosion, and there is a raging fire. The SS are still roaming around that area and I almost fell into their hands."

I didn't care. I said, "I am going. I want to see for myself." But as I stood up to leave, Kazik grabbed me and begged me not to go, not to leave him. "We are the only ones left," he pleaded. "Let's stay together. There is nothing else we can do except look for revenge before we get killed."

I was in total despair. My mother—my wonderful, loving, suffering mother—was gone. First Father and Mietek, then Mina and now Mother—my whole family was dead, murdered. Where was God? What had we done to deserve such horrors? I cursed Him. Kazik and I lay on the roof silently sobbing. We had both lost all we had. "Your mother and all the others in the bunker died instantly from the bomb explosion," Kazik said, trying to ease my pain.

In these few paragraphs, Adam Boren captures the horror, the helplessness, the inner conflicts, and the utter randomness of fate that epitomized the Holocaust. Most important, as we read the moving and dramatic story of Adam Boren's life, we stand in awe at the power of the human spirit that emanated so forcefully from the depth of the Warsaw ghetto, Majdanek, and Auschwitz and that permeates every page of this heartrending book.

—Menachem Z. Rosensaft, Director and Editor-in-Chief,
Holocaust Survivors' Memoirs Project

DEDICATION

This book is dedicated to my family who perished in the Holocaust: my father, Israel; my mother, Sara; my sister, Mina; my brother Mitek. Their love sustained me on my journey.

This book is also dedicated to all the untold thousands of my fellow slaves, who were not as fortunate as I was and perished in Krzemieniec Prison and Majdanek, Auschwitz, and Sachsenhausen concentration camps. May peace be with them on their last journey.

This book is devotedly dedicated to my wife Claire, my daughter Sari, and my son Johnathan, who prodded me to complete this work.

ACKNOWLEDGMENTS

I would like to express my appreciation to all those who guided me through this difficult task: Marion Landew, my professor of writing at New York University, who instructed me and kept my spirits up; Menachem Rosensaft and Mary Morrison, without whose encouragement this work would have never been published; Jeanette Friedman, the nagging editor who battled me for every word and won; and to all the friends who encouraged me in this endeavor and whom it would be unfair to name, in the event I inadvertently missed one.

CHAPTER 1

In early August 1939, my family returned from vacation in Sfider to our home in Warsaw, Poland, a city that was especially beautiful that late summer. The warm, golden sun cast a fairy-tale glow on the old sculpted buildings, and the atmosphere was deceptively peaceful and serene. It was an eerie quiet that hung in the air. Radio broadcasts and newspapers reported German saber rattling and Hitler's ultimatums. Would there be a war? Would they dare attack? What would England and France, our allies, do if Hitler carried out his threats? The constant barrage of martial music on the radio only heightened the tension.

My friends and I, all of us adolescents, had these old people's thoughts in our heads and wondered if we would be going back to school. Then, the mayor of Warsaw broadcast a request for volunteers to dig antitank ditches on the main thoroughfare. With spades on our shoulders, my young friends and I marched through Warsaw like soldiers. We dug and dug all day, with no food and only a bit of water to drink. We were dead tired, hungry, and covered in mud, but we proudly marched back to our homes. A few days later, the mayor ordered everyone to secure their windows in case there was a bombardment. We ran through town to find tape and crisscrossed our windows. The adventure of "preparing for war" and not having school was very exciting—we thought and talked about how to destroy the German enemy.

By this time, the grocery stores in our neighborhood were nearly empty. Our family was running out of food and Father sent each of us into a different part of

Warsaw to find some. My brother, Mietek, who was four years older than I, went to the east of town; my sister Mina, seven years older, went north; Father and I went looking around our area. Mother stayed home. Our search met with some success—a couple of kilos of rice, some beans, some cooking oil, and little bits of other food. That evening, Mother and Mina prepared rice and beans and baked a cake.

Father, a chemist by profession, was a successful businessman who owned and operated a food processing plant and sawmill in Novojelnia in northeastern Poland. Father traveled extensively in Europe on business, so we hardly saw him, though he always came home for holidays. He was tall and good-looking, with a little square moustache. He spoke several languages and was—others told me later—quite a ladies' man. At home he was strict but caring with us, and fascinated us with his stories about traveling across Europe and the people he met. We loved him dearly, and he would often bring us little gifts from different countries.

Mother took me to the park and read fairy tales and poetry to me. She also took me to marionette shows whenever they came to town. Sometimes, she took me along to the theater and concerts with her friends, and she never, never scolded me—no matter what I did! She never nagged me to eat like other mothers did, either. As far as I was concerned, Mother was a terrific cook and baker, who created special dishes and baked tasty cakes and pastries just for me.

My mother was full of life; she sang and danced almost all the time. She had many friends for whom she would throw small parties, and I would be allowed to sit in the corner and listen to their conversations, which sometimes dealt with Zionism and the growing antisemitism in Poland. Zionism, the idea of the creation of a Jewish state, was Mother's and her friends' primary interest and activity. A large portrait of Theodor Herzl, the movement's founder, hung prominently on the living room wall.

Most of all, I loved my sister Mina. She had just graduated from gymnasium and was deciding which university in Europe she would attend. Many times I would fall asleep at the table while reading a book, and Mina would undress me and put me to bed. At other times she would play games with me. I was always able to confide in her. She taught me to dance and, to prove what a great dancer I was, would show me off to her friends. When I was older, she secretly let me read her books on sex, like *The Perfect Marriage* by Van Der Velde, a book that was off-limits for boys my age.

My brother Mietek was still in gymnasium. He always tried to impose his will on me, so we didn't get along too well. He seldom got the better of me, even when he complained to Mother, who always took my side. I was constantly in trouble. I would beat up kids who called me a dirty Jew; I would be arrested for jumping on and off trolley cars; I would jump from one house roof to another on a dare and was never afraid of anything or anybody.

The grown-ups around me, including our neighbors, began to worry about what would happen to the Jews if the Germans came. Father told us that a Jewish family, recently arrived from Germany and now living in our apartment house, described the terrible situation for Jews in Nazi Germany. They told Father about the *Kristallnacht* pogrom in Berlin, their hometown. It painted a very scary picture of the future: mass arrests of Jews, who were sent to Dachau; rioters who burned down Jewish homes, synagogues, and businesses. Father told us it would be dangerous, especially for Jewish men, to stay in Poland under the Nazis, and that we would have to get out.

CHAPTER 2

In the early morning of September 1, 1939, a loud, martial voice on the radio informed us that the German army had crossed the Polish border and that we were being invaded. A little later, air-raid sirens began blasting and the radio announcer ordered people to take cover. "Attention, attention. Enemy air force planes headed for Warsaw. Take cover."

Everyone ran to hide in the cellar of our apartment building except a couple of my friends and me. We ran to the roof to see what was happening. Soon we spotted a squadron of Luftwaffe Stukas on the horizon; one after another, they dive-bombed Warsaw's buildings. The sirens attached to their wings screamed as they dove toward the buildings and released the bombs. The sirens and the falling bombs made a horrifying noise followed by explosions. Later, we learned that the Germans especially designed the sirens to terrorize their victims.

We lay on the roof, fascinated and a little scared, watching the bombs fall. Our building shook from the explosions; windows were breaking despite the tape; buildings not far away were set afire; black smoke was billowing into the sky.

Our street was not hit yet, but two streets away, I saw people covered in blood running from buildings that were collapsing. You could hear screams for help. Finally the Stukas flew away, and except for the crackling of the fires and the crying of the wounded, there was silence. Slowly people came out of the cellars, dazed, looking bewilderedly at the destruction around them.

Polish soldiers told us how the army was defeated and of the rapid advance of the Germans. The mayor of Warsaw, Stefan Starzynski, broadcast a plea on the radio, urging all men of military age to leave the city for the eastern part of Poland, where the Polish army would try to reorganize and fight back. He also urged everyone to build barricades around the city to stop the German tanks.

Trolleys, cars, and buses were set across streets to form barricades. We all tried to help. On the eighth day after the start of the invasion, the Germans were at the gates of Warsaw. The heavy artillery shelled the city all night, while the Stukas, in wave after wave, dive-bombed during the day. It was Hell on Earth. Everything around us was crumbling; there was no electricity; our only water was what we had managed to save in our bathtub.

On September 10, my friends and I were lying on the metal roof of our building when the Stukas appeared on the horizon, flying in our direction. Suddenly they were over us, diving; the screaming sirens on their wings were tearing at our eardrums. It looked as if they would crash into our building. Just before they pulled up and released the bombs, we saw one pilot's face.

A couple of small, foot-long canisters fell onto our roof. We ran toward them and, with long sticks we had, pushed them off the roof into the garden below, where they exploded into a shower of phosphorous sparks meant to set the building on fire. In the garden, the sparks were harmless. Later, we were praised and congratulated by our neighbors for saving the building. No other bombs fell on our house, but three or four buildings away, fire burst from roofs and broken windows. No fire trucks or firemen appeared because there was no water. The blowing wind sent the raging fires into adjoining buildings, away from us, but the sound, the smell, and the smoke that engulfed us made us feel like we were in the depths of Hell.

We all wondered, "Who are the barbarians burning our city and killing our people? What will they do to us once they enter the city? What will they do to Jews?"

In mid-September, on the first day of Rosh Hashanah, the aerial bombing intensified. The heavy bombardment continued straight through Yom Kippur—the timing was deliberately chosen by the Nazis.

Though Father decided to flee with the family, we couldn't get out. The city was surrounded by the Germans, and we would have to wait. All our food was gone, and the few bakeries still operating had breadlines hundreds of people long. Standing for hours in the open, Mietek and I took turns on those lines to get one loaf of bread, while the bombing and shelling went on around us.

Several Polish cavalry soldiers and their horses were standing in our building's garden when shrapnel hit one horse and killed it. In minutes the soldiers used their knives and bayonets to skin and butcher the horse. They shared the meat with us and the other tenants of the building, asking only that we cook it for them. That evening, Mother prepared the meat for us and the four soldiers. It was the first meat we had eaten in weeks and it tasted terrific.

To keep our spirits up, Mina and I set up our old RCA phonograph, turning the crank until it was fully wound, and played old tangos and waltzes as we danced with abandon around the living room table. Between German bombing runs, the neighborhood kids and I played soccer, cowboys and Indians, and war games. We paid no attention to our scolding parents. But conditions around us deteriorated by the hour. Water was in short supply. No one had enough water to wash themselves or do laundry; everyone stank.

During air raids, the cellar shelters were the worst. The smell and atmosphere were so thick, you could hardly breathe. No matter how intense the bombing was, I would run outside to get some fresh air.

The telephones worked only sporadically; it was almost impossible to reach relatives and friends to find out if they were alive. Assuring Mother I'd be very careful, I ran down the street to my Uncle Sojnek and his family and found out their building was partially damaged by bombing. Thank God they all were okay and managing. He was happy to hear that our family and my grandparents, who lived in the same building with us, were all well. Some others were not as lucky—those who discovered their relatives or friends had lost their homes or were wounded or killed were in shock. Mother and Mina tried their best to console them.

Everyone was tense and on edge, tempers were frayed, and fuses were short. People blew up at the smallest provocation, at times without reason, screaming at me for things I hadn't done or said. I tried to be very careful not to upset them.

The continuous bombing during the day and the shelling at night gave us no respite. Some of us, though, got used to the noise and shock. I would wake up at night bewildered when the shelling stopped for a while and things got quiet.

On September 28, 1939, Warsaw capitulated and the guns and bombardments stopped. Two days later, on a clear Indian summer day, the victorious German invaders marched into our city in their stiff and arrogant posture. The boots of the iron-helmeted soldiers beat out a martial rhythm on the pavement. The thud of their goose steps echoed in the hollow, bombed-out buildings, as their right arms swung in meter to the tattoo of their feet. Their left arms held the rifles that made them look like evil robots.

Then the giant tanks rolled in, with their crews sitting up top, semiautomatic guns in their hands; large, dark goggles stuck out from the tops of their steel helmets. The troops' green uniforms, the same color as the tanks, blended men and killing machines. The power they projected was overwhelming and scary, like thick storm clouds threatening. In our building and around it, a heavy silence prevailed. "What next?" we wondered. "How would they treat us?"

It didn't take us long to find out.

The following day a fully armed platoon of Germans marched into our building's garden. An officer was screaming in German, which none of us could understand. He unsnapped the flap on his holster and reached for his gun. We stood there paralyzed with fear. A man from our building, who spoke German, came out and said something to the still-screaming German, who was looking for a specific place in our building complex. Among the several buildings, there was a small one that had formerly housed a private Hebrew high school, Hinukh Yelodim.

The German officer, holding a map, demanded to know which building housed the former Jewish high school. Our neighbor calmly pointed out the building to him. In guttural, loud German, with his hand still resting on the butt of his pistol, the officer ordered our neighbor to lead him to it. As they marched toward the school with troops, our hearts stopped pounding and we started breathing normally.

The German platoon settled into the school and put everyone in our building on edge. Kids could no longer hang out in the garden or roam the streets. The Germans were everywhere, strutting on the sidewalks with their arms swinging, forcing everyone to step off the pavement and into the gutters.

While all of this was going on, Jew-hating Polish hooligans were having a field day. Under the amused laughs of the Germans, they identified Jews who stood for hours in the breadlines, pulled them out, and beat them; four or five of them would jump one elderly, bearded Jew, hitting him with bats until he fell to the ground bleeding, while they spit out hateful curses. Not one of the Poles watching this scenario came to the old Jew's help or tried to stop the gangs. Some stood watching with smirks on their faces.

I grew up as a patriotic Pole and could not fathom how any Pole could, in the face of the enemy, attack his fellow citizens or just stand by without reacting to it. Were not the Germans our common enemy? Had they not brutally attacked our country and destroyed our city? I was shocked to witness those terrible actions by my fellow Polish citizens. I remembered my stern, Polish-language teacher in grade school reminding her Jewish students that we were not Jews, but Poles who believed in Moses' teachings.

Soon placards appeared everywhere, with orders in German and Polish: No Jews were permitted on the streets after 6 p.m. or before 7 a.m., except with German permits. A Jew must step off the sidewalk into the gutter and bare his head when a German soldier approached. No Jewish business was allowed to function unless it was transferred to German or Polish ownership. Schools were closed to Jews. Every day new orders were issued to forbid the Jews this or that, making our lives more and more unbearable.

Food and medicine became scarce. We sold our possessions to the Poles to buy food on the black market at exorbitant prices. Just getting around the city became dangerous. Polish gangs sought out Jews to rob, even stealing the clothes off their backs and beating them. The Germans, with the help of Polish gangs, apprehended Jews on the streets and carted them out of town as slaves for the German army.

Secretly, under penalty of death, we listened to the BBC [British Broadcasting Corporation] for any news. We heard that France and England had declared war on Germany. But it seemed no action took place, and we felt abandoned by the rest of the world. We quickly learned that the Nazis had no mercy. Hatred and terror guided their actions and lives.

There were 29 people, including my grandparents, aunts, and uncles, in our immediate family. On my father's side, my grandparents Godel and Pesha lived in a large apartment two floors below us. Many times, when my father wanted to discipline me, I would run downstairs to seek their protection. Uncle Sojnek and his wife lived with their two-year-old son, Adam, two blocks down the street. Fredek, my youngest uncle, had been married for about a year to Marysia, and they had a newborn daughter, Miriam. Tofila, Rena, Manya, and Cesia were my four aunts. Rena, who was divorced from her husband, lived with her four-year-old daughter, Betty, at her parents'. Tofila and her husband lived on the other side of town with a daughter and son, also named Adam. A third aunt, Manya, and her husband lived in Katowice, in the southwestern part of Poland. Cesia and her husband Peter had two daughters, Lusia and Ruth. On Mother's side, there was her sister Rosa, Rosa's husband, and their three children—Mietek, Bobek, and Hanka. They lived on Żelazna Street, about three streets away from us.

My Aunt Ruth, a widow of Mother's brother, lived with her two sons and two daughters—Michal, Salek, Boba, and Halina—on Dzielna Street, not too far from us. There was also an Aunt Adela, Father's sister, who married an American and lived in the United States with her son, Moe.

Father kept insisting we leave Warsaw and, if at all possible, smuggle ourselves into Lithuania. From there, he was sure we would somehow manage to get to his sister Adela in the United States. I heard later that Mother did not want to leave her sister. So it was decided that only Father, Mietek, and I would leave, because it was most dangerous for Jewish men in German-occupied Poland.

We began our preparations for the trip; we had only one backpack and needed two more. I traded a football and a chemistry set for a rucksack from one of my friends. Mietek managed to find one, too. We packed one change of underwear, one shirt, some basic medications and bandages, a couple of bars of chocolate that we had saved for emergencies, a shawl and gloves, and a bottle of vodka each—in case we had to bribe somebody.

No one outside our family and close friends could find out that we were planning to leave. The German authorities strictly prohibited Jews from traveling anywhere. It was the last week in October 1939. We were ready to go, but saying good-bye was hard for all of us. First, we went to our grandparents' apartment, where all our uncles, aunts, and cousins were waiting for us. The hugging and tears would not end. I had to promise over and over to be careful, to watch out for Father and Mietek, and never, never to forget to write letters. All of them promised to watch out for, and protect, Mother and Mina. Then I went out to find my two best friends, Henry and Itzhak. We hugged a lot, but there were no tears, and we promised we would remain true friends come hell or high water.

Leaving Mother and Mina was most traumatic. I didn't know then that I would never see Mina again, but deep inside me I felt a foreboding. To be brave and not to cry, I suggested that we set up our old gramophone and have our last dance together. With great abandon we twisted and jumped to polkas and waltzes, laughing like two lunatics. Mother hugged us all but kept her composure and didn't cry, like the trooper she always was. Father promised that we would return as soon as things settled down and the situation became safe.

That afternoon, we left for Warsaw's Eastern Railroad Station. The station was full of people who stood around or sat on their luggage. Old peasants in babushkas were holding large baskets; mothers held infants in their arms, some of them breast-feeding their babies; old men and young kids ran about, but there was no train. Father asked around but got no true answers. Some people had been waiting for the train for two days; others said they heard from railroad workers that a train was due to arrive that evening and would leave either that night or the next morning. We could do nothing but wait. Father moved us to a dark corner, so we would not be recognized as Jews and denounced to the Germans by antisemites. Sitting on the ground and leaning against the wall, I fell asleep.

I was suddenly awakened by the sharp, long blasts of the steam whistle on the incoming train and the noisy tumult of the waiting crowd. Hissing, the train came to a slow halt. Without waiting for the train passengers to disembark, the crowd rushed to the train, pushing and shoving. Mietek and Father lifted me to a half-open wagon window; I slid into the compartment and leaned back out for them to hand me our packs. Then Father helped Mietek lift himself into the compartment.

All this commotion took no more than a couple of minutes. People around us were pushing, screaming, and cursing at each other. Mothers were shouting their lost children's names. It was bedlam. Meanwhile we lost sight of Father, who was trying to get to the wagon door. Our compartment was rapidly filling up with all kinds of people: women with children in their arms, men with children on their shoulders, old and young. Suddenly I heard Father calling my name from inside, so I stood on the bench seat and waved to him. Pushing and shoving, he worked his way through the crowd toward us.

Mietek and I gave up our hard-won seats to two mothers with babies, and we stood packed like sardines in a can, with no room to turn around. That tight pack made it safer for us, since no German or Polish police could possibly get into the wagon. For more than two hours the train didn't move. The air got thicker and people's tempers shorter, as more people tried to push their way into the car. Fights broke out in the corridor. Suddenly, with a jerk, the train began moving. Fresh air filtered through the open windows, and tempers calmed. We were headed east, we hoped away from the Germans. Night was closing in, and I was so tired I fell asleep standing up.

The train clickety-clacked slowly through the night, stopping at each small town, disgorging some of the people aboard. Each time it approached a station, the engineer blew the whistle and woke me up, but once the train began moving again, I would fall back asleep. In the early morning, as the train moved through the countryside, I saw a beautiful, dreamy picture. Green pastures were partially covered by low fog, and now and then a cow's head stuck out of the mist. The newly harvested wheat stood in bundles on the fields, like castles on a chessboard, and the early sun threw long shadows off the trees. As the train stopped at each station, it slowly emptied. At last, after standing for more than five hours, we could sit.

People around us struck up conversations about the war and the Germans. One man described the devastation the German Luftwaffe caused in his village, and how people escaping from their burning homes were machine-gunned by the German air force. A woman told us how the Germans confiscated all grain, flour, and animals in her village, and no one could explain to them that the grain seed was needed for next year's sowing. They talked about the random shootings of people who put up the slightest opposition. The stories grew more and more depressing. When I could not bear it any longer, I walked out to the corridor to watch the countryside's surreal beauty unfold.

Finally, with a long, sorrowful sounding of the steam whistle, the train came to a stop in a small nameless town. A stationmaster announced this was the train's last stop, and everyone had to get off. We disembarked, tired, bleary-eyed, and hungry, not really knowing where we were. We were told that the village sat on the river Bug, and we would have to find a way to cross it.

CHAPTER 3

The bridge across the river was destroyed. Father found a fisherman who agreed to take us across the river in his boat for a bottle of our precious vodka. It was late afternoon when he rowed us across the Bug, and as we stepped on the supposed safety of the shore, a soldier in a strange uniform, wearing a peaked hat with an emblem consisting of a hammer and sickle on a red star, approached us. His rifle had a long bayonet attached to it, and he said something in a language I didn't understand. Father replied in the same language and told us they were speaking in Russian. The soldier was in the Red Army of the Soviet Union, but it was all strange to me. What was a Soviet soldier doing in Poland? We soon discovered that the Soviet Union and Germany had signed a pact, later known as the Molotov-Ribbentrop Pact, to divide Poland between them.

The Soviet soldiers were very friendly, offering us black bread and Father Soviet cigarettes. He lit one cigarette and started choking, it was so strong! It was made from *machorka,* which is the stem of a tobacco leaf and very strong. Looking at Father choking and coughing while he tried to smoke, the soldiers laughed and said that capitalists from Poland were too weak to smoke strong Soviet cigarettes. In a nearby village, Father traded some clothing with a friendly farmer for the use of his house to wash up and for a meal. His wife served us hot soup and bread, while the farmer asked us about conditions in the German-occupied part of Poland and how the Germans treated people. Before we left, he gave us a large loaf of home-baked bread and a bit of butter.

That evening we walked to the railroad station in the next village, where we learned that there might be a train the next day. We were told that all the available rooms in the village were taken over by the Red Army troops, so we settled for a seat on a bench in the railroad station. We were happy to be out of German control, but Mother and Mina were still trapped. We missed them terribly and worried about what would happen to them. Father decided to take Mietek and me to a Jewish fruit farmer with whom he once did business and to ask if we could stay at his farm, while he would try to get back to Warsaw and bring Mother and Mina out.

To reach my father's friend, Mr. Gold, owner of the fruit farm, we took the train for about three hours to another small town, the name of which I cannot remember. Then we climbed into an old, creaky farmer's wagon pulled by one poor horse. It took us, by wagon and foot, another four hours to reach the farm.

Mr. Gold was very surprised but pleased to greet us. From the doorway, in a cheerful voice in Yiddish, he bellowed to his wife, "Sara, we have honored guests; make a samovar of hot tea," and invited us inside. The house was essentially a log cabin with a thatched roof and fascinating to me, as I had never seen one like it. It was built from full-length tree logs, placed one on top of the other, interlocked at the corners. Dry moss was stuffed into the cracks between the logs to prevent leaks. The little windows had red-painted shutters attached to them. It evoked the gingerbread houses in my mother's fairy tales.

We walked into a large room. There was a 3.5-meter-long table right in the middle of it with a thick wood top that was partially covered by a crocheted tablecloth. The two sides of the table were lined with wooden benches, and carved chairs stood at opposite ends. The floor in the room was made of thick wooden planks stained a deep brown. A large, tall stove/oven of mortar and stone stood against the wall at one end of the room. Something cooking in its hearth smelled delicious, like baked beans.

We hadn't eaten anything that day, so my stomach rumbled loudly as I stared at the red glow of the coals, and my mouth began to water. Mrs. Gold set a shiny, copper samovar on the table and poured boiling water and tea essence into tall glasses, passing each newly filled glass to us. Mr. Gold brought out a plate of rock sugar with a small hammer, like a small tomahawk. I was about to pick a sliver of the rock sugar and put it in my tea glass, when Father laughed and explained that to use sugar sparingly, one breaks away a small chip of the sugar with the hammer, puts the chip into one's mouth, and sips the tea through the sugar. It was an old Russian custom called *na prikusku*.

When there was no sugar available, Russians would take a small piece of sugar they had saved and look at it while they sipped their tea, that they called *na priglyadku*. Mrs. Gold must have noticed the sad, hungry expression on my face as I kept looking at the oven. Without saying a word, she pulled a large steaming pot out of the oven and served us a thick soup of potatoes, beans, and meat. Then she brought out a large, round bread that must have weighed nearly three kilograms, and gave each of us a 30-centimeter-long slice of it. It was delicious. When we finished eating, we were shown to a small room wide enough to hold two narrow beds with a night table between them.

"This will be your bedroom," Mrs. Gold said in Polish. "I will make up the beds for you this one time, but then it will be your responsibility." Tired as we were, Mietek and I went right to sleep in our new room. Father remained at the table with Mr. Gold and a couple of his neighbors, drinking tea and talking about the Germans and the Red Army. I listened for half an hour before I fell asleep.

CHAPTER 4

It seemed I had slept only an hour or two when the farmer woke us up. "Get up," he shouted. "It's six o'clock in the morning, time to feed the animals and milk the cows."

Outside it was still dark and the house was cold. First, the farmer started a fire in the large oven to warm up the house and fired up the samovars for morning tea. He then pointed to an attached shed. "Go in there and wash," he said.

"There's a pitcher of water and a wash bowl. Don't waste the water," he cautioned. "You have to carry it from the pump in the center of the village."

Stripped to the waist I washed myself, using as little water as possible. I dried myself and dressed in the one pair of pants I came with. Mr. Gold walked into the room, looked at me, and started laughing. "You don't plan to work in the barn with the cows and horses dressed in those pants and wearing those shoes, do you?"

"It's the only pair of pants and shoes I have," I answered.

"Go have a glass of tea, and I'll get some work clothing for you," he said.

Dressed in old work pants and rubber boots, Mr. Gold and I marched to the barn, about 30 meters from the house. It was built from wood logs sawn in half and was two stories high. The bottom level contained the stables for his horses and cows. The loft was used to store hay, straw, and grain for the animals below.

A tall ladder led to the loft and a wooden chute led from the loft to the barn below, so that hay, straw, and grain could be easily tossed down. We began our first day by mucking out the horse and cow stalls. Mr. Gold did the shoveling, and I rolled the filled wheelbarrow to the compost site, turned it upside down, and dumped the contents. Then I was told to climb up the ladder to the loft and shovel straw, hay, and grain down the chute. The work was hard, but I enjoyed standing up to my knees in beautiful-smelling hay; rolling in the straw; and at the end of the chore, sliding down the chute. Then we shoveled the straw and hay into the stalls and spread grain on the floor for the chickens, which had free run of the barn.

Mrs. Gold came into the barn carrying an empty tin bucket and a low stool. She placed the stool next to the first cow, sat down, and started milking. It was fascinating to watch her alternately and rhythmically pull on the cows' udders and see the sharp stream of milk shoot into the bucket she held between her knees. The stream of milk made a modulating, almost musical sound as it hit the metal side of the bucket, and changed pitch as the bucket filled up.

I crouched next to her and she asked me to open my mouth wide; when I did, she directed the stream of warm milk into my mouth, splashing some over my face as well, and we laughed. It was delicious.

After filling the bucket with milk, she asked me to carry it outside and dump it into the large milk can standing by the barn door. She repeated the milking process with each of the four cows, and I carried the full buckets to the milk can. It was well past eight o'clock when we finished the work in the barn. Then it was time for breakfast.

Father and Mietek were in the house when we came in from our chores. We took off our muddy boots, washed our hands, and sat down to breakfast together. Mrs. Gold brought out a large loaf of home-baked sourdough bread, a dish of homemade butter, a dish of farmer cheese, and the samovar. Before we began eating, Mr. Gold recited a short, thankful prayer in Hebrew, and then we ate. I was starved, and to me, the fresh bread and butter tasted better than any cake, and the tea with sugar *na prikusku,* made the breakfast perfect.

We started planning Father's trip to Warsaw. We agreed that Father should take any train going west toward the new border between the Soviet and German zones and find a guide to get him safely across the border. Then he should try any way possible to get to Warsaw, traveling light and hiding money and valuables in his clothing, in case he needed them to bribe someone.

It was the first week in November 1939, and the weather was getting cold, especially in the evenings and at night. Mr. Gold brought out a short, warm coat for

Father. Mrs. Gold cut up a large loaf of bread to make sandwiches with chicken fat and salami and some with butter and cheese, wrapping them separately in old newspapers. She packed some fruits, some homemade candy, and stuffed it all into Father's rucksack, with a clean shirt, underwear, socks, and a half-liter bottle of homemade vodka.

Father was ready to leave. We embraced and wished him a safe, successful trip and a fast return with Mother and Mina. The farmer's wagon had been hitched to two horses and was waiting to take Father to the nearest railroad station. We loaded Father's rucksack on to the wagon, embraced and kissed him once more, and stood there with tears in our eyes, waving good-bye as the wagon pulled away.

Our family was being torn apart; Mother and Mina were in Warsaw under Nazi rule. Father was on a perilous mission with unknown consequences, and Mietek and I were left in Soviet territory. Mietek and I feared for Father's safety and were scared of being left alone on the farm, though Mr. and Mrs. Gold were very nice and caring.

When Mr. Gold returned that evening, he told us that nothing untoward had happened on the way and that a train going west was expected to leave the next day. Father had his ticket and a room in the town's inn, where he would spend the night.

Winter was fast approaching. The weather was getting colder, and the temperature dropped lower each day. In mid-November it snowed heavily for several days and the drifts created by the fierce winds reached more than a meter in height. Mr. Gold, Mietek, and I shoveled snow all day to clear a path to the water pump in the village center. The pump was covered in straw, except for the pumping wheels on each side of it and the water-discharge spigot. The water would flow from the spigot when we turned the pumping wheels, and each of us carried water home in two tin pails suspended from a horizontal wooden bar that rested on our shoulders.

The first day without Father had set the pattern. Each day we got up before the sun did, washed in cold water, made up the beds, and then helped Mr. Gold clean the barn and feed the animals. After breakfast, when the sun came out, we would go outside to cut up tree trunks and split them into chunks for firewood.

Mietek and I set up two wooden sawhorses, placed the tree trunks on them, and using a 1.5-meter-long double-handled saw, cut them up. We worked in rhythm. I would first pull the saw toward me, and then Mietek pulled the saw toward himself until we cut through the trunks. With a large axe, we then split the trunks into smaller pieces and stacked them against a barn wall. Even though the weather was below freezing, we sweated as we worked, dressed only in our undershirts and pants.

We cut and split wood until midday, when Mrs. Gold would call us inside for dinner. After we washed and gathered around the table, Mr. Gold would make a blessing to which we replied "amen," and then Mrs. Gold would remove a large stone pot from the oven and dish out our meal, first to her husband, then to us, and lastly to herself. Usually she served a thick soup with pieces of chicken floating in it. After a hard day's work on the farm we ate with gusto, and then we had two hours of rest. Mr. Gold usually took a nap. I read some old Polish books I found until I, too, would fall asleep. Mrs. Gold cleaned up. Several times I offered to help her, but she always refused. "This is women's work," she would say.

Afternoons were spent working around the house. Attached to it was a shed where the Golds stored large stone jars full of milk. After a few days, the milk would sour and the sour cream would float to the top. My job was to skim the cream from the sour milk and pour it into the butter churn. The wooden cylinder was about 20 centimeters in diameter by 76 centimeters tall. The top, a removable cover, had a 5-centimeter hole in the middle for a 2.5-centimeter-thick wooden rod with a small paddle at one end that was inserted into the wood cylinder. I would half fill the churn with the sour cream and beat it into butter by moving the rod up and down through the cream in the cylinder. Mrs. Gold would scoop the floating globules of butter into a wooden bowl and press them together with a large spoon while running cold water over it. After several rinses in water she would press the butter into freshly squeezed carrot juice to give it a yellow color.

The sour milk left in the jars was turned into farmer cheese by pouring it into triangular linen pockets hung to drain from hooks in the shed's roof beams. Nothing was wasted. The whey left in the churn was mixed with animal feed and given to the horses.

When darkness fell, all outside work and work in the shed stopped. We returned to the house to wash and change our sour-milk-splattered clothes. Mrs. Gold lit kerosene lamps that hung from the center ceiling beam over the big wooden table and brought out the food for our supper. After Mr. Gold recited his evening prayers, Mrs. Gold would cut long slices of home-baked bread, spread thick layers of fresh butter and farmer cheese on them, and hand the first slice to Mr. Gold; then she would give one each to Mietek and me. Only after she had cut a few more slices of bread and brought out a jar of marmalade would she sit down to eat. The sour rye bread with fresh butter, marmalade, and hot tea was, to me, a royal feast.

After we all ate our fill, Mrs. Gold would clear the table, except for the samovar in the middle with the small teakettle sitting on top of the samovar flue. She would place a dozen tea glasses around the table. A bit later, two farmer neighbors walked in with their wives. Greeting and shaking hands with everyone, we sat down and began the tea-drinking ceremony. Mrs. Gold filled everyone's tea glasses with boiling water and the tea essence from the samovar and then passed around the plate with the rock sugar and small hammer. Each of us held our very hot tea glasses by the top and bottom rims, between our thumbs and center fingers, and lifted the steaming brew to our mouths to sip the tea through the sugar between our teeth. I was shocked to hear the farmers sip with so much noise. I tried to drink the tea in silence, as I was taught to do by my mother, but I burned my tongue. After that, I drank the hot tea as noisily as the farmers did.

Sitting around the table, the farmers and their wives drank untold glasses of tea, until the large samovar was empty. While they drank, they sang folk songs in Yiddish, Polish, and Russian. Mietek and I knew some of the songs, so we sang lustily along with them. Later, when the guests left and the table was cleaned, Mrs. Gold took one of the hanging kerosene lamps off its hook, I took the other, and we all went to sleep.

On the first day of December, the snow began to fall and didn't stop for three weeks. When it finally stopped, the thatched roofs of the farmers' houses were covered with a sparkly, pristine white blanket, 60 centimeters deep. The branches of the evergreen firs and pine trees were bent to the ground, some of them breaking under the heavy, frosty load.

It was a constant battle for us to keep a path cleared between the house and the barn so that we could feed the animals and bring milk and firewood into the house. The advantage of so much clean snow was that we didn't have to get water from the village pump. We gathered the snow in buckets and melted it on top of the stove. It was the sweetest and softest water, great for washing oneself.

During the third week of December, when the snow finally stopped and the sun came out, the temperature dropped to -40 degrees Fahrenheit. The panorama before our eyes was like a fantasy, a vision in crystal, white, and blue. The tree branches were covered in clear ice; long icicles dangled from roof gables and sparkled in the sun like diamonds. For as far as the eye could see, the green and gray fields were now covered with a thick, glossy white eiderdown of melted and refrozen snow that glittered in the bright light like a huge, virgin skating rink.

The farmer's wife dressed us in sheepskin coats and heavy felt boots and sent Mietek and me out to play in the snow. The thick snowy silence was broken by our squeals of joy, the thud of a snowball meeting its target, and the occasional snap and crack of a tree branch breaking under the weight of its beautiful coat. The snow was 90 to 122 centimeters deep, white and pure. The air was crisp, and even though the temperature was way down, I was warm from jumping around and rolling in snow that was as fluffy as a featherbed.

Late in December, we heard on a Soviet news broadcast from Moscow that Finland had threatened Leningrad and the Red Army was responding to the threat by invading Finland. We all knew that tiny Finland would never start a war with the vast Soviet state, and that the news was pure propaganda to cover up the Soviet invasion. We expressed our thoughts among ourselves with great caution; otherwise, the farmer told us, it would be a straight ticket for the whole family to the gulag in Siberia.

In the village that year, winter was the coldest in anyone's memory. At night, the temperatures dropped to well below −40 degrees Fahrenheit. In the mornings, the walls of the room we slept in were frosted white from our breath. We slept under huge goose-down quilts and allowed only our noses and the tops of our heads to stick out. Until the house oven was fired up, the temperature in the house was well below freezing. Later in the day, as we worked outside cutting the firewood, we had to check our faces for white spots, a sign of frostbite.

On most Wednesdays, Mr. Gold harnessed two of his horses to a large wooden sled and filled it with hay and produce. We would be covered from head to toe in sheepskins, and ride to the next large village to the market. Mr. Gold traded the potatoes and apples we brought for salt, rock sugar, and an occasional live duck or goose. When it was time to go home, Mr. Gold, using a long wooden pole, broke the sled runners away from the frozen ground so the horses could pull the sled.

Despite the overwhelming power of the Red Army, it was stopped by the tiny, but well-trained Finnish army at the so-called Mannerheim Line. People at the market told us that they saw trains returning from the front, full of Red Army soldiers suffering from severe frostbite on their hands, feet, and faces, and that most of them were not wearing proper winter clothing.

In late December 1939, Father returned to the farm, alone. He tried several times, at different points, to cross the border into German-occupied territory, without success. Each time he and his guide tried to cross, they were stopped by the Soviet or German border guards. Twice, they were captured by Soviet soldiers and bribed their way out of trouble with money and vodka. Once they were shot at by the Germans but managed to crawl away and escape.

We were heartbroken that Father had failed to rescue Mother and Mina from the Germans and reunite us, but he promised he would try again as soon as he could.

Our stay at the Golds' farm was coming to an end. As much as Mietek and I loved the safe and simple life on the farm, now that Father was back, we had to leave. Before the war, Father purchased apples from the Golds and other orchard farmers to process in his factory. Now he was afraid that someone in the farming village might recognize him as a capitalist and denounce us to the Soviets.

We loved the Golds, who were like loving grandparents to us. They taught us to work around the farm and the animals and how to make butter, bread, and cheese for simple meals and drink tea from samovars. The memories of the nightly singing and tea-drinking ceremony will stay with me forever.

The day we parted was sad for all of us. We packed our meager belongings into our rucksacks, and Mrs. Gold pressed on us a large bag filled with bread; butter, rolled in large leaves; farmer cheese in linen wrappings; a jar of honey; a fruitcake she baked specially for us; and a bag of tea leaves. We had tears in our eyes as we left for the railroad station in the horse wagon with Mr. Gold as our driver.

We arrived at the railroad station and found that the next train north would not get in until late that night or early the next morning. We thanked Mr. Gold for all he and his wife had done for us and said good-bye. I walked over and kissed the two horses I had taken care of during our short stay on the farm. I whispered to one in his ear that I would miss them terribly and never forget them.

Then we settled down on a bench in the station and prepared ourselves for the long wait in the already crowded waiting room. We made ourselves sandwiches from the food supplied by Mrs. Gold, and I, tired from the long ride, stretched out on the bench and fell asleep. It was midnight when Father woke me to say the train had arrived, and we'd better hurry and get aboard.

CHAPTER 5

Our destination was Białystok, a city in northeastern Poland that since October 1939 had been under Soviet control. Father had been to Białystok several times before the war and felt we could blend in with the large population without his being discovered as a "capitalist" and enemy of the Communist state. We arrived in Białystok in the morning, after a five-hour train ride. We found a room in a small, old hotel, occupied mostly by Soviet army officers and their orderlies. The room had one large bed that Father and I shared and a narrow cot for Mietek. Against one wall was a tiled, wood-fired stove; next to another wall stood a washstand with a porcelain bowl and a water pitcher. A narrow window opposite the bed looked out at an inner garden. We unpacked our meager belongings, put the butter and cheese on the outside windowsill to keep it cool, and fired the stove to warm up the room.

After we ate the wonderful bread that Mrs. Gold had given us, I ran out to see the town. Białystok was less than a quarter the size of Warsaw, but after living on an isolated farm, it seemed huge. The buses, military trucks, and bicycles brought back memories of the Warsaw I missed. The open stores, even though they had only a few things to sell, the movie houses showing Soviet films, and the music floating from windows were all very exciting to me.

The supper we ate at the hotel restaurant was nothing compared to what we had eaten at Mrs. Gold's house. We ate it anyway, and too tired from the trip and excitement of the first day in Białystok, we went to sleep.

The next morning when we got up, we noticed a curious thing in the hotel corridor. There was a line of Soviet soldiers in front of the only toilet. Every five minutes or so, two soldiers exited from the toilet and two entered the toilet and closed the door. The interior of the toilet was no more than 122 centimeters squared, just enough space for one person. What were two of them doing in there at one time? We soon found out. While the Soviet army officers used the only washroom and bath on the floor, the soldiers—simple peasants from the Soviet kolkhozy, the collective farms in the boondocks, who had never seen a toilet before—were using the toilet bowl as a wash sink. One soldier pulled the toilet chain while the other washed himself. There was no way we could use this toilet for its intended purpose. Luckily, we found another toilet in the basement.

We were told that the schools in Białystok were open, and that there was a school just around the corner. After breakfast, Father, Mietek, and I went to look the school over and find out if Mietek and I could become students there.

Before the war, the school program in Warsaw was a 12-year program with 6 years of public school and 6 years of gymnasium. The Soviet school system, we found out, was a 10-year system called *dziesiatiletka,* with no public school, gymnasium, or high school. In September 1939, I was supposed to start gymnasium in Warsaw, but the war broke out. In Białystok, after I took oral and written exams, I was assigned to the eighth grade in the Soviet system. The curriculum in that school was taught in Polish, with daily classes in Russian, Marxism, and History of the Soviet Communist Party. All other subjects were standard: math, physics, French, Polish and Russian literature, and chemistry. Most of the teachers were Polish, except those who taught Russian, Marxism, and History of the Communist Party. They were Russians from the Soviet Union.

The subjects were not difficult for me and, except for the class in Communist Party history, I got top marks. My favorite subjects were math, the sciences, and classic Polish and Russian literature.

Mietek was assigned to the tenth grade, with subjects similar to mine but on a higher class level. After graduation and after the war, he planned to enter a technical university in Warsaw or in France or England. Father found a job in a fruit and produce cooperative as a manager in the production of dried fruit, sour cabbage, and sour pickles. He found us a large room in town, not too far from our new school. The room was on the first floor of an apartment house that faced a dark, inner courtyard, but it was larger than the hotel room and had a toilet and a bath adjacent to it. In the room were two beds, a large double bed and a narrow one; a wooden table with four chairs; a wardrobe; and a storage bin under the window for perishable food. Across from the apartment building was a small dairy farm with a barn and five cows. The smell of the hay and the mooing of the cows reminded me of the Golds' farm.

Father's job pickling tomatoes and cabbage gave him access to salt. Salt, for whatever reason at that time, was in very short supply, if available at all. Instead of cash bonuses that were worthless, the cooperative gave its workers and managers a few kilos of salt. Because we had salt, we were rich.

We traded salt with farmers for butter and homemade sausages, with shoemakers who resoled and repaired our shoes, for linen pillows and blankets for our beds, and for almost anything else that was not available on the open market. Such trading was not perfectly legal, and if we got caught, we would land in jail, but that was how the Soviet economy was run. We had learned how it worked very quickly.

Our daily activity became routine. We got up every morning at half-past six, washed ourselves, made the beds, and cleaned the room. On a small electric plate (which we had obtained for salt), we boiled water for tea, and then we sat down to a breakfast of bread, butter, and jam. After breakfast, Father took a trolley to work, and Mietek and I walked to school. School started at 8 in the morning and ended at 2:30 in the afternoon. At midday we would lunch at the school's cafeteria and have our only hot meal of the day. Usually it consisted of a thick potato soup and bread, and sometimes, if we were lucky, a sausage or two and tea. After going to school and doing homework, I sought part-time work to earn pocket money for movies or sweets, if and when they were available.

The Soviet soldiers and civilians bought everything from the stores that were still open. Evidently the goods that were still available in Białystok were not available in the Soviet Union. On the local black market, townspeople and refugees like us sold their possessions to the Russians, who bought almost anything being offered, even if it was old—broken watches, old clothing, and Jewish prayer shawls that were sewn into shirts. Lingerie and nightgowns were bought for the Soviet women. Later, we saw them wearing them on the streets and we were all amazed. Was this the worker's paradise they kept telling us about?

Still, for us, it was a safe haven from the Germans. As long as we kept our mouths shut and kept up the pretense that we were from a worker's background, they left us alone. We kept telling each other that if we could bring Mother and Mina from Warsaw, we could safely sit out the war.

CHAPTER 6

As winter turned to spring in 1940, the Soviet government ordered all refugees to register at the local militia station to obtain internal passports. The passport we were issued had a stamp that stated the owner was restricted from living less than 100 kilometers from Soviet borders or in cities of more than 100,000 inhabitants. We could not live or travel near military installations, under the 11th paragraph of this Soviet law. Suddenly, we became second-class residents. We wondered if that meant we could no longer live in Białystok.

A week after these "11th-paragraph passports" were issued, Soviet militia and military started rounding up refugees and arresting them. No one knew where they were sent. At work, a Soviet director with whom Father had become friendly told him that the transports of refugees were shipped to either Siberia or Kazakhstan, into the Soviet gulags.

One day we came back from school to find Father packing our few belongings and foodstuffs into our rucksacks. He told us that when it got dark, he would move us to the loft above the barn at the dairy farm across the road.

Two hours after we moved into the barn, we peered through an opening between the barn planks and saw a truck filled with Red Army soldiers stop in front of our apartment building. They ran into the building and about 20 minutes later returned to the truck and drove away. We knew they were looking for us, because we were the only refugees living in that house.

The farm manager brought us some food, and Father paid for it with a sack of salt. We stayed in the loft for a week and only relieved ourselves in the outhouse late at night. At the end of the week, the farm manager told us things had quieted down. That's when Father decided we had to escape from Białystok and travel south to some small town in Ukraine.

Late one night we left the barn and walked to the railroad station. Father had gotten our tickets by bribing the stationmaster. Hardly anything could be gotten in the Soviet Union without the *protyanut' bratskuyu ruku,* the outstretched brotherly hand—the hand waiting for its bribe.

We were nervous when we boarded the train to Lvov, which was now in the Ukrainian SSR. The Soviet secret police, the NKVD, were always inspecting and searching trains for illegal travelers, smugglers, and anyone who could possibly be perceived as a Soviet enemy. We heard that a traveler with a valise full of sugar was caught by the NKVD. The traveler probably bought the sugar in a town where sugar was easy to get and was trying to smuggle it to a town that had none and sell it at a profit. Buying, selling, and trading were considered serious capitalist crimes that could cost him ten years in a Siberian gulag. He told the NKVD he had stolen the suitcase from a train station. Instead of ten years in the gulag for selling, he got three months in the local jail for stealing. Such was justice in the Soviet Union.

Besides clothing and food for the trip, we were carrying a nine-kilo bag of salt Father had gotten as a bonus from the pickling plant director. If the NKVD had searched us as we headed to Lvov and found the salt, nothing would have saved us from the gulag. Luckily, we thought then, no one paid attention to us.

We took a local train from Lvov to Krzemieniec, where people were likely to get caught because the NKVD knew that passengers headed from big cities to villages usually smuggled in wares that were not available locally. Instead of selling or trading the salt in bulk, and to avoid getting caught, Father decided we would split the nine kilos into several smaller bags and hide it in our coat pockets. In the darkest corner of the train station, we poured the salt into several clean socks. The salt was the only valuable commodity we had, and we were not about to give it up.

The train finally arrived, late and crowded. We pushed and shoved to get ourselves into a car with standing room only, and after about two hours, the train finally started moving. Mietek and I stood close together in the aisle. Father stood pressed into a corner, about three meters away. The train ride to Krzemieniec was supposed to take about five hours, but who knew for certain?

Mietek and I agreed to try to sleep in shifts, jammed among the others for one or two hours, while one of us would watch that no one stole anything from us. The swaying and clickety-clack of the train wheels soon put me to sleep. I woke up suddenly when I felt someone pulling on my coat pocket.

"What the hell are you doing in my coat pocket?" I screamed at a big, gruff-looking character standing next to me.

"Oh it is your pocket?" he asked with an innocent look on his face. "I was looking for something in my pocket, but it's so crowded here I made a mistake."

"You sure did, just don't do it again or I'll call for the Militia," I snarled.

"Don't you dare accuse me of anything or I'll break your neck," he threatened, and pushed himself against me. This was about to explode into a fight, the big bully against little me, when Mietek pushed himself between us and looked directly into the guy's eyes. He said quietly, "Let's cut out the crap and relax."

Everyone nearby was looking at us and some were taking sides. I figured that before something developed that might bring in the Militia, I would move away. The wagon was so tightly packed with people it took me a while to get to the other side of Mietek and away from the bully.

"You shouldn't start a fight with a guy twice your size," Mietek admonished me.

"But he was about to rob me. What was I supposed to do, let him?" I said. "Anyway I can't sleep any more, so I'll watch and you go to sleep." Father, in his corner, was dozing off, totally unaware of what had just happened.

The train made its way slowly through the night, sometimes stopping for a short while for no discernible reason. Then the steam whistle would blow and the engine would start again with a jerk, jostling all of us in the wagon. It was still dark when we finally arrived in Krzemieniec. Stiff and tired, we got off the train, and with our few bags walked into the small station's empty waiting room. The people who filled it earlier were now on the train that had brought us. Father was going to walk into town to inquire about renting a room for us and told us to stay in the empty train station, rest, and wait for him to return.

We placed our bags on each end of the bench to use as pillows, but first I told Mietek that I was going to look for a place where I could wash up and relieve myself and that when I got back, it would be his turn. I soon discovered there was no toilet in the waiting room, but there was a filthy-smelling outhouse nearby. I pinched my nose and held my breath while I used it. Attached to the waiting room was a tiny shed that contained a small water pump mounted to the floor, with a well dug out under the spigot.

Pumping with one hand, I quickly tried to cup my palms under the spigot to catch some water as it began flowing. The water was ice cold. Nonetheless, I tried to wash my face and my hands. I had to repeat this several times to feel a bit cleaner, and my palms were stiff with cold. I wiped my face in my shirttail because I had no towel.

The smart way to handle a situation like that was to have Mietek pump the water while I washed and then pump the water for him, but that would have meant leaving our bags on the bench, a good way to have them stolen. When I got back to the bench, I told Mietek about the fancy outhouse and the water pump and told him it was my turn to watch the bags.

"I'll wait till Father gets a room and then I'll wash," he said. We lay down on the wooden bench and promptly fell asleep. It seemed only moments before Father was shaking me awake.

"I found two nice rooms in a Jewish house, and we can move in now," he said. "First they offered only one room as a bedroom for the three of us, but after I offered them two kilos of salt in addition to the rent, they gave us a second room. You will like the people and the rooms."

We picked up our bags and dragged our tired bodies toward the town. It was already midmorning and the sun was shining. Though I was tired, cold, and somewhat hungry, the panorama of Krzemieniec surrounded by snow-capped mountains gave me a happy feeling. Father had rented our rooms from the Rosen family, who owned a house in the middle of town, two streets up the hill from the main street. The house was constructed of thick, rough-sawn, wooden planks and had a porch the full length of the house. The roof was covered with thick thatch, giving the house a warm look.

In fact, the Rosens greeted us warmly as we entered the house. Mr. Rosen was about 168 centimeters tall, a muscular man with bushy, dark hair and a flowing mustache. His powerful physique contrasted with smiling eyes that projected a warm and friendly personality. Mrs. Rosen, also of medium height, was slim, with a long swanlike neck and a finely chiseled face. Her light brown hair was tightly wound on top of her head, giving her additional height. Even without makeup and in a simple, straight peasant dress, she projected the dignity of a royal figure. I fell in love with her at first sight.

They had a daughter, a shy 10- or 12-year-old named Sara, who hid behind her mother when we entered the house. Mrs. Rosen asked us to drop our bags and sit down at the large table, which we did with a sigh of relief. She then poured each of us a large glass of tea. After we rested a bit, Mrs. Rosen led Mietek and me to a small room about 2.5 meters by 3 meters with one narrow window. It looked out at a hilltop, on which stood a large house. Between the two houses there was a large pear orchard. Mrs. Rosen saw me looking out the window and said that the orchard was theirs. There were two narrow wooden cots standing against opposite walls, and against the wall, across from the window, stood a tall mirrored wardrobe.

She told us we could put our belongings away, so we began unpacking our rucksacks and the battered valise the Golds had given us. When Mrs. Rosen came in carrying bed sheets, pillowcases, and blankets, she told us sternly, "You'll get a fresh set of linen once a month, fresh towels once a week, and you must keep the room neat and clean."

"Yes, Mrs. Rosen," both Mietek and I meekly responded. She sounded so much like a drill sergeant, we burst out laughing and she looked at us with bewilderment in her eyes.

The only artificial light in the room came from a single bulb hanging from the ceiling. There was no room for a table or chairs, yet it was a cheerful room with flowerpots on the windowsill and the view of the orchard. Father's room was a bit larger, with a full bed, a closet, and a small round table with two chairs. There were flowerpots on the windowsill in his room, too, and he had a pair of pretty curtains on the window. Father's arrangement with the Rosens included eating breakfast and dinner with them, which was great for Mietek and me, because otherwise we would have lived on cold sandwiches.

We had just finished arranging our meager possessions when Mrs. Rosen walked into the room, looked carefully around and smiling, said, "It looks like you'll keep your room neat. Come, we'll have something to eat together," and led us to the main room of the house, one that served both as a dining and sitting room.

In the center of the room stood a large oval table covered with a flower-embroidered tablecloth. The table was large enough to seat eight people in comfort. Opposite the entry, in one corner, stood a small square table with four chairs that we later found out was used for nightly card games between the Rosens and some of their friends. In another corner was a small, round, lace-covered table on which stood a large, shining, copper samovar. The floor and the ceiling in the room were made of large wooden planks—the ceiling was painted white and the floor was stained dark brown.

There was a simple electric fixture with one bulb and a green metal shade suspended over the center of the large table. On the large wall opposite the entry, the Rosens hung a multicolored handwoven rug that depicted a biblical scene, and several framed family photos. Above the family photos, they hung a large portrait of Stalin, a "must" in every home in the Soviet Union. The two windows looking out at the back of the house were partially covered in pretty, colorful drapes, and again, the windowsills were covered in flowerpots. The whole room was very cheerful and warm.

Mrs. Rosen directed us to the chairs around the table, with Mietek and me on one side, and Father sitting opposite us. I felt that she did that so Father could make sure we behaved. Two chairs away from me sat Sara, her shy daughter, but Mr. Rosen had gone back to work and could not join us. Mrs. Rosen moved her chair to the end of the table and indicated that was her seat. We settled down, and she brought a large stone soup pot out of the kitchen and placed it on the table next to her. The smell of the soup filled the room.

"It's a potato 'burn' soup!" I cried out. "My favorite!"

Of course the soup was not burned, but it was so named for the slightly burned chopped onions in it, which gave it a particular aroma and taste. My mother used to make it for me.

We passed our soup plates to Mrs. Rosen, who ladled the soup into each plate, and then went back to the kitchen to bring out a large loaf of farmer bread, which she cut into generous slices for each of us. The bread, she told us, came from the town bakery. After I tasted it, I said the bread was very good, but to myself I said it was not as tasty as Mrs. Gold's home-baked bread.

The potato soup was thick with large potatoes and aromatic "burned" onions that tasted wonderful and nicely filled my hungry belly. For dessert Mrs. Rosen brought out a bowl full of apples and pears. "They were all washed; you can eat them with the skin, it's healthier," she told us.

After the meal, Father, Mietek, and I went to scout around the town. Mrs. Rosen told us that the town had about 5,000 inhabitants. Compared to the neighboring village, it was considered a large town, which before the war had an elected town council and mayor. Now it was ruled by a Soviet-appointed party boss and the NKVD secret police. The town lay in a valley at the foot of the Biała Góra (White

Mountain) range. The houses, including the Rosens', were set on a slight slope rising from Main Street. As we walked toward the thoroughfare, we were surprised to pass several houses that had mezuzot nailed to their doorposts, indicating to us that they were Jewish homes.

Main Street was a wide road surfaced with large round river rock we called "cat's heads." Each side of the street was lined with a row of houses built of timber with thatched roofs. Old evergreen trees were planted in front of them. A few storefronts were scattered between the homes facing the street, and the whole presented a peaceful, postcardlike view. Walking down the street, we passed a town photographer's shop, a small grocery, a pharmacy, and a Soviet store that sold used clothing and other used items on consignment from townspeople. Other storefronts stood empty. Main Street ran from a high wall that enclosed the town's prison to the foothills of the Biała Góra, about three kilometers away.

We were somewhat tired but pleased with what we found in the peaceful, colorful town. We returned to our new home just in time for supper.

The Rosens were not very religious, so we didn't have to put on our yarmulkes, and Mr. Rosen didn't recite prayers before a meal. That night, the light meal consisted of a vegetable soup with bread and butter. Afterward, Mrs. Rosen and Sara cleared the table, leaving the tea samovar and tea glasses. We sat down, and Mrs. Rosen filled each of our glasses with hot tea and placed a small chunk of rock sugar on a plate in front of each of us. From the kitchen, she and Sara brought out two heaping bowls of cookies. We waited until Mrs. Rosen sat down at the table before we started eating the cookies, and slowly and carefully sipped the boiling tea through the rock sugar held in our mouths. Except for the sound of crunching cookies and the wet sound of tea being slurped through the sugar, there was silence.

I was itching to ask Mr. Rosen and Sara about the town. Did the school teach in Polish or Russian? Was there a sports club? Were there movie theaters? But I kept quiet, not wanting to be the first to break the silence. After clearing his throat a couple of times, Mr. Rosen turned toward Father.

"How was your trip here? Did you have any problems?" he asked.

"Not really," Father replied, "except the train was very crowded and very slow."

"Where do you come from now, and where are you from originally?" he asked turning toward me. "Please tell us about it."

"We come from Warsaw," I started bragging, letting them know that we came from a big, sophisticated, capital city, not some little village. Then I proceeded to describe how the war started, how Warsaw was bombed and shelled by the German invaders, how Warsaw capitulated to the Nazis, and how the victorious Germans marched into the city. Then I told them Father's decision that we men head east. He had heard that the Nazis would persecute the Jewish men and leave the women alone. I told them that we left Mother and my sister Mina in Warsaw and hoped to get them out soon. Then I told of our journey from Warsaw to Białystok and how we came to them. While I talked, I kept eating the cookies until I couldn't anymore, and that was when I stopped talking.

The Rosens sat as if hypnotized, listening to my story. Neither one of them had eaten a cookie or taken a sip of tea as they listened to me.

"Oy vey," whispered Mr. Rosen, after I stopped talking. "It's like a film or an adventure book," he said. "You are lucky to be alive. We have not experienced anything like it. One day we were a part of Poland, and the next the Red Army marched in without a shot being fired, and we became a part of the Soviet Union."

Father talked about his failed effort to bring out Mother and Mina from Warsaw. Mietek and I had no chance to ask the Rosens about Krzemieniec. Tired from the trip and the excitement of the day, we decided to go to sleep.

It took us about a week to settle into the new house and town. Father secretly told us never to tell anybody that he was once an owner of a factory before the war. In the Communist Soviet Union that was a crime, and all of us, if we were discovered by the NKVD, would be arrested and deported to a gulag in Siberia. We were to say Father was a simple worker in the food industry, and that we came to the Soviet Union as workers, to escape from the Nazis.

Both Mietek and I were registered for classes in the local school. The school was housed in a large, beautiful building, and many stone steps ran its entire length, leading to a columned entrance. High ceilings and large, tall windows made an impressive sight, and the school was named after the classic Polish author, Juliusz Slowacki. Talking to new friends, I had to be very careful and invent new scenarios about my life in Warsaw before the war. We said that our family was poor and that we were always discriminated against for being Jewish.

Father found a job in the local food production plant as a manager in the pickling of cucumbers and tomatoes. It was run by the Ukrainian state enterprise for fruit and vegetables.

The classes I attended were held in Polish, with the addition of daily classes in Marxism, Russian, and Ukrainian. Once a week after regular classes, we assembled on a field for military training, marching to orders as we carried wooden rifles, singing Soviet patriotic marching songs.

We heard no news from Mother and Mina and this worried us most. The scraps of news we heard from Jewish people who had recently escaped from Warsaw and the German occupation was that the Germans were about to set up a ghetto in Warsaw and herd all the Jews into it. How would Mother be able to deal with this? Would the family there be able to take care of them? There was nothing we could do to help them.

Once Father got hold of a smuggler who claimed that he could ship food packages to Warsaw for a large sum of money. We prepared a large box with jars of melted butter, flour, dry cereal, sugar, and dry cookies that Mrs. Rosen baked for us and gave the box to the smuggler. We never heard from the smuggler again, and most likely he never delivered the package to Mother.

Days, weeks, and months went by in 1940, with Father working in the co-op pickling plant and Mietek and me going to the Soviet school. I did pretty well in school, getting top grades in math, science, and Polish and Russian literature. I especially loved and memorized many Polish poems by Adam Mickiewicz and Russian works by Pushkin and Lermontov.

To earn some pocket money for movies, on the days off from school I worked at nailing together wooden crates for fruits and vegetables. The pay was meager, hardly enough to earn a movie ticket a week. Each day after work, we had to attend a political meeting and listen to the *politruk*'s [political leader's] repetitious Soviet propaganda. At one such political meeting, the *politruk* stated that he had received a proposal from one of the workers to donate one of our working days a month to the Red Army. "Who is against this proposal?" he asked, and no one dared to answer.

"We will send a telegram to our dear Comrade Stalin," he said, "to let him know that our working team has donated, with 100 percent approval, one day a month to the glorious Soviet Red Army."

I had made a few friends among the students, but I considered only one, Heniek, my best, true friend. Heniek; a non-Jewish Polish girl named Hanka, whom we both admired; and I would often go for long walks in the evenings to the top of

Biała Góra while we recited our favorite Polish and Russian poems. Heniek and I had a gentleman's agreement not to make any advances on Hanka, but to maintain platonic relations with her.

The winter of 1940 was very cold, and there was lots of snow. The roads were covered, and transportation was limited to horse-drawn sleds. The school loaned the students wooden skis, so no matter how cold the weather or deep the snow, we had no excuses not to go to school. On our days off, the three of us would ski down Biała Góra to our heart's content, or until our strength gave out from climbing the hill—there were no ski lifts.

The skiing was rather hazardous because our old wooden skis had no safety bindings to fasten them to our walking boots, just a single leather strap. If you fell and twisted your leg, the ski would not release. The terrain down the mountain was covered with deep snow powder that hid fallen trees and large rocks. Many times we fell, luckily without any major injuries. It was great fun.

To get home we would ski down the middle of Main Street, dodging the horse sleds and singing some of the Russian songs we had learned in school. Some of the sleigh drivers cursed us in Polish, Ukrainian, and Russian because we scared the horses and caused them to rear, which would almost toss the sleds on their sides.

The sad side of being in the Soviet Union was that we could not celebrate our Jewish holidays. All synagogues and prayer rooms in the town were closed. Some had been converted to stables or warehouses, and observance of religious holidays at home was frowned upon and could lead to arrest. Although we weren't Orthodox in our religious beliefs, I had always loved the festivities. Going with Father to synagogue, having large dinners with the whole family, especially on Passover, Purim, and Hanukkah, were my favorite parts of the year.

Now that the family was broken apart, the future was unknown. Though I felt safe, I also felt suspended in time, with no present or future.

As the winter of 1940 turned into the spring of 1941, my thoughts were more and more on Mother and Mina. The little news from Warsaw that was filtering through to us was scary. The Germans were indeed herding the Jews into a ghetto, an area a quarter the size of their former neighborhood, forcing two or three families to live in one room. We heard that widespread hunger and contagious diseases were rampant. How were Mother and Mina managing? Were the other members of our family, uncles and aunts, helping them? Father, as the oldest son of the seven children, always helped those in need. Would his siblings be as kind?

Father and Mietek were equally worried. We talked about it every day but were frustrated because we could do nothing. The border between the Soviet Ukraine and German-occupied Poland was now heavily guarded by the German and Soviet armed forces, and it would be impossible to cross to rescue Mother and Mina. We could only hope that the war would soon end.

Unfortunately, even that hope slowly evaporated as the news got worse, and we heard about concentrations of German troops nearby and on the border. That could only mean potential hostility was growing between the Soviet and German forces.

I dreamed about Mother nightly, and sometimes I had nightmares from which I woke up screaming. Mietek and I would sit on our beds for the rest of the night and futilely talk about how we would smuggle them out of Warsaw. Perhaps one of us would somehow get to Warsaw to help them, but that was impossible, too. Krzemieniec was 100 kilometers from the border, and we had those cursed "paragraph-11" passports that prevented us, under heavy penalties, from getting closer to the border. The whole 100-kilometer strip between us and the border was heavily guarded by the NKVD.

CHAPTER 7

Early on the morning of June 21, 1941, we suddenly heard and saw hundreds of German warplanes flying over the town, and radio loudspeakers on the streets blared announcements that the Fascist German Luftwaffe was bombing the city of Kiev. The war was on, and panic spread through the town like wildfire. People were running in all directions trying to find extra food. Within a couple of hours, there was none left to be gotten. Because we had been through this before, we went outside the town to buy or trade for flour, cereals, butter, and other food from the local farmers.

Such dealings were strictly illegal in the Soviet Union, but with the war at our door, we didn't care anymore. We hoped the might of the Red Army would quickly defeat the Germans and we could return to Warsaw. The streets in town were full of Soviet army soldiers, trucks, and tanks, but we couldn't understand why their disorganized movement was all headed east, away from the Germans. Was the mighty, gallant Red Army retreating? All we got on the radio was martial music and propaganda. Over the next few days it became clear that the Soviets were beating a hasty retreat with the Nazis on their heels. Now we had to worry how long we had before the Nazis made it to Main Street. The Jews were terrified. Those who were perhaps smarter and preferred to take their chances with the Soviets moved east with the army. We decided to stay until the Germans came, hoping perhaps that would give us the opportunity to return to Warsaw and find Mother and Mina. We had no clue what was in store for us, but we didn't have to wait long for the Nazis.

Four days after the start of the war between the Germans and Soviets, the Red Army was gone. So were the political officers and the secret police. The town became quiet and the streets were deserted. Early the next morning, German scouts on powerful motorcycles rode into town and gunned their loud engines. Behind them came the giant tanks that squealed, clanked, roared, and crunched over Main Street, making horrible noises as they rolled over the paving. Suddenly, the empty streets were filled with large numbers of Ukrainians who ran toward the Germans, waving Ukrainian flags, throwing bunches of flowers at them, and pressing breads, fruits, and other goodies into their hands, welcoming the German army as their liberators.

Knowing how the Ukrainians harbored murderous antisemitism in their hearts, the Jews were alarmed. The combination of the virulent strains of Nazi Jew-hatred and ingrained Ukrainian antisemitism was terrifying, and it didn't take long at all before the devil came knocking. Early the following morning, bands of Ukrainians, mostly teenagers in groups of three or four, ran to Jewish homes and dragged out whomever they could find, cursing and beating them all the while. We all hid in the attic. We could hear the Ukrainians running into the house and searching the rooms. We heard them curse when they didn't find any Jews, and they finally left. When things got quiet outside, I went down to investigate.

Just as I opened the door a crack to see what was going on, a band of three Ukrainian teenagers ran from the side of the house and grabbed me. They were 16 or 17 years old, and I knew one of them from school. They grabbed and twisted my arms and forced me to run in front of them toward Main Street and then to the town jail. While I ran, they kept hitting me, cursing and laughing, telling me that when we got to the jail, they would kill me. There were other Ukrainian gangs herding other Jewish men and women in the same direction. Some of the Jews had blood pouring down their faces. The older Jews, who could not run, were dragged by their hands or feet down the street, with their heads banging on the fieldstones.

Halfway down Main Street, we were stopped by a gang of four Ukrainians on their way back from the jail. They were bragging to the gang leading me that they had captured and herded three Jews—two women and one man—to the jail. Pointing to me they laughed that my gang had only one Jew.

"What's happening at the jail?" the Ukrainian who held me asked. They laughed, "We make them dig the graves with their bare fingers where the Soviets killed our prisoners, and then we kill them with bats and chains."

While they were talking like that, the guy holding my arm let go of me. I instantly pulled away from them, ran up an embankment, and jumped over a tall wooden fence into a potato field. The potato stalks were about one meter high and growing densely together. After running through the crop for about 15 meters, I dropped to the ground and was instantly covered with the potato stalks. I could hear the gang running around and looking for me. There was a woman sitting on her porch who had seen me jump the fence. One of the gang asked her, "Did you see a running Jew?"

I held my breath as I listened for her answer. "No, I didn't see anybody," she said. Some of the gang jumped over the fence and started looking in the potato field. They passed just three meters from me, then went down to the river at the other end of the potato field. I could hear them cursing and saying what they would do to me when they found me, and it was nothing pleasant. After about half an hour, I heard them give up the search for me and go back to town to get more Jews.

It was already dark when I left the potato field to walk toward the river. Along the way I found an old abandoned barn where I spent the rest of the night without sleeping. Early the next morning, tired and shivering from cold, I walked along the river toward the town. On the main road that led from the jail toward the town, I saw several horse-drawn wagons loaded with corpses of Jews tortured and killed at the jail. The blood was dripping from the wagons into the road. I sat down on the ground and shook with sobs and hoped that Father and Mietek had escaped the pogrom. As I got closer to town, I could see gangs of Ukrainians roaming Main Street, carrying bundles of goods probably looted from the Jewish homes, as small groups of German soldiers stood in the middle of the street and watched the Ukrainians.

Even from where I stood hidden near some wooden structure, I could hear the Germans laughing and pointing to the Ukrainians. It would have been too dangerous for me to get to the house through the streets, with all those itchy antisemitic killers around, so I decided to stay where I was and figure out the best and safest way to get there.

Several hours later, about midday, Main Street was emptied of Ukrainians. The German soldiers remaining on the street were not yet capable of distinguishing a Ukrainian from a Jew, so were less dangerous to me than the Ukrainians. I took a chance and crossed Main Street to get to the Rosens' house.

I made sure I walked slowly and with dignity, and smirked at the Germans as I passed them. It seemed to me that they smirked right back and let me through. When I got to the house, I found Father, Mietek, and the Rosen family still hiding in the attic. They were shocked to see me. Father and Mrs. Rosen were both trying to stem the flow of tears down their faces. Father embraced me and whispered that they were sure that the gang had killed me.

Mietek watched through an opening in the attic for approaching Ukrainians while I told them how I escaped from the gang—and what I had seen and heard about the fate of the hundreds of Jews they dragged to the jail. I also told them what I found in the wagons that morning. Mr. Rosen said several Ukrainian gangs had broken into the house looking for the inhabitants and, not finding any, had stolen anything they could carry. We expected to be discovered momentarily and dragged to our deaths.

We spent that night, sleepless, in the attic, and nothing more happened. Later, we found out the Germans had taken control of the town and set a curfew from six in the evening to six in the morning, thus forcing the gangs of Ukrainians off the streets. In the morning, a loudspeaker mounted on a German truck announced that the town was under German control, and that anyone who did not obey the German orders posted on the City Hall's walls in Ukrainian and German would be shot on sight. The laws were addressed to the Jews.

> No Jew without special permit is allowed on the street between six o'clock in the evening and six o'clock in the morning.
>
> All Jews, including Jewish children, must wear a yellow circular patch on the left breast and top back of their outer clothing.
>
> All Jews must submit all their fur coats, fur jackets, fur hats, and fur gloves to the German authorities in the City Hall.
>
> No Jew is permitted to deal with any Poles, Ukrainians, and Germans without a special permit from the authorities.
>
> No Jew is permitted to attend any school.
>
> Any Jew not obeying those orders will be shot.

In the following days more orders for the Jews were issued:

All male Jews aged 16 years to 55 years must register with the Labor Department of the German administration to be assigned to work for the German armed forces.

Any Jew not complying with this order will be shot.

We all lived in fear of what would happen next. How and where would we be able to get food? How would we survive? Luckily, the Rosens had hidden sacks of rice, beans, and potatoes under the floorboards and offered to share their food with us. It was a relief, but what would happen when their supplies were gone?

The German command ordered Jews whose family members had been murdered in the pogrom to bury them. The corpses I had seen earlier, more than 200 of them, had been dumped on the grounds of the local Jewish cemetery. Some of the dead were butchered beyond recognition, and their families could identify them only by their clothing. Eyewitnesses told me that the weeping mothers and sons who were digging graves to bury their husbands, fathers, and sons were surrounded by grinning German soldiers.

Every new day was another revelation in brutality. Jews hurrying on the street were stopped by laughing Germans who kicked them and spat on them. The Orthodox had their beards and side locks pulled and sometimes cut by soldiers with bayonets. The Ukrainians, likewise, showed their hatred of Jews, attacking any they could find. Constant terror ran through the Jewish community—when we had arrived, there were more than 3,000 of us in the town.

About a month after the Germans occupied Krzemieniec, they announced the formation of the Jewish ghetto. Two streets, less than half the size of the former Jewish residential area, were declared the ghetto and surrounded by a high wooden fence. The Germans forced the Jews living outside the ghetto into it and herded Jewish families living outside Krzemieniec in small neighboring villages into the ghetto, as well. It didn't take long for conditions inside the ghetto to become unbearably crowded. Families of five or six persons were forced into one room, if they were lucky to find one. Otherwise, they were forced to live in the former synagogue or warehouses with 100 or more people to a room.

In the meantime, the German command designated one man of the leading Jewish family in town as the *Ghettoälteste* (the ghetto elder), to relay German orders and demands to the Jewish community. They obtained his name, I was told, from prewar synagogue documents they found in the Soviet archives.

The *Ghettoälteste* was responsible for the distribution of food. Food ration cards were printed and distributed to each Jew in the ghetto. This action forced each person in the ghetto to register and gave the German command the exact number of Jews in the ghetto, their names, age, sex, and location.

The Germans used their data to demand that the *Ghettoälteste* deliver a specific number of Jews to work at designated job sites. They would be required to repair damaged railroad tracks, load and unload supply trucks, wash command cars and trucks, and do all the heavy and dirty work the Germans could find. The work commandos, as the Germans used to call them, worked 12 hours a day and got only a bowl of thin soup to eat. They were constantly pushed and beaten to work faster. In the evening, they would return to the ghetto, hungry and exhausted. They could hardly drag their own feet.

Weeks, then months, went by without any relief for the tormented ghetto inhabitants. Good news of German victories over the Red Army from the eastern front was blasted from loudspeakers in the streets. It was the only news we heard, and it depressed us. Would the Nazis conquer the whole world?

Father told us to start planning a possible return to Warsaw to reunite with Mother and Mina. We heard that the Germans had a border guard between the so-called General Government, the western part of former Poland, and the conquered Soviet lands. We would need a guide to smuggle us across the border and lead us to Warsaw. Despite the grim situation, life in the Rosens' house returned to a somewhat normal routine, except that a family of four, parents and their two sons from a nearby village, moved into the main living room of the house. They told us how German soldiers and the newly formed Ukrainian police ordered the Jews in their village to leave their homes in two hours, with whatever they could carry, and head to the Krzemieniec ghetto.

September and October of 1941 were still very warm, and on sunny days, the older boy and I would sneak out of the house to the pear orchard in the back of the house to play ball and pick pears off the trees. The large house above the pear orchard had been requisitioned by the Germans and occupied by some of their officers. Several times, while the older boys and I played in the orchard, we had to hide behind the trees when we saw the Germans leaving or entering the house.

Once, while I was in the orchard picking pears, I heard a German soldier yell at me in German. I jumped out of the tree in a hurry, spilling the pears on the ground, and ran behind our house.

One rainy afternoon in October that year, I was sitting in the house, reading a book at the table in the main room, when two uniformed Germans walked in. I remained where I was, pretending to read, when one of the Germans started screaming in German and reached for his pistol. At that moment, Father entered the room and, in Polish, told me to stand up immediately. Then he turned to the Germans and in German told them that I understood only Polish.

The soldier screamed at my father that a Jew must stand up when a German soldier enters. He then put the pistol back in the holster. They walked through the house while everyone stood at attention, and then they left. It seemed to us that they wanted to see how Jews lived. Everybody breathed a sigh of relief, and then we made bad jokes about learning the different makes of the Germans' pistols—the hard way.

CHAPTER 8

Daily life in the ghetto became more and more unbearable. We finally ran out of food, and the food we obtained with the ration cards was not enough to keep us alive. We were forced secretly to sell our meager possessions to the Ukrainians, to see if we could get potatoes and carrots for one meal a day. Several times Father, Mietek, and I were forced to work for the Germans outside of the ghetto for 12 or more hours a day. All we got to eat was a small bowl of watery beet soup and a slice of bread.

The work was backbreaking. They made us unload heavy cases of ammunition, while the German and Ukrainian guards screamed at us to move faster and faster. By November, Father had enough and decided we should take our chances and return to Warsaw as soon as he could find someone to smuggle us across the border and guide us to the city. A week later someone introduced Father to a Pole who claimed to be an expert smuggler and said he had crossed the border many times. The price he demanded was more than we had, so Father agreed to pay him half when we started on our trip and half when we reached the Warsaw ghetto.

By the middle of November, winter had set in. Heavy snowfall covered the whole area, and temperatures dropped to below freezing. We had no wood to fire the stove, and the house was very cold, so we sat and walked around wrapped in our sleeping blankets. Whatever scraps of wood we could find were used to boil water and to cook some meals. To keep up our spirits we sang songs, told funny stories and jokes, and sometimes played dominoes or chess.

Father searched for warm winter clothing and boots for us. He found me a pair of leather ski boots with heavy waterproof soles and square toes. He also bought a sheepskin coat, a couple of heavy wool sweaters and wool socks, sheepskin gloves, and hats. We were ready for the long trip. The guide instructed us not to take any of our possessions with us and warned us to take only what we would be wearing on our backs. Whatever we had, we gave to the Rosen family and the family that moved in with us. We planned to leave the second week in November by marching out of the Krzemieniec ghetto with a working commando. When it got dark, we would escape into the adjoining forest. A couple of hours later, we would walk about three kilometers to the Krzemieniec railroad station to board the nine o'clock train to Lvov. From Lvov, we would board a train to Warsaw.

It was Wednesday before we could volunteer for a working commando unloading German war material. We took as much food as would fit into our pockets without being noticeable, and we said good-bye to the Rosens, to whom we had become attached. Mrs. Rosen and Sara cried and wished us a safe and successful trip back home. At seven o'clock in the morning, we marched out the ghetto gate toward the German army depot about two kilometers from town. At the depot, a German assigned Mietek and me to pulling loaded wagons from the unloaded army trucks to the depot barracks. Father, because he spoke German, was assigned inside the barracks to inventory the incoming supplies.

Pulling a loaded cart was not terribly hard work, except that it was cold. At noon, the Germans rolled out a large soup kettle and ladled out bowls of watery soup with a few slices of beets floating in them to each of us. Eating it with a few bites of Mrs. Rosen's bread lessened the hunger that was beginning to pain me. It was five o'clock in the evening and already dark when Father came out and told us that it was time to sneak into the forest. We would leave five or ten minutes apart and make sure that no one noticed. I made believe I had to urinate and nonchalantly walked toward the forest. When I saw that no one noticed me, I ran into the forest and hid behind a large pine tree while I waited for Father and Mietek to join me. Within ten minutes we were together and began to walk deep into the forest.

The interior of the pine forest looked mysterious to me. The earth was covered with white snow, and the tree branches were bent from its weight. Occasionally, a light blast of wind would shake the branches, sending a shower of snow floating to the ground, and sometimes a bird would announce its presence, or sometimes a grunting of animals could be heard from afar. Otherwise there was silence.

We rested on a fallen tree trunk and congratulated ourselves on our successful escape. We removed the yellow patches on our clothing that identified us as Jews, or we would not be able to travel anywhere, especially by train. Then we headed through the forest to Krzemieniec railroad station, to wait for the nine o'clock train to Lvov. The station had not changed from the time we arrived there from Białystok. There were half a dozen people sitting and sleeping on the benches, and no one paid any attention to us. Half an hour later our guide arrived but stood against a wall opposite us. None of us attempted to meet or even look at him, because we had previously agreed to make first contact after we reached Lvov.

We sat on a bench with our heads down, the collars of our coats up, and our hats down on our foreheads, pretending to sleep. We still had a two-hour wait, provided the train arrived on time. Every minute we spent sitting in that station felt like an hour. Every time someone came in or left the waiting room, I shivered. I remembered the Germans saying that Jews found not wearing the yellow patch would be shot, and the same fate would befall any Jew traveling outside the ghetto. We knew the German Gestapo was offering a liter of vodka and money to those who brought in or denounced a Jew for whatever offense the Gestapo described. Many Ukrainians knew me and Mietek from school, and they knew Father from work during the Soviet regime. It was very dangerous for us.

By eight o'clock that morning, the waiting room was filling up with Ukrainian farmers carrying sacks and baskets of varied products, and most of them were smoking *machorka*. Harsh smoke filled the waiting room and made some of us choke and our eyes tear. We overheard them say that the Germans would create an independent Ukrainian state for them and get rid of the Jews.

Suddenly the entrance door to the waiting room was thrown open, and four uniformed German SS men and two Ukrainian policemen marched in, their heavy boots striking the floor with a noise like gunshots. In the middle of the room they stopped and looked around. All conversation in the room stopped, and a weary silence prevailed. *"Wo sind die Juden?"* screamed one of the SS men, and the Ukrainian translated: "Where are the Jews?"

The blood drained from my head as I looked up at the Germans. Father put his hand over mine and held it tight. One of the Ukrainian policemen looked in our direction, and pointing a finger at us said in Ukrainian: "There are the filthy Jews."

Two of the SS men pulled their pistols from their holsters and pointing them at us, screamed in German: *"Auf und raus"* (Get up and get out). As we all got up, fast, the two Ukrainians grabbed my and Mietek's coat sleeves and pulled us toward the exit door while Father was pushed by the two SS men who were pointing their pistols at him. Outside the door stood a large farmer's sleigh with two horses harnessed to it. The Ukrainians pushed us and Father to the sled while they and the four SS men, pistols drawn, sat on the sled's two benches.

The sled took off on the snow-covered road toward the town, the small bells hanging from the horses' necks ringing merrily, but to me it was the sound of doom. A thousand thoughts were running through my head. Who was it that recognized and denounced us? Was it our guide who got paid half of the money before we even started on the trip? He was not arrested with us.

The sled stopped in front of the former station house of the Soviet secret service. We were ordered to get out of the sled and forced to run into an interior room of the house. Except for a table in the middle of the room and a few wooden chairs, the room was empty.

We were made to stand against a wall and waited to find out what would happen next. A heavy-set SS officer entered the room, holding a short leather whip in his right hand. He walked very close to Father, their faces only inches apart, and looked directly into his eyes. In a soft whisper, he asked Father, "Are you a Jew?"

Father replied in a positive voice, "No, we are Polish," and handed the SS man our forged Polish identification papers. The SS man made a swift hit of his whip across the outstretched hand holding the documents and knocked them out of Father's hand.

"Don't you lie to me, you dirty Jew, or I'll kill you right here!" he barked at Father and reached for his holstered pistol. "Drop your pants. Let's see if you are a Pole or a Jew," he ordered.

Seeing that there was no way out of it, Father quietly stated, "Yes, we are Jews from Warsaw, trying to get back to our family in the Warsaw ghetto."

The SS man laughed and hit Father with the whip across the face. "You tried to lie to me, you dirty Jew, and thought that you'd get away with it," he barked. "No Jew will ever succeed." He looked at all of us with a hateful smirk on his lips and then left the room. After the SS man left, I stood there shaking, tears running down my face, seeing Father's bleeding face. Mietek stood there quietly crying. In a whisper,

Father tried to cheer us up, reminding us that they hadn't yet killed us and that as long as we were alive we had a chance to survive.

Soon we were pushed into a brightly lit cell that held only one wooden bench. We sat down on the bench in total silence. Though the hour was well past midnight, we could not sleep. Every half hour a Ukrainian would enter the cell to check on us and curse us for keeping him awake. What would happen to us? What would these beasts do to us?

Early the next morning, a Ukrainian entered the cell and took away our sheepskin overcoats and gloves; he ordered us out into the cold, where we stood shivering for about an hour. Then a large, horse-drawn sled with two uniformed Germans sitting on the driver's bench pulled up. One of the Germans screamed at us to get in and sit on a middle bench. Two Ukrainian guards sat on the rear bench, so that we were sandwiched between them.

The sled, with its merrily ringing bells, started running up Main Street in the direction of the jail. Suddenly I saw Hanka, my school friend, walking on the side of the road, and as the sled came near her, she must have seen me. She stopped and looked at me, bewildered. That was the last time I ever saw her.

We entered the gates of the same jail where the Ukrainians had murdered hundreds of Jews and were ordered out of the sled. We entered the building, where guards searched us and took away everything they found. They made us run along a corridor into a cell, about six meters by six meters, packed with other Jewish prisoners, most of them standing. There were no benches or beds of any sort, and only a few prisoners sat on the floor or leaned against the wall.

There were 40 prisoners in that cell, in a space that should hold no more than 10. The cell had one small window with steel bars and a part of the glass was broken, letting in the cold. The walls of the cell were bare concrete and so was the floor. From the ceiling hung one bare electric bulb that threw dim light around us.

When the cell door closed, the prisoners questioned us. Why were we arrested? We told them, over and over again, and asked others why they were there. One man was captured outside the ghetto for picking frozen potatoes from a field. Another was arrested for being a few minutes late for work, and others were in for being on the street after curfew. All had committed minor infringements, but by German order, we were all guilty of capital crimes. Some of the prisoners, who had been held for several months, looked starved.

The food for the day was a bowl of thin beet soup and a slice of black bread. The Germans had taken all our extra food away after they captured us. All the prisoners were dirty and smelled of stale perspiration. In one corner stood a metal bucket full of urine, with some spilled on the floor around it, adding to the stink that made me sick.

Suddenly from the back of the cell someone called out, "Adam!" The person who called my name was my former Soviet high school French teacher. I pushed my way through to him and we embraced.

"Why are you here?" I asked.

He told me, "Coming from work outside the ghetto, I tried to get some potatoes and carrots from a farmer when they captured me." I cannot recall his name, but I remember his high spirits and the black sense of humor he used to cope with our situation. He told the story of a young Jew in Czarist Russia about to be inducted into the Czar's army who thought aloud:

> If they will reject me, that will be fine, but if they induct me into the Czar's army, I'll have two ways out. Either they'll send me to the front, or they'll keep me in the rear. If they keep me in the rear that will be fine, but if they send me to the front, I'll have two ways out. Either I'll kill the enemy, or the enemy will kill me. If I kill the enemy, that will be fine, but if the enemy kills me, I'll have two ways out. Either I'll go to heaven, or I'll go to hell. If I go to heaven that's fine, but if I go to hell I'll have two ways out. Either I'll eat the devil, or the devil will eat me. If I eat the devil that'll be fine, but if the devil eats me, I have only one way out.

He was trying to keep me from sinking into depression and despair in the dire situation we were in, as if there were two ways out, even in our situation. There wasn't enough space in the cell to lie down, so we sat on the concrete floor, back-to-back, to support each other while trying to doze off. As hard as it was, after a while, I fell asleep.

About six o'clock early the next morning, our daily routine began. We were awakened by the Ukrainian guards, who were banging on the metal door and screaming, "Wake up now you dirty Jews, or I will teach you a lesson!"

Half dead, we were run out of the cell into the long prison corridor, where the guard gave each of us a large, empty glass bottle and ordered us to our knees. Holding the bottle at an angle, we were told to press the bottom edge of the bottle into the wooden floor, and by moving the bottle back and forth, leave a shiny streak on the wood. By repeating this movement, millimeter by millimeter, the floor began to shine, but after four hours of this work, the pain in our backs and knees was unbearable.

While we worked, the guard screamed and whipped us. About noon, the work stopped and we were given a small bowl of watery beet soup and a slice of bread. Then we were allowed to urinate into the bucket in the cell.

Half an hour later, the guard opened the cell door and ordered us to bring the overflowing urine bucket to the outhouse. Woe to the two prisoners ordered by the guard to carry it. Inevitably, urine would spill on them as they rushed to the outhouse, while the Ukrainians hit and kicked them to make them move faster. When they returned to the cell with the empty bucket, the prisoners would form a line in front of it, and in minutes, it was full again. We would bang on the door for the guard to let us empty it, and we would have to repeat this two or three times before we could empty the bucket again. Some men, unable to hold back, urinated on the floor, adding to the misery of body lice eating us day and night.

Then we were locked back in the cell for the rest of the day. The floor "bottling" routine, as it was called by the guards, continued day after day. After a week, most of the prisoners, including Father, could hardly stand up from the pain.

Trying to sleep on the concrete floor through the cold nights, we would often wake to help others stand up—they were so weak, they had no strength of their own and would fall when they tried to get up on their own.

No one in the cell had any idea what would happen to us, or how long they would keep us there. The hard, painful work, lack of food, and the lack of sanitary conditions began to work on our psyches, and we grew more and more depressed. Would we ever get out of there alive? There was not even an iota of hope among the prisoners.

From outside our small window, we could hear noises of hammering and digging. Climbing on Mietek's shoulders to peer through the broken window, I saw prisoners using heavy wooden beams to create a structure similar to a frame for a child's swing. No one could figure out what they were doing.

Yet.

Father, despite his constant pain, tried to cheer up Mietek and me by reminding us how we always managed to survive dangerous situations and that we must have hope. He reminded us of the Warsaw bombardment and our escape from the city, through the country and across the river. As hard as it was to believe him this time, Mietek and I always trusted Father and knew that somehow, he would get us out of this, too.

CHAPTER 9

In our cell, the days dragged by. The cold wind, sometimes carrying snow, blew into the cell through the broken window, adding to our misery. There was no place we could wash ourselves and we felt like caged animals, unable even to lick ourselves clean. The smell of the unwashed bodies was overwhelming, even though we got somewhat used to it.

The "bottling" routine, repeated day after day in the cold, made our lives unendurable. Even my former French teacher, who had tried so hard to cheer us up, went silent. There was noise from the construction project directly outside the window until one day, the noise stopped.

In the last week of November 1941, just as darkness fell on a bitter cold night, the door to the cell was thrown open and an SS man entered the cell with two Ukrainian guards. He referred to a sheet of paper and called out names of prisoners, ordering them to step outside. Twenty people were called out, and then they all left.

No one knew what was happening. Would there be a trial? Would we find out how long we would remain in confinement? As tired as we all were, we stayed awake wondering. A strong, nasty wind blowing across the metal roof of the jail made loud, vibrating, whistling sounds.

Two hours howled slowly by until the door of the cell was suddenly opened and the guard ordered us all out. Two SS men and several Ukrainian guards screamed at us while they hit us with whips and rifle butts to force us out of the building, on the run, into the prison yard, which was surrounded by high stone walls. As we rounded the corner, four of our cellmates stood before us, naked in the relentless cold. There was a heap of clothing before them.

The SS men continued to scream. Four more of our cellmates, all naked, were hanging on ropes from the gallows they had built beneath our cell window. Under them lay several more naked bodies, with lengths of the hanging rope still attached to their necks.

Still screaming their guttural German, the SS men ordered us to pair up and get hold of the dead corpses' legs, drag them about 61 meters to a pit near the prison wall, and throw them in. The Ukrainians whipped and kicked us back to the gallows and forced us to pick up the remaining corpses, which now included the four cellmates we had seen standing there when we first came around the bend.

The SS and Ukrainians forced us to the other side of the building, where we were ordered to the undressing point. When I turned the corner, I noticed a small shed with an open door and ducked inside as our group ran past it. I held my breath, waiting, but no one noticed, and the whole group, including Father, Mietek, and the guards, ran past the shed.

I didn't know if Father or Mietek had seen me hide. I was terrified, and my heart beat so loud and fast, I could hear it. The shed was about two meters by two meters, and about two meters high. In the middle of the ceiling was a 60-centimeter by 60-centimeter opening to the attic. I reached for the edges and pulled myself up into the space and waited. No one followed or came looking for me.

I heard the muffled screams of the SS and Ukrainian guards, and then the cries of the victims, as they called out in Hebrew, *"Shema Yisrael Adonoy Eloheynu Adonoy Ehod"* (Hear O Israel, the Lord Is Our God, the Lord Is One). It was the ancient prayer of our people; we said it at least four or five times a day, for thousands of years, in our daily lives and when we faced death at the hands of our enemies.

That cold night, it was the last cry of the murdered, including my Father and my brother Mietek. Except for the malicious wind that continued its bizarre noise through the corrugated tin roof, it was still for a while. Then I heard women's voices that grew in volume as they realized their fate. The SS and the Ukrainians screamed even louder, but the women's cries of *Shema Yisrael* pierced through the pandemonium.

I lay, shaking, on the attic floor. I don't know how many women prisoners they executed, but the shouting lasted a long time. Again, at last, except for the wind, it became quiet.

Between the slanted roof of the shed and the attic floor was an opening large enough for a body to slip through. I looked through it and saw the top of a brick wall no more than a foot away. I thought it was the prison wall, and crawled out, only to discover that it was some unfinished construction inside the prison proper. The prison wall was another 12 to 15 meters away. As I looked around from my vantage point, I realized that no one was out in the open, and that the lights in the guard towers were out. I quietly slid down the wall to the ground and looked around.

The prison wall was about 4.5 meters high and built of large fieldstones. Without a ladder or rope, it would be impossible for me to escape. Looking down, I noticed a wooden wheelbarrow partially buried in the snow nearby. I dug it out with my bare hands and noticed it was missing its wheel.

Crawling, I dragged the wheelbarrow to the prison wall. The noisy wind covered any sounds I made and the wall under construction hid me from the guard tower. I stood the wheelbarrow up against the wall and set the two long handles in the snow, with the barrel box against the wall. On my first try climbing the box, I slid and fell. I lay in the snow for a few minutes and held my breath as I waited to see if anyone saw or heard my fall. Nothing.

I climbed the box again, more carefully, but I wasn't tall enough to reach the top. I needed to lift myself at least another 30 centimeters. I crawled around in the snow, looking for something I could use. I found a bucket filled with some frozen substance. I brought it back to the wall, waited to see if anyone noticed me, and then carefully lifted and placed the frozen bucket on top of the barrel box. Then I tried to climb the contraption, but fell, with the bucket, back into the snow. I was gripped with fear, as again, I held my breath and prayed I hadn't been caught. Obviously, the wheelbarrow/bucket combination would not work. I noticed a pile of dirt had been dumped against the wall during construction. It was close to a meter high and fully exposed to the guard towers and prison yard. I had an idea and I had no choice. I had to take a chance.

On my knees, I dragged the wheelbarrow to the exposed wall and placed it on top of the dirt heap. I slowly climbed the wheelbarrow box and stood up, stretching my arms to the top of the wall. My hands gripped its edge and with all my strength, with my leather, square-toed ski boots scrabbling for an edge, I hoisted myself to the top of the wall and lay there for a moment, listening. Then I flipped over to the outside of the jail wall and dropped down.

The open field in front of me was bare of any growth and covered with snow. There was no way could I cross that field and not be noticed. The only way out was to stay low and close to the wall and make my way to the front gate, then to crawl or run through the evergreen trees that grew on both sides of the road that led to Main Street. I don't know how, but I made it.

I crossed the main road and headed toward the woods and the river. I ran on the river ice in order not to leave footprints in the soft snow. A few miles downriver toward the town, I spotted a barn and climbed into the loft, where I buried myself in the hay. My fingers, ears, and nose were completely frozen and the tips of my fingers felt like wood, but no amount of rubbing relieved them. Exhausted, I fell asleep and suddenly woke from a terrible nightmare at dawn. I realized I had to get out before the farmer came in to do chores, so I sneaked back to the forest and, shaking from the cold, continued running along the river toward the town and the ghetto.

Sneaking into the ghetto was easy. The fence surrounding it was made of wooden boards that were easily removable, and I lifted one up and squeezed through the opening. Then I went to the house of the ghetto leader, my father's friend. He was shocked when he saw me without my coat, shivering on his doorstep. He quickly pulled me inside, covered me with a coat he grabbed off a hook near the door, and yelled for his wife to boil some water and bring food.

Everyone knew we'd been arrested by the Gestapo and brought to the jail. He asked me how I made it back and what had happened. I told him how they had tortured us and how I had hidden when they came to hang us. He and his wife cried for the loss of their friends and my father and brother. Though they themselves did not have enough food, they had sent food packages to the prison. I had to tell them the sad truth—that the Ukrainians had probably stolen the food, because the packages had never been distributed.

I was able to take a warm bath and was given an overcoat, a woolen hat, and a pair of old eyeglasses to disguise my appearance. His wife threw away my vermin-infested clothing, cooked me a thick potato soup, and gave me a slice of bread. For me, it was a feast. After I ate, we talked some more, and after I described the horror of the prison, he told me what had been going on in the ghetto.

Things had gotten worse since my arrest. The Jewish men doing forced labor for the Germans were constantly beaten, and if a German didn't like someone, he could shoot him on sight. We decided that staying in the synagogue's crowded main room was probably my safest bet. I agreed to stay there for a day or two, until I worked out a plan to get to Warsaw and my mother and sister.

The synagogue was almost as crowded as the jail cell. Families with small children lay on the bare floors, protected from the cold by the few pieces of clothing they were able to salvage. It was pitiful. Small babies cried, clinging to their mothers. Old men and women squatted on the floor, their heads sagging with despair; sick people were moaning, and no one had hope.

I could not sleep. I lay on the bare floor and the pictures of the execution ran through my head. Twice I dozed off from sheer exhaustion but woke up shaking. I had to get out of there fast, or I would go crazy. I was too close to the jail. The next morning I asked several men how to get to the railroad station beyond the one in Krzemieniec. One of the men had worked for the railroad under the Soviets and sketched a map to a secure railroad station about 20 kilometers away. A train to Lvov usually left the station nightly at 9:10. I began to plan my escape from the ghetto.

By midday, the forced-labor working commandos were gone from the ghetto. I left the synagogue wearing the glasses, pulling the knit cap low on my face to make it harder to recognize me. In full daylight, I went to see the ghetto leader, whose frightened wife let me in and admonished me for not waiting until dark.

"If the Germans find out we hid you, they will kill us. What do you want?" I told her I wanted to get out of the ghetto but needed some money to purchase a railroad ticket, and I didn't have any. She said she would speak to her husband as soon as he got back, but that I needed to return to the shul immediately. I didn't tell her how and where I planned to go, in case she was questioned. Before I left, she gave me a few slices of bread and some farmer cheese.

As I ran back to the synagogue, I hid my face in my collar, pretending that I was cold. I divided the bread and cheese into four chunks and gave three pieces to the poor mothers holding their hungry babies. I ate my piece as I sat in a corner against the wall, totally exhausted from the sleepless night, and promptly fell asleep.

I woke up when someone pulled on my coat sleeve. He asked me my given name, and making sure that no one could hear him, whispered that he came from the ghetto leader and handed me a small package. He also told me that the ghetto leader said that my name was now Abe Goldstein and I had been assigned to a working commando that would leave the ghetto the next morning at eight o'clock. I was to meet the rest of the group at the ghetto gates.

I unwrapped the small package under my coat and I found a few banknotes that I stuffed inside my boots. The enclosed note read: *"Mit mazel"* (with luck). I wrapped myself in the overcoat and went back to sleep, trying not to think about the risks I was taking. It was still night when I woke up. Without a watch I couldn't tell what time it was. The few small lightbulbs threw a foglike atmosphere over the multitude of bodies lying curled up on the floor. The only sounds were the whimpering of children and the soft moaning of the old and sick. Carefully, I climbed over the people and made my way to the door. A Jewish guard posted outside leaned against the wall, half asleep. He jumped awake when he heard the door close with a whining sound and saw me.

"Who are you, and where are you going? You cannot leave the synagogue during the night," he said.

"What time is it?" I asked. "I have to be at the ghetto gate at eight o'clock." He looked at his watch. "It's only five o'clock, go back to sleep."

"I can't sleep anymore. Mind if I stay here with you?" I asked. "I don't have a watch and I don't want to miss the eight o'clock assembly." I said.

"OK," he said, "what's your name?" "Abe, Abe Goldstein," I said. "What's yours?"

"Moyshe, from a little shtetl next to Krzemieniec. I took the job of a watchman for an extra portion of bread for my family," he said. For the next two hours he told me about family life in the shtetl before the Germans came, and how the Germans and the Ukrainians forced them out without giving them time to take any possessions. He sounded depressed, had nothing for his family, and had no way of knowing, any more than the rest of us, what would happen next.

My mind was wholly occupied with planning my escape from the labor commando and my trip to Warsaw. The train travel, I was told, was very dangerous, especially for me. There were constant document checks on those trains, and I had no documents. At best I could say my wallet and my papers had been stolen at the station while I slept. I didn't think it would work because I didn't look, or dress, like a Ukrainian peasant, nor did I sound like a Ukrainian native. In my mind I had no choice but to take the chance and go.

At eight o'clock in the morning, the working commando marched out of the ghetto. As we approached the gate, I realized the Ukrainian guard facing us and counting the column was the guard who participated in the hangings at the jail. I pulled the woolen cap almost over my eyes and lowered my head; then I breathed a sigh of relief as we marched through without being stopped. My luck held.

We stopped on the road next to a forest, were given spades and ordered to fill potholes on the road caused by heavy tanks. The work was not too hard for me, but I was just waiting for the right moment to flee. As night fell, I pretended I had to relieve myself, walked into the woods, and disappeared. I hid, flat on the ground behind a fallen tree, and waited to see if anyone would look for me.

After about an hour, I heard the commando ordered to leave the roadwork and marched back to town. I tore the yellow star off my coat and, in almost total darkness, walked in the forest along the roads mapped out for me by the Jew in the synagogue. Tired and cold, I finally arrived at the station and carefully peered through the window. The big clock in the waiting room said it was half past eight, and the room was almost empty of passengers. I decided it would be safer to wait in the woods and board the train at the last moment, as it pulled out. In the woods I tried to stay warm by running in place.

At last I heard an approaching train and the sigh of its whistle as it came into the station. It was already full of passengers, and the few Ukrainians waiting there had to jump on the steps leading to the wagons and hang on to the handrails. As the train slowly began moving, I ran toward it and landed on a step next to a huge Ukrainian peasant woman who hung on for dear life with one hand and held a large basket in the other.

As the train picked up speed, the woman, in carefully selected Ukrainian, described the passengers inside the wagon and demanded they squeeze together a little more and make room for her or they would be sorry later. Laughing, the people managed to create a space, and she then pushed me in front of her and we were in.

I was in the safest place on the train, pressed up against this woman. No Ukrainian police or German SS could ever get inside the wagon to check anyone's papers. The huge Ukrainian woman talked without stopping during the entire trip to Lvov, telling funny stories and jokes, and everyone laughed and egged her on. She stopped only to eat. When she reached into her basket for a large piece of bread and cheese, she looked at me.

"You are so skinny, you must be hungry," she said. She broke the bread and cheese, and gave half to me. I thanked her for her kindness, and hungry as I was, I swallowed the bread and cheese in a few bites, then pretended to fall asleep to avoid conversation. After two stops at small villages, the train arrived at Lvov's main railroad station. I jumped off and mixed with the hundreds of people who had luggage or boxes of all sorts. I noticed several German and Ukrainian police milling about and looking at the people. Near me sat a Ukrainian family with two children and a large wooden box. Slowly I moved toward them and asked if I could sit on the box for a while to relieve the pain in my sick hip. The father looked at me carefully.

"Sit down, but don't touch my children," he said, perhaps thinking I might infect them. I sat on the box and faced them, pretending I was part of his family. Hundreds of thoughts ran through my head. How could I find out which train was going to Warsaw, and when, without being noticed by the police? Should I get up and get the ticket to Warsaw now, or get on the train without it? Either way was dangerous for me, so I decided to wait and see.

As I sat on the wooden crate, a station loudspeaker announced, first in German, then in Ukrainian and Polish, over and over, that the express train on track number five was leaving for Warsaw in 15 minutes, and that it was only for Germans. Only for Germans.

I was sitting on the crate no more than 15 meters from track number five and looking at the train. When I heard the engine let off a blast of steam that signaled the train was ready to start, I jumped off the box and, limping slightly, moved as quickly as I could toward it. Just as it moved out of the station, I jumped on the running board that ran the full length of the car and squatted on it, hoping not to be seen by the police.

As the train picked up speed, I stood up on the running board and looked through the door window into the cabin. It was empty, but I decided to hang on a little longer. The train was now running at full speed and I was being buffeted by a fierce cold wind. The cabin was still empty, so I slowly turned the handle and opened the door. Again my luck—and my strength—held, when a strong wind suddenly swung the door open and could have knocked me off the train.

I climbed through the door and, with all my strength against the wind, pulled it shut. I was in a first-class cabin, with soft upholstered benches and footstools. I sat on a soft bench in a corner near the window and dozed off. I started awake when the door from an adjoining cabin opened and a uniformed man with a large briefcase came in and sat down opposite me.

I looked at him with half-open eyes and expected the worst. His uniform sleeve had a black band with the description in German "Organisation Todt." From the little Yiddish I had learned, the word *toyt,* or *todt* in German, means dead. In my mind he belonged to a German Dead Organization.

The German opened his briefcase, took out a newspaper and a sandwich, and calmly proceeded to eat while he read the paper. Not once did he speak or look from behind the paper at me. Just before we reached the Warsaw station he got up, put the newspaper back into his briefcase, and left the compartment. I was concerned he might report me to the police, but nothing happened.

Later I found out that the Organisation Todt was a German labor battalion named after the Nazi armament minister, Todt. Luckily for me, the "for the Germans only" train didn't have a conductor to check the tickets, because Germans traveled free. As the train pulled into the Warsaw station, just before it stopped, I opened the door and jumped off.

The station was packed with people—Poles and uniformed Germans. It was easy for me to mix in and get out on the streets; it was midday and they were full of pedestrians. I knew Warsaw because my friends and I had often roamed the city before the war, looking for innocent adventures. I quickly oriented myself and headed toward Ogrodowa Street, where we used to live.

As I walked, I saw a large group of men marching down the street, wearing white armbands with blue Stars of David. Realizing they were a Jewish working commando, I joined their column and asked the fellow next to me where they were headed.

"To the ghetto," he said, "after 12 hours of road building. Why are you trying to join us?"

"I want to enter the ghetto, and I can't tell you why," I answered.

"Stay with us and you'll get in. Most Jews want to get out of the ghetto, but you want to get in. I don't understand, but it's your business," he said.

We were approaching the gate on Leszno Street when I saw the wall of the ghetto for the first time. It was made of red bricks and was at least 4.5 meters high with glass shards embedded on the top. At the gate, a booth was manned by a German SS guard holding a rifle and by two Polish policemen armed with guns. On the other side of the gate, inside the ghetto, stood two men with armbands that read "Jewish police"; they held wooden sticks. The column was stopped at the gate while the German SS man and Polish police walked between the rows of the column and looked at each man to see if he was trying to smuggle food or other products into the ghetto. Because they didn't find anything, they let us in.

How would I tell Mother about Father and Mietek? It was tearing me apart. It was a very cold, gray, and nasty day in December 1941, and dirty snow covered most of the streets. The atmosphere reflected the grim situation of the Jews.

CHAPTER 10

The labor column marched into the ghetto and dispersed. As I walked toward Ogrodowa Street, I was shocked by what I saw. The sidewalks and the roadway were full of people, some in rags, cocooned in remnants of blankets, their shoeless feet wrapped in newspaper, their thin and shaking hands outstretched as they begged for food or help of any kind. Others, men and women reasonably well dressed, walked swiftly, as if trying to get off the crowded, depressing street. Others walked by like lost souls, constantly on the watch for unexpected danger.

On the sidewalks, little children and babies lay covered in rags, shivering, holding each other and crying. Everyone—men, women, and even children—wore the white armband with the blue Star of David. Everywhere, homeless families huddled with their children against the buildings, starvation on their faces. In shock, I ran toward our apartment house. It was only two blocks away, but I couldn't bear seeing what was going on in the streets.

I was home at last. I ran up the staircase, three steps at a time, to the third floor, to our apartment. For a moment I stood in front of the door I had not seen for more than two years. I was home. With some hesitation, I rang the bell, but nothing happened. I rang it again, but I couldn't hear the ring, so I softly knocked on the door a few times and waited. The door opened a crack and an older woman I did not recognize peered out suspiciously and asked in a raspy voice: "Who are you, and what do you want?"

"I am the son of Sara," I said. "I have come back after two years. Does she live

here, and is she home?" I asked. "Yes, she lives here," she said, "but she is out selling handkerchiefs. Come in and wait. She should be back soon."

I followed her into Mina's bedroom.

"This is your mother's room," she said. "You can wait here. By the way my name
is Celina."

"Is it also my sister Mina's bedroom?" I asked her.

"You will have to talk to your mother," she said. As she walked away I suddenly
felt something was wrong. I'd have to find out from Mother what was going on
and where Mina was.

The room I was in had always been Mina's bedroom. I had fond memories of
it. As a child of six, I had fallen asleep in there many times as I read my books and
would wake the next morning, tucked into her bed. When she was away, I used to
sneak in there and read books that were forbidden to me. When we had parties in
the apartment, she would ask me to dance, even though I was at least seven or
more years younger than her friends. She always coached me in my Latin homework,
in French, and in writing Polish compositions. She was beautiful, full of life, and
had a sparkle in her eyes. Before the war, when we walked together on the streets
of Warsaw, or during vacation in some summer resort, I was proud when I noticed
men stopping to look at her, to tip their hats or wave a hand in greeting. She was
my favorite and I adored her.

Mina's bedroom was located at the end of a long corridor that led to the master
bedroom, Mietek's and my bedroom, the living room, and the dining room. Each
of the rooms was now occupied by different families.

Mina's room contained a narrow metal bed, covered by a blanket. Next to it was
a small round table covered with a tablecloth Mother had crocheted a long time
ago. On top of it sat framed photographs of Father, Mietek, Mina, and me. Against
one wall stood a long narrow table partially covered in a white sheet; on top lay
several pressed handkerchiefs. The walls were bare of any pictures; the floor was
partially covered by an old, worn rug.

I walked to the window and looked down at the street below. The view brought
back memories of my carefree childhood there. Other kids and I used to play soccer
on that street, and I often skinned my knees when I fell on the stone. I remembered
how we raced our bicycles down Ogrodowa Street while we dodged autos and
horse carriages. Sometimes on Sunday nights, when no one was home, a couple of

friends and I would lie stomach-down on our third-floor balcony and drop water-filled paper bags on the sidewalk in front of walking couples, splattering them. That had been the extent of our mischief.

Once I unwittingly dropped a water bomb in front of someone who turned out to be a high police official, who figured out from which balcony it had been tossed. Within minutes he was ringing our bell, banging on the door, screaming to open up or he would break it down. We were too scared to move. Finally he threatened to be back the next day and he left. He showed up the next day, as promised, and our parents punished us.

I would often get into fights with the Polish kids who called me a "dirty kike," and threw stones and empty bottles at me. I would come home to wash off my bloody nose and my other cuts. Mother never asked how I got myself so bloodied. She only helped me clean up. Now, when I looked down, I saw our bedraggled, starving people. The walls of the apartment building fronts were lined with carts filled with old books and housewares that children were trying to sell. Starved adults held items in their hands and tried to sell them to passersby. Skinny boys pedaled rickshaws carrying one or two passengers down the middle of the street, threading their way through the masses of people. The suffering was palpable; it was everywhere. Among the crowds I saw the ghetto militia. They wore military hats and held truncheons in their hands. I could not stand looking at the shocking scene any more and turned away from the window.

Mina's room contained some of its original furniture. The armoire in light blue lacquer still stood in its place, and next to it stood her narrow writing desk, reminding me of all the times she had helped me with my homework. My favorite place used to be at her desk with my elbows supporting my head in my hands while I was totally engrossed in some book. When I looked into the closet, besides a couple of Mother's dresses, were Mina's favorite summer flowered dress, Father's brown business suit, and Mietek's sport jacket and pants. I was surprised to find my old school uniform. I tried on the jacket, but it was much too small for me—I had grown substantially in those last two years. I held the jacket on its hanger in front of me and thought again of better times.

During the school semester we had to wear our uniform in and out of school. It was navy blue, with a double-breasted jacket and silver buttons. The pants had a light blue narrow band running down the side seams and along the jacket cuffs.

A small light blue shield was sewn on the left sleeve near the shoulder, with the school number, 94, embroidered on it. You got into trouble if you were caught out of uniform or out after the 10 p.m. student curfew.

It was getting dark when I heard the outside door close, and then Mother walked into the room. For a moment she stood stock-still and silent, staring at me. My once beautiful, vivacious, always smiling mother stood there before me, bent with grief, her once shiny brown hair now totally white and pulled back tightly. A long, gray, nondescript dress hung on her thin frame. The small package she held in her hand fell to the floor, and handkerchiefs spilled out of it.

Tears streamed down her face as she stood there looking at me. After what seemed to me an hour she whispered softly: "God, is it really you Adek?" We ran toward each other with tears on our faces and silently hugged. I felt the thinness of her body pressed against mine and felt her silent sobbing.

After a while she stepped away from me and looked me up and down, "You have grown a lot. You look like a man," she said, "not the little boy I remember. What has happened to your hair? Why is it cut so short?"

"I had hair lice," I lied, "so I cut it to get rid of them. I am fine now." Suddenly she looked sharply at me and asked, "Where are Father and Mietek? Why aren't they here?"

"They could not get out of the Krzemieniec ghetto with me," I said. "I escaped. Soon perhaps they will be able to get out. Meanwhile they send you and Mina all their love." As I answered her, I pretended to fix a shoelace. I couldn't look into her eyes. To change the subject I asked her, "Where is Mina? Is she working late?"

Looking down at the floor she whispered so softly that I could hardly hear her, "Mina is dead."

"What happened to her?" I cried out. "How did she die?"

"She died of typhoid fever last year," Mother said. "There was an epidemic in the ghetto and thousands of people died. We had no medicine. The rumor was that the Germans had purposely infected the ghetto to kill our people."

She began to cry again. "I sat with her and held her hand, while she was fading away from me," she whispered. "I never thought that I would ever see any of you again."

"I am here Mama," I said. "We will go on together, no matter what." We sat on the edge of the bed and held each other as it became dark. I was torn up by the news that my vivacious Mina was dead. And yet how great must have been my mother's pain, all alone in this horror, watching Mina get sicker and sicker, unable to help her. From then on, I determined I would be her total support system and her ray of hope. Together we would do the best we could to survive.

Exhausted, I lay down and closed my eyes but couldn't fall asleep. Mother lay down next to me and held me tight. Not a word passed between us. Finally I must have fallen asleep. I woke up startled with the morning sun on my face and Mother lying next to me, still embracing me. We got up, washed up a bit, and sat by the desk for a bite of bread and ersatz tea. The black bread tasted like it was filled with sawdust, which it probably was, but on my empty stomach it felt good. Mother asked me about our life in the Soviet zone, and why we did not write. She had tried very hard to find us, but without success.

I told her we had written letters to her and Mina, and that we'd also sent food packages. Evidently the Germans never forwarded them. There was no other way for us to communicate from the Soviet zone. I told her about how we had to be very careful not to let anyone know that Father had been a factory owner. We could not travel to our factory in Novojelnia, now a part of the Soviet republic of Belorussia. I said that was why we settled in Krzemieniec in the Soviet Ukraine, where we were safe. Father, I told her, was working in a state-managed fruit-and-vegetable combine, in charge of a sauerkraut and pickling plant. Both Mietek and I went to school.

"The life for us was not hard there except that we missed you and Mina terribly," I lied. "Our only dream and wish was that the war would soon end and we would be together again. News from the German-occupied part of Poland, and especially from Warsaw, was very rare. We only heard that the Germans were forcing the Jews into ghettos, including in Warsaw, and that the life in those ghettos was very hard. It made us very worried about you and Mina and the rest of our family."

I made up a story of how I escaped from the Krzemieniec ghetto and traveled on a German train to Warsaw. I told her how Father and Mietek would try again to get out and come to Warsaw. I asked her then what was she doing. Mother smiled and said she was in the handkerchief business.

"What do you mean 'in the handkerchief business'?" I asked.

"I buy used, dirty handkerchiefs from street urchins who steal them from Polish pedestrians and smuggle them into the ghetto. I wash and iron them and these same kids smuggle them over the wall and sell them to the Poles. We split the profits. Sometimes they bring me small pieces of kielbasa or a couple of eggs I cook and share with them."

"What about grandfather and grandmother, uncles, aunts, cousins?" I asked her. "How are they doing? Are they all well?"

"Everyone is around, thank God, except that we are diminished and broken up. I hope and pray that some day soon we'll be together again. You cannot imagine how happy I am to see you and be with you again. At least a part of my prayers are answered," she replied.

The weather was very cold. No one, including Mother, had any heating fuel, and the room was ice cold. She gave me some of Mietek's old winter clothing, which made the cold a bit more bearable. My solidly frozen fingers and earlobes began to thaw, causing me terrible pain. But I would not let Mother know.

"Let's go out outside," I said. "I feel stifled. I'd like to see what's going on in the street. Is that okay, is it safe?"

"Yes we can go down," she said, "but we must be careful."

It was still early morning, but the streets were full. In addition to the rickshaws, there were pushcarts loaded with personal possessions pulled by stooped men in harnesses. Despite the masses of people, it was silent except for the pleas of beggars and children peddling small possessions. I noticed the only open stores were a shoe-repair shop, a tailor, and a small tearoom that offered ersatz tea and small cookies.

Though some of the people on the street were neatly dressed, their faces showed the stress they were under. Suddenly from an open window came a beautiful sound of a violin playing a Chopin Polonaise. It seemed as if it came from another world. Everybody looked toward the window. It was dangerous to play music. Then the sound stopped and someone closed the window. We came back to the apartment in the early afternoon to be greeted at the entrance door by a woman in a very aggravated state, telling us that an hour earlier, two Germans from the Gestapo came and hounded her with questions about me. She told them that she did not know me, nor had ever seen me, which was the truth. We had never seen each other before.

In a great hurry, Mother and I packed Mietek's few belongings and left the apartment. I would stay with my Aunt and Uncle Iberkleid on the other side of the ghetto. On the street, mother asked me why I was being hunted by the Gestapo. I lied and told her it was because I had escaped from the ghetto, not from my execution.

We arrived at the Iberkleids just before the curfew. Uncle Peter and Aunt Cesia were still living in their old apartment with their two daughters, Lusia, who was about two years younger than I, and Ruth, an infant. Aunt Cesia was my father's sister.

Uncle Peter was now managing a knitwear factory that he had owned before the war. Schultz, a German company, had taken it over according to Nazi law. Before the war, his factory produced silk stockings, high-end sweaters, and socks. Under the Germans, Mother said, all they manufactured were socks and sweaters for the German army.

Aunt and Uncle Iberkleid were surprised but happy to see me. They wanted to know when and how I had returned to Warsaw; where were Father and Mietek? On and on. I promised to tell them all, but first Mother and I told them what had happened and why we were there so suddenly. Aunt Cesia said that it would be fine for me to stay for a while with them, but I would have to sleep on a couch, because they didn't have an extra bed.

Uncle Peter said that he would take me to the factory in the morning and find me a job. That, he said, would protect me from being sent to a forced-labor commando and would get me a food ration card. I told them how I escaped from the ghetto. By then it was late, too late for Mother to return home, so she slept on the couch, and I slept on the floor next to her. The next morning, as we ate a breakfast of bread and margarine with tea, my aunt and uncle continued to ask about the ghetto in Krzemieniec and my escape from it. They wanted to know why I didn't wait for Father and Mietek to get out and why we didn't come to Warsaw together.

I kept repeating the story I had told Mother and added that after escaping, I had waited a whole day and night in the woods for them to get out, but they didn't. It was very dangerous for me to wait any longer, I said, but I was sure that shortly they would escape and come to Warsaw. Mother returned to her apartment and promised to come over again the next day. Uncle Peter told me to rest and the next day we would go to his factory. After Mother left, I asked Aunt Cesia to assemble all the uncles and aunts, but not grandfather or grandmother, because I had something important to tell them. They both became very concerned at my request and kept asking what it was about. I insisted that I wanted to talk to the whole family when they got here and not before. Finally they gave up questioning me and Aunt Cesia got dressed and left to get the family.

While we waited for them to arrive, I told Uncle Peter and Lusia about our life in the Soviet Union. I described how we traveled from Warsaw, Mietek's and my life on the Jewish farm, and life in Białystok and Krzemienec. I told them how we hoped and prayed that someday the war would end and we would return home, and how, when the German army invaded the Soviet Union, our hopes were shattered. I told them about the pogrom by the Ukrainians, the daily persecution by the Germans and Ukrainians, and then about the life in the ghetto.

"I can imagine that your life in the Soviet zone was full of fear that your father could be found to have been an industrialist and in the eyes of the Communists an enemy," Uncle Peter said. "We, here, were from the first day of the German occupation threatened with annihilation, especially since the establishment of the ghetto in October 1940. The Nazis forced tens of thousands of Jews then living outside the ghetto area to leave their possessions behind and move into the ghetto. Then in November 1940, they closed the gates.

"You cannot imagine the tragedy of whole families left on the streets unable to find any housing with the cold winter weather approaching. All the Jews were forced to live in an area of the ghetto that at best could hold maybe a quarter of that number. People moved into attics, cellars, sometimes two families to a room, if they were lucky enough to find one. Still many families couldn't find anything and became homeless, living on the streets."

I listened, depressed by the story. Living in the Soviet zone we had heard of the establishment of the Warsaw ghetto but did not imagine it had been as brutal as it was. I realized how much Mother had suffered living alone after Mina's death, being separated from us, and not knowing if we would ever return. She was always a strong person, but now I realized how brave she was in carrying her burden.

In the early afternoon the family started arriving. First came Fredek, father's youngest brother. Fredek was just a few years older than Mina and very close to us all. He married Marysia a year before the war, and they had a baby girl. We ran to each other and hugged and kissed; he held me while explaining that Marysia had to stay behind to take care of the baby. Then Uncle Sojnek arrived, also alone, because his wife had to care for their baby son, Adam. Again we hugged and kissed. Sojnek was always my favorite uncle. He used to take me to the zoo, play games with me, and always brought packets full of candies whenever he came to visit. Last to arrive were Aunt Tofila and Aunt Rena, my father's sisters, and Aunt Cesia. Rena lived with her parents and had a baby daughter Betty, whom I used to call Betty-Boop, a little blond, blue-eyed doll. They all hugged and kissed me, and asked about Father and Mietek and why they did not come with me.

I asked everybody to sit down and told them that everything I said must be kept confidential, away from Mother. Everyone in the room tensed up. Sojnek was the first to ask, "What happened? Tell us."

"Father and Mietek are dead," I whispered.

Choking with tears both Aunt Rena and Aunt Cesia shouted, "How did this happen? Where? When?"

Sojnek tried to calm them down, though he himself was shaking. "Let him tell us the whole story," he pleaded. Everyone quieted down, except that all my aunts were sobbing.

I described the events of our attempt to return to Warsaw from Krzemienec; our capture by the Gestapo; the subsequent execution of the whole Jewish cell, including Father and Mietek; and my escape. For a while there was silence; everyone was looking at me in bewilderment.

"How do you know they were killed?" Sojnek asked. "You were hiding in the shed and could not see it, isn't that so? They may be still alive in the jail."

"No, I don't think so. I heard from the last group of men. Father and Mietek cried the *Shema Yisrael,* and then I heard the cries of the women being led to their execution."

"But you did not see them for yourself being executed, did you?" Fredek asked. "So how can you be so sure?"

"No, I did not see it," I said, "and I cannot be 100 percent sure."

"It is my opinion that we shouldn't accept the worst as a fact and try to find out directly if they are still alive," Sojnek stated in a strong, positive voice.

"But how can we find out?" I asked. "We are in the Warsaw ghetto, and they were in a Ukrainian jail."

"We'll get Gancwajch to find out; he's got connections to the Germans."

"Who is Gancwajch?" I asked Sojnek.

"Gancwajch is a Jewish agent for the Warsaw Gestapo. For a bribe he can get his friends in the Gestapo to look into it. I know how to get to him, so let's not lose hope yet. But I agree with Adam. Let's not tell Sara, except what Adam told her."

Even though I believed that Sojnek's attempts would fail, and that there were no Jewish survivors in that jail after the execution, when I saw the relief on their faces, I went along with their scheme to find out what happened.

CHAPTER 11

Everyone asked me why we hadn't written to anyone; they said some people in the ghetto got letters from the Soviet zone, but nothing had been received from us. I repeated again how we sent letters and packages to the family, but evidently either the Soviet censors or the Germans did not forward them. We had no way of knowing what happened to the mail and had wondered why we weren't getting replies.

Everyone left while it was still light.

Worn out, I lay down on the couch, fully dressed, and promptly fell asleep. At midnight I suddenly woke up drenched in sweat from a nightmare about the execution, and I couldn't fall asleep again. Thoughts of all the horrors that had befallen our family were running through my mind, especially how my mother was suffering alone in this living hell.

As day broke, I drank a glass of some ersatz tea and ate a slice of bread; then Uncle Peter and I left for the knitting factory. It was located on the second floor of a large commercial building on Leszno Street.

There were several rows of manually driven knitting machines in a large room. Some were round; some, called "sleds," were long. Uncle Peter sat me behind a round knitting machine and proceeded to show me how it worked. The round machines manufactured socks. When the crank was turned, a thread was pulled through a circular row of knitting needles, forming a tubular sock. I soon mastered the process and spent the rest of the day making socks for the Germans.

Getting the job from Uncle Peter gave me legal status in the ghetto, with the right to obtain a *Lebensmittelkarte* (a food ration card) and a certificate stating that I worked for a German enterprise, to protect me from being sent to some labor camp. The amount of food obtainable with the ration card, I soon found out, was not enough for survival.

Then there was the painful fact that, after our years apart, I was still separated from my mother. I hoped that after a while the Gestapo would forget about me, and we could be together again. Every day, as I walked to and from the factory, I saw the misery on the streets. Corpses covered with newspapers lay on the sidewalks, waiting to be picked up by the ghetto burying squads, the *hevre kedishe,* who dumped them into mass graves in the Jewish cemetery. Everywhere I looked I saw the ghetto wall, like a cage. One sadistic German guard at the ghetto gate, for his amusement, would take aim at the masses of people on the street and pull the trigger on his rifle, indiscriminately killing one or more people, simply to create panic.

On a Sabbath in mid-April 1942, the SS started a massacre in the ghetto. They ran from house to house pulling men from their beds, dragging them into the street, and shooting them. About 60 innocent men were murdered that night. The SS picked the victims from a list they had, and when they did not find the desired victim, they killed his wife or his son in his place. The rumors were that a German had been killed in the "No Man's Land" between the ghetto wall and the Aryan side. The massacre was a form of corporate punishment.

The massacre became known in the ghetto as "The Night of Blood." Fear ran through the ghetto. Who were those on the SS list? What would the murderers do next? Who would they pick to kill? In the following months, individuals on the SS list were removed from their homes and murdered, and the Nazis always performed those killings on the Sabbath. In June of that year, 110 Jews were arrested, put in prison, and executed. The terror continued unabated and fear consumed our family. Would they come for any of us? What could we do? Where could we hide? No one had an answer.

One day Sojnek, who had trained with the Polish army, told us he was joining the ghetto fighters' underground. He said he would fight before they killed him. Because the Gestapo was looking for me and perhaps had my name on a list to capture and kill, it was decided I should move out of the apartment and into the factory. I was given a tiny storage room with no room for a bed, but several sacks of discarded cotton and woolen thread would serve. Mother was terrified the Gestapo would find me. I tried to tell her they had more important matters to attend to. The proof was that they never came back, but I was careful anyway. To make her feel safer we met just once a week.

Information was going around the ghetto in May and June 1942 that the Germans had built an extermination camp in Chełmno, northwest of the city of Łódź, where they were mass-murdering Jews. Stories about the killing commandos, the Einsatzgruppen, came from the conquered Soviet territories. Almost no one in the factory wanted to believe those horror stories. "It's exaggerated," they said. "They're probably only killing the Soviet communist *politruks*. Maybe there were some Jews among those. One cannot believe that they mass murder people."

Even when escaped witnesses from Chełmno and the former Soviet zone returned to the Warsaw ghetto and confirmed those horrors, most did not want to believe them.

Young Jews, who believed that the Germans planned to exterminate all Jews, formed resistance groups. Sojnek joined one of those. Daily, we heard more rumors about an impending deportation of Warsaw's Jews. The news of the mass deportations of Jews in Lublin and Lvov reached the Warsaw ghetto. Though the Judenrat and its chairman, Adam Czerniakow, tried to calm down the population, the fear was everywhere. The SS terror in the ghetto increased in mid-July 1942. Hostages were taken and sent to prison, and people were shot on the streets.

I begged Uncle Peter to bring Mother to the factory. She was all alone and helpless, and I felt we must be together. He said there was no place in the factory, but he agreed to let her come. Early the next morning while it was still quiet on the streets, I ran to our old apartment and took Mother and a handful of her possessions, including photos of Father, Mietek, and Mina, to the factory. We were happy to be together again and shared the closet as a sleeping space.

Uncle Peter put Mother to work sorting socks, as there were no spare knitting machines available. Still, everyone working in the factory felt somehow safer, because they thought that the Germans would not harm the workers who produced socks needed for the German army. And the workers were at least assured of one plate of soup and a small piece of bread per day.

I asked Sojnek if he'd heard anything from the Gestapo Jew Gancwajch, about the fate of Father and Mietek in the Krzemieniec jail. Were they by any chance alive? I knew that they had not survived the execution, and it was a false hope to rely on Gancwajch. Sojnek told me he'd heard nothing from that Jewish traitor, except a demand for more money. Mother and I worked 10 to 12 hours a day. We didn't venture out on the streets because they had become dangerous.

On July 22, 1942, early in the morning, when we looked out the factory window, we noticed a large number of uniformed military personnel outside the ghetto wall. (Later we learned they were Ukrainians, Latvians, Lithuanians, and Polish police.) At the Leszno Street gate was a large group of armed SS.

Fear ran through our veins. What was happening? What did the Nazis intend to do? We had never seen so many armed men surround the ghetto. We stopped working and expected the worst. At about one o'clock in the afternoon, placards appeared on the ghetto wall across the street from the factory, and a large crowd gathered trying to read them.

I and another worker ran out to read them, but we couldn't get near them. At last we pushed our way to the front. The placards were printed in bold letters, half in German and half in Polish. By the order of the German command, all Jews in the Warsaw Jewish quarters (ghetto) not employed in German or Polish enterprises must report immediately, under penalty of death, to the Umschlagplatz, the plaza in front of the railroad station. They could bring jewelry, cash, other valuables, and seven kilograms of personal belongings. Each person at the Umschlagplatz would be given bread and marmalade for the trip to a labor camp in the East. The Germans called it the *Umsiedlung Aktion* (resettlement action).

On the next corner, Jewish policemen grabbed people and led them off. We ran back to the factory and reported what was going on. I tried to calm down the workers who had left their families at home, and said that even though something terrible was happening, according to the placard, the families of those employed in German or Polish enterprises were excluded from deportation. Almost immediately after the placards were hung, men came to our factory and begged Uncle Peter to give them jobs. Uncle Peter could take in a few workers, but only those who could bring their own knitting machines. Within hours, a few men came back lugging various knitting machines and were given jobs. Others had to be turned away.

Meanwhile, on the street the Jewish policemen corralled whomever they could catch. If someone tried to escape from their clutches, two or three of them jumped on the unfortunate and subdued him. In anguish, we watched the hated Jewish police collaborate with our oppressors. Later we discovered that the SS demanded that, by the end of the day, the Jewish police deliver 6,000 Jews to the Umschlagplatz for deportation.

We also learned that many of the starving homeless gave themselves up for the price of a piece of bread and marmalade. The Jewish police continued without respite. People ran in all directions, trying to escape their clutches. I saw a man trying to bribe a policeman. I saw them arguing, and then the man took off his wristwatch and handed it to the policeman, who finally let him go. Those bastards! If I'd had a gun, I would have killed those collaborating traitors, and I promised myself never to forget or forgive them.

The atmosphere in the factory was intense. At 5 p.m. everyone ran home to see if their families were all right and to bring the documents that proved they worked in a German factory. Our factory was overcrowded with people seeking to escape deportation. Some workers tried to bring their families into the factory, especially elderly parents who were not protected under the law. Arguments and fights erupted between newcomers and the regular workers, who were afraid the Germans would find out what we were doing and deport everyone.

That same day, July 22, we learned the shocking news that Adam Czerniakow had killed himself. The people in the factory kept asking themselves "Why? Did he know what was going to happen to the Jews of the ghetto? Then why didn't he warn us?"

Perhaps he preferred to die, rather than cooperate with the SS and the Gestapo in deportation actions against the Jews. We never did find out the answer.

In the morning, some workers brought their wives and children to the factory, because they were afraid to leave them home to be caught in the ongoing *Aktion*. With the factory floor already crowded, Uncle Peter let the women and children stay in the attic and cellar. We were all on edge. What was next? Where were the Jews really headed? Why not let them work in Warsaw? There was no hard news from anywhere, just rumors.

Outside, the scene was worse than the day before. The police were rounding up the poor and homeless, those most recently herded into the Warsaw ghetto from Germany and Czechoslovakia, and those caught on the streets without German work papers. The busy street in front of the factory was now deserted, except for the Jewish policemen, the sick or crippled who cringed against the building walls, the starving little orphans, and the corpses.

We heard that the captured people were being herded to the Umschlagplatz and being loaded into the freight wagons like sardines by the SS and Ukrainian soldiers. No one knew where they were going. In the knitting factory things were desperate. Again our work stopped, as some laborers walked around in despair, worrying about their families. Had they been captured and deported? Mother and I lost all contact with my aunts, uncles, and cousins.

Mother continued to ask me for details of Mietek and Father. "How was the life in the Krzemieniec ghetto? How did the Germans and Ukrainians act against the Jews in the ghetto? How was their health, and did they have enough food?"

I tried to calm her with invented stories that they were doing well, and that the Germans did not bother the Jews in the ghetto, but I don't think she fully believed me. She kept asking me the same questions over and over. Not knowing they were dead allowed her to hope they would not try to return to Warsaw.

I kept asking myself why, after escaping execution, I returned to hell in the Warsaw ghetto. I could have escaped to Romania or Slovakia, not that far from the city of Lvov, but how could I have left Mother and Mina alone in the Warsaw? Now that only Mother and I had survived and were together, I had to find a way for us to survive the deportation. First, I thought we could try to escape to the Aryan side and hide with a Polish family who were our friends before the war. After questioning several people, I was told that we were totally surrounded by the SS, Latvians, Lithuanians, Ukrainians, and Polish police and that escape was impossible. The only safe thing to do was to stay at the factory. Mother had to be hidden in the secret room behind our sleeping closet, and I worked at the knitting machines, hoping the SS would not find her and capture me.

A few days after the Germans ordered the first deportations, those Jews who worked for nonmilitary factories were no longer exempt from deportation. New rules were constantly being issued, and we were confused. Only those who could prove that they worked for German military enterprises and factories could remain in the ghetto. All others were deported. Then later, only those Jews who worked for German factories that directly supplied the German army received papers exempting them from immediate deportation. Because we knitted socks for the Wehrmacht, my luck held.

There were rumors that the SS planned to issue 100,000 food ration cards to the remaining Jews in the ghetto, supposedly proving that the deportations would stop. But few people believed it. To save themselves, Jewish girls and women without the latest documents tried to marry men who had them. Uncle Peter asked me to sign a wedding certificate that stated I was married to a girl I never met. Of course I signed as requested, and perhaps she would be safer. I was then legally, if fictitiously, a married man at the age of 13. The wedding certificate said I was 18 years old. I often think about my fictitious wife and hope she survived.

It wasn't long before we started running out of food. The little store of flour, grits, and rice we had amassed was rapidly diminishing, and the rations became smaller with each day. What would happen when the food ran out? How would we get more food?

A few days later, the SS announced that any one who voluntarily showed up at the Umschlagplatz would be given three kilos of bread and a kilo of the ersatz marmalade. Thousands of starving men, women, and children went to the Umschlagplatz to get the bread and marmalade and were all deported.

From the end of July until mid-August 1942, a new phase was initiated by the SS. Together with the Ukrainian, Latvian, and Lithuanian collaborators, the SS surrounded several blocks of apartment houses in the ghetto and searched the buildings from top to bottom for hidden Jews. Those who were sick or unable to move fast enough, they shot on the spot.

One day during the first week in August, they surrounded the housing block where the factory was located. We heard the Germans scream, *"Alles raus, alles raus,"* and then the Ukrainians screamed in broken Polish, "All get out, those who hide will be shot."

Through the window we saw the SS and their cohorts herding people, like frightened cattle, to the middle of the street. We also heard gunshots coming from the next building, where they were most likely killing those unable to move or those attempting to hide. The SS and Ukrainians mercilessly beat the slower-moving old men and women with their rifle butts and truncheons, while they continued to scream. Those who fell were brutally kicked. Running blood covered the victims' heads and faces. Mothers, in panic, looked for their children in the melee.

Mother and several of the workers' wives hid behind a false wall in the closet where she and I slept. The rest of us sat behind our machines, pretending to work.

The workroom door was suddenly thrown open, and several SS and Ukrainians burst in with their guns aimed at our heads. We immediately scrambled to attention, because the law required that we come to attention at the sight of a Nazi. One of the SS walked between us and demanded our documents. Although they had papers, the SS man pulled several older workers away from their machines and pushed them toward the wall. The SS man walked toward me, looked at me with contempt, and pulled my papers out of my hand. For a moment my heart seemed to stop beating. In rasping German he barked something at me. I didn't understand and someone quickly translated. He wanted to know what we were making. I answered in Polish, and the same worker translated what I said into German. I told him that we produced woolen socks and sweaters for the German army. He picked up a sock from the table in front of me, looked at it for a moment, then threw it back and moved on. I exhaled a sigh of relief.

He stayed for ten interminable minutes, and when he and his gang left, they took with them a quarter of our workforce, most of them older men. The SS officer did not care that they claimed to be expert knitters and punched several of them in the face, hard, while screaming at them to shut up. The others pushed them out. The door slammed, and we were stunned silent. Soon some of the men started sobbing.

Suddenly we heard the cries of the women and children hidden in the attic and the screaming of the SS and the Ukrainians, *"Raus! Raus!"* Men in the shop froze. Those were the voices of their wives and children. The murderers also found the women and children hiding in the cellar, and we could hear their screams from downstairs. The men whose families had been caught ran to the door to get to their loved ones, but as they opened the door a Ukrainian soldier standing there hit them with his rifle butt, spit at the desperate and crying men, pushed them back into the shop, and slammed the door.

They were on their knees, pleading with the Ukrainian to let them go to their families. They tore at their hair and hit their heads with their fists in frustration and grief, but to no avail. The Ukrainian opened the door and in broken Polish yelled that if they did not stop, he would shoot us all. Others tried to embrace the stricken men and held them tight, trying to calm them. The whole shop was in tears and shaking. Some said they would prefer death to witnessing the horror and living from day to day in constant fear. Others, with hate in their eyes, cried out in Yiddish that we must resist and kill the murderers before they killed us. Finally, the SS left the area.

I stood frozen with despair. Even the brutal executions of my father and brother in Krzemieniec, hearing them as they went to the gallows, and the pain of losing my loved ones, did not harden me to what I saw on the faces of those men. I began to choke and a worker standing next to me slapped me in the face, trying to stop me. I fell to my knees and sobbed uncontrollably. In my heart I felt fortunate that they had not found my hidden mother or selected me for deportation.

Mother and the few women hidden behind the false wall came out. We ran to each other and hugged with tears in our eyes. Mother whispered that it must be God's will to protect us and maybe we would survive. I told her that just before my escape from the Krzemieniec ghetto, the Jewish leader of the Judenrat assured me, that no matter what, I would survive and had wished me good luck.

The sounds of screaming Germans and crying Jews drifted through the factory windows from the streets. An hour later we heard them move out. When I peered out, the SS and their collaborators led several hundred bent and broken people, holding on to each other, to the center of the street. Mothers carried their babies as their other children clutched at their skirts. I wondered what we had done to deserve such bestial treatment. Where were our Polish neighbors? I felt totally abandoned.

Letters and postcards supposedly arrived in the ghetto from some of the deported, stating that they were well and working in the fields somewhere in eastern Poland. No one we knew saw such letters themselves—it was always some third person who saw them. Later we discovered those letters were German forgeries—or written by deportees, on order of the SS, before they were gassed in Treblinka—to deceive the remaining Jews. In the second half of August, we learned that everyone was being deported to the extermination camp Treblinka, where they were gassed and burned.

More news of mass slaughters in Treblinka reached us. Some of the reports came from eyewitnesses who escaped from the transport trains near Treblinka and from escapees from the extermination camp. The stories of their escape were un-believable. I heard them from my Uncle Sojnek, who spoke to one of the escapees. The man, a Hasid, son of the Parzerver Rebbe, Yaakov Rabinowicz, Uncle Sojnek told me, was near nervous collapse. He could hardly speak, choking and breaking out in tears as he described the process of mass killing in Treblinka. He escaped from Treblinka by hiding in a railroad wagon packed with the clothing of the mur-dered Jews.*

The news from Treblinka was staggering. It meant the Germans planned to an-nihilate us and were doing it in stages to confuse the population and avoid resis-tance. Although some workers were in denial, the majority accepted the appalling news. We decided we could not, and would not, be taken by the SS without resistance. We all agreed that if we had to die, we would go down fighting and not in the gas chambers.

A resistance movement was forming in the ghetto. Young people—men and women, boys and girls, of all political ideologies—Labor Zionist, Socialist, Betar Revisionist, Communist, and others—joined together in a fighting organization that was named Żydowska Organizacja Bojowa (Jewish Fighting Organization), ŻOB for short. It was led by a young Zionist, Mordecai Anielewicz.

First the ŻOB smuggled several fighters who could pass for Poles out of the ghetto, so they could confirm or deny the ghastly facts about Treblinka. When the facts were confirmed, they sent an appeal to those who remained in the ghetto ask-ing them not to give themselves up but to build bunkers and hiding places.

The deportations continued on a daily basis. From the factory window we watched the SS and their collaborators herd the Jews, mostly those who were emo-tionally broken, the sick, and children trying to hide in crevices between buildings, or those who were sprawled on the sidewalks, half dead, to the Umschlagplatz.

During the second week of August, the ŻOB dropped leaflets on the streets, accusing the Jewish ghetto police of collaborating with the SS in the murder of more than 200,000 Jews. The ŻOB found all members of the ghetto police guilty, and later they posted placards that said the leader of the Jewish police had been executed, and that other executions of the guilty would follow. The ŻOB also con-tinued to urge people to hide and not to give themselves up.

---

*His testimony is in Hillel Seidman, *The Warsaw Ghetto Diaries* (1997).

Sometime in mid-August, Soviet planes appeared over Warsaw and bombed the city. Though some bombs fell on the ghetto, we cheered and hoped that help was finally coming. Unfortunately, there was only that one attack. More surprising to us, for reasons unknown, the SS never entered the factory again. We workers sat at our knitting machines, but hardly any work was done.

After dark, some men sneaked out to pick up the ŻOB leaflets and returned with the stories they heard from others on the street. One story was that the SS was about to stop the deportation, another, that the BBC had reported the Soviet Red Army was defeating the Germans on the eastern front and the Wehrmacht was in retreat. We used to say the source of the stories was the "YVA" telegraphic agency, in Yiddish, *Yidn vilen azoy* (Jews wish it that way). None of the stories were true.

More important, we were running out of food and water. What water we had was what we had been able to store in a bathtub and all available containers, and we rationed it for drinking only. None of us had washed in weeks, and a stench permeated the factory. The toilets no longer functioned, and we relieved ourselves into containers we emptied out through the windows, into the street. It all added to our misery.

Sometimes we sneaked out at night to search the adjoining empty buildings for food. We occasionally found rice, dry beans, flour, dried-out bread, and marmalade that had been hidden by the former occupants. Once we even found a large bottle of vodka and cautiously carried it back to the shop.

When we had discussions, we wondered about what life was like on the outside, for the Poles. Did life go on in a normal way? Didn't they know what was happening in their midst? Didn't they care? We heard about the organized and armed Polish underground army, the AK (Armia Krajowa), the Home Army that operated against the Germans. Why didn't they sabotage the railroads leading from Warsaw to Treblinka, to stop the transport of Jews, or attack and destroy the Treblinka gas chambers? Why couldn't they at least provide hiding places for Jews escaping from the ghetto or provide arms for the ŻOB?

They didn't help because the Polish army and the AK were made up of former Polish officers and soldiers who were extremely antisemitic. They were not willing to help Jews, and most of them were pleased the Germans were making Poland *Judenrein*. Uncle Sojnek told me the ŻOB had information from Jewish partisans that the AK was dangerous to the Jewish partisans and killed many of them, doing the work of the Germans, because the Germans seldom entered the forests. Their behavior was beyond my comprehension.

For 44 days and nights the deportations continued. Later, the ŻOB told us the SS had succeeded in deporting and murdering 90 percent of the ghetto's Jewish population, more than 300,000 men, women, and children. The deportations stopped abruptly in mid-September 1942, and by some unexplainable luck, Mother and I escaped them. We noticed from the shop windows that the SS and the Ukrainians were suddenly gone, and that the Latvian and Lithuanian guards around the ghetto walls had also disappeared. Word of mouth had it that the deportations had stopped, if only temporarily.

Then the Germans "shrank" the ghetto, and we had to leave the shop because it was outside the designated area. We, the workers who remained, were herded into a small part of the former central ghetto, which included the enclaves housing German factories and their Jewish workers. The Schultz, Többens, and Landau brush-making shops and several German-owned factories and shops that produced military uniforms and other military goods for the German army used Jewish slave labor.

The areas between the enclaves and the rest of the central ghetto consisted of empty streets and buildings, which we were forbidden to cross under the threat of death. Mother and I moved the few possessions we still had to Niska Street, now controlled by the Germans, the Werterfassung, whose job it was to collect and sort valuable items and furniture left in the apartments of the deported and ship them to Germany.

First thing next morning, Mother and I went looking for our relatives, grandparents, uncles, and aunts from both sides. Uncle Peter, Aunt Cesia, and their daughters Lusia and Ruth somehow had managed to leave the ghetto when the deportations began in June. We didn't know where they were. We looked for Aunt Roza Benderman, my mother's only sister, with whom she was close; her husband Ignatz; and their children Henia and Kuba. Before deportation, they lived in an apartment house on the corner of Leszno and Żelazna Streets, but we found the building deserted. A crippled old man hiding under a staircase told us that the Benderman family had been captured by the SS and herded to the Umschlagplatz. We knew immediately they were dead. Mother burst into tears. I tried my best to calm her.

Dejected and disheartened, we went to Dzielna Street, where Mother's widowed sister-in-law, Aunt Fela Gold; her sons, Michal and Salek; daughters, Mina and Boba; and their husbands used to live. That building was also empty. When we asked bystanders what had happened, we were told that everyone in that building had been rounded up, marched to the Umschlagplatz, and deported. Only Salek, Aunt Fela's youngest son, who had escaped from Warsaw to the Soviet zone, might still be alive.

Then we gathered enough courage to go to our old house on Ogrodowa Street, where we all lived with Father's parents, Godel and Pesha, and several uncles and aunts. Our building was deserted. By pure chance, we ran into Uncle Sojnek, who tearfully told us that his wife and baby son Adam had been deported to their deaths.

Except for Sojnek and Uncle Fredek's baby daughter, whom he gave to a friendly Polish family for safekeeping, no one survived. From a total of 70 family members, only eight were still alive at that time. We couldn't talk any more and silently returned to Niska Street, where we busied ourselves by unpacking and putting away our meager belongings.

Sojnek came over the next day and told us he was a member of the ŻOB fighting group, and as a former soldier in the Polish army, instructed other ŻOB fighters in the use and operation of available weapons, hand pistols, and grenades. He told us how much he hated the murderers of our family and swore that before he died, he would avenge their deaths.

I soon returned to the shop to pick up what few remaining items belonged to us. The atmosphere was morbid. Some people had gone looking for their loved ones and found out they were gone forever. "What is the purpose of living?" they asked. "Everyone we loved is gone and we are like hunted animals about to be caged and killed."

I clamped my hands over my ears and ran out of the shop into the street.

In mid-October 1942, Mother and I began working for the Werterfassung. The work, carried out under the watchful eye of the SS, consisted of looting the now-empty apartments of the murdered Jews. We removed all valuables, including furniture, and assembled them on the street, where they were loaded into German trucks and shipped, I later learned, to Germany.

Often, as we did the Germans' dirty work, we came across personal effects, like family photos, letters, books with dried flowers between the pages, and other memorabilia. Especially painful to look at were photos of smiling babies and children, now dead, murdered before their potential could be realized. Occasionally we found small amounts of money hidden in a bedpost, or some leftover food, which we hid in our clothing and smuggled out. As much as we hated the work, we did it for the meager food ration cards and what we could smuggle out, or we would have starved.

Sojnek wanted me to join the ŻOB. They told him I was too young to be in the ranks, but that they did need couriers to deliver orders and messages to different posts and to act as casual observers of the Germans and their movements around the ghetto. I told my uncle I was ready to join, to do anything demanded of me. Sojnek told me that he would relay my message to the commanders and would let me know what to do next.

Mother and I continued working for the Werterfassung until the first week of November when my temperature soared to 105.8 degrees Fahrenheit. A doctor in the Niska Street building said I had typhus and there was nothing to be done except wait and hope. My temperature might go down after several days and I would recover, or not. Meanwhile, I was to be given nothing to eat.

Most of the time I lay bathed in sweat as Mother cooled my hot body and head with wet rags, sitting by my bed day and night without sleeping. After five days, my body temperature finally dropped and I slowly started to recover. Mother managed to get in touch with a Polish friend, a Madam Pasternak, on the Polish side—where life went on more or less as usual—and arranged to smuggle us out of the ghetto to a barn on the outskirts of Warsaw.

Madam Pasternak used to live in our apartment house before the war and was a good friend of Mother's. Her father was the superintendent of our building, and she risked her life and her family's lives to hide Mother and me in the barn for several weeks. Except for our two narrow folding cots, the barn was empty. Every day, Madam Pasternak brought food and news. At one point, she told us we would have to leave the barn in a few days, because the danger was growing. The Polish police were beginning to snoop around the area.

I was still too weak to get to the forest outside Warsaw and join the partisans, so we were forced to go back to the ghetto, to our old room on Niska Street. Mother went back to work for the Werterfassung, and I stayed in our room, trying to regain my strength. The only person who came to see us was Sojnek, who brought the latest news from inside and outside the ghetto, and some food. He told us the Red Army had stopped the German advance and was forcing the Nazis back on several fronts.

In the ghetto, he said, the ŻOB was organizing resistance in case the SS restarted the deportations. He told us how tough it was to get arms from the AK, and that the ŻOB had set up secret shops to produce explosives and Molotov cocktails. He and other fighters had built a bunker underneath the basement on Ogrodowa Street. Sojnek said that when there was an emergency or a deportation started, we should hide there. He described the small entrance to the bunker behind a pile of trash and said he'd make sure it would be kept open for us. Several days later Sojnek came to tell me that I and another young boy, Sewek, were now ŻOB couriers and spies for the Jewish fighters.

The ŻOB continued to distribute pamphlets that announced the execution of several Jewish collaborators and traitors, and asked everyone to contribute money and valuables for the purchase of arms from the Poles. The remaining Jewish police stayed out of sight, afraid for their lives. Now Jewish life in the ghetto was run by the ŻOB, but everyone sensed that the Germans would not leave us in peace and would attempt to deport us to Treblinka.

I continued to heal because Mother traded her remaining pieces of jewelry for food, or sometimes found bits of hidden food at work. As I got stronger, I was able to walk around and visit with friends. My favorite was Itzek, son of a large, but very poor family that before the war lived in a two-room basement apartment in our old house. As little boys, we were best friends. We were afraid of nothing and no one, though we were usually in trouble.

Another good friend was Halinka, a tomboy almost 15 years old. Itzek and Halinka used to come over as often as it was safe while I recuperated. Halinka was very beautiful, and I especially liked the freckles that covered all of her face. We used to tease her by saying she had been suntanned through a colander. With her great sense of humor, she didn't mind it at all. Whenever we three met, we talked about how we would avenge the Jewish people for what had been done to us and what we would do when we survived.

Halinka's dream was to be a ballerina, and she would take off her shoes and socks and pirouette with deep bows to our applause. Itzek was an ardent Zionist who belonged to Betar, the paramilitary Zionist organization led by Vladimir Jabotinsky. Itzek dreamed of going to Palestine to fight for the creation of a Jewish state. I wanted to study engineering before I moved to Palestine and joined Itzek. We swore to each other that if we survived, we would meet at a designated place and time and have a party to celebrate our victory over the enemy.

It was a cold and nasty December in 1942 and it was freezing in our room. We used our broken furniture as fuel to cook our paltry rations. We slept with our clothing on and covered ourselves with a blanket and all the clothing we possessed.

The ŻOB continued to urge people to hide if there was another *Aktion*. According to Sojnek, the AK refused to pass substantial amounts of arms to the ŻOB. They believed it would be a waste, because Jews were not capable of fighting. They gave the ŻOB a few pistols and grenades, some of which were rusted. Fortunately, the ŻOB was able to purchase some munitions on the black market with the monies and jewelry collected in the ghetto. There were still not enough arms to distribute among the fighters. The ŻOB supplemented the shortage with Molotov cocktails and explosive powder to make bombs. Morale among the ŻOB fighters was high. They all were ready to die in the battle and take a German or two with them. Sojnek assured me that when I got back to normal, he'd take me to his fighting cell for training. The work Mother was doing for the Werterfassung was hard and grim. Several times she came home in tears.

On December 31, 1942, Itzek, Halinka, a couple of other friends, and I decided to celebrate New Year's 1943 as the new year of our survival. With the permission of Halinka's parents, we set up a table with some snacks in their two-room apartment with a bottle of samogon, homemade vodka. At midnight we embraced each other and, with small glasses of vodka in hand, wished each other, not a happy New Year, but a safe one, and prayed that all of us would survive. We sang happy Polish and Hebrew songs and danced the hora. Halinka, a little drunk, did some ballet steps and pirouettes.

In the beginning of January 1943, it was rumored that a large contingent of Ukrainian soldiers had arrived in Warsaw. That could mean only one thing, that the Germans were planning a new deportation.

Tension mounted. Sojnek told us to prepare to move into the bunker and not to bring anything with us, except what we could carry in our pockets. Mother stopped going to work, and, on edge, we both waited for news. The hope the SS would leave us alone evaporated.

Mother and I discussed the idea of smuggling ourselves out of the ghetto to the Polish side, to join the partisans in the forest. We did research to see if it was possible. First, we needed documents that identified us as Catholic Poles and asked Sojnek how to go about obtaining them.

CHAPTER 12

The second week in January 1943 began with the news that Heinrich Himmler, chief of the Gestapo, was coming to personally inspect the remains of the Warsaw ghetto. We knew deportation always followed visits of high-ranking Nazis. Two days later, Sojnek took us, via underground passages and narrow alleys, to the bunker. Its entrance was camouflaged behind a large pile of junk. The bunker was dug out below a cellar and was a room containing several narrow bunk beds lined up against the walls. Wooden crates filled with varied provisions also served as stools and a table. In one corner, behind a hanging curtain, was a toilet, ingeniously connected to the building's sewer pipe. Several large farm-type metal milk cans, filled with water, stood around. The bunker had a dirt floor and was very cold and damp. The ceiling was about 1.5 meters high. We sat on crates, dressed in all the clothing we had, and wrapped ourselves in blankets.

In the middle of the bunker ceiling, dangling from a loose wire, was a single light bulb that threw eerie shadows around the room. Six people were already there—four men and two young women, to whom Sojnek introduced us. They were all members of the fighting unit, discussing the situation in the ghetto and their readiness to fight. We were to remain in the bunker for at least a week, to see what developed. Sojnek told me that as soon as he had any information about pending deportations, I would become their courier. In order not to reveal its whereabouts, none of us were to leave the bunker except in an emergency.

The atmosphere among the fighters was enthusiastic. Over and over, the young women and men said their main mission, before they were forced to die, was to kill as many Germans as possible to restore Jewish honor and avenge the crimes against the Jewish people. The third week in January, on Monday, at about seven o'clock in the morning, Sojnek burst into the bunker and excitedly announced that a large contingent of armed Germans had entered the ghetto, searching for Jews and arresting them. According to Sojnek, this was a surprise to the command of ŻOB. They had not expected an *Aktion* so soon. Armed resistance would commence immediately.

Sojnek and several fighters left the bunker in a hurry. Before they left, he told me to stay in the bunker until he came back for me. I was disappointed not to be able to participate in an avenging action, but I was not alone. Mother and five others were in the bunker, three older men and two women. In silence, we sat around the crate that served as our table, not knowing what to expect next. By late afternoon, none of us in the bunker had anything to eat. We were all too nervous even to think about food. We fretfully waited for any news. It seemed like days before Sojnek and some of the fighters returned to the bunker that night.

They told us how they and other ŻOB fighters attacked German soldiers who were leading Jews to the Umschlagplatz. The ŻOB killed two of the soldiers and wounded several others. Four Jewish fighters were killed in the German crossfire, one of them from our bunker. Sojnek and the others expressed satisfaction that they, for the first time, were able to inflict casualties on the Germans with their meager arms and were able to capture a German rifle and pistol. Other returning fighters told us other cells had killed two Germans but lost three of their own, two men and a girl. They told us how the once arrogant, strutting SS were ducking from nook to nook, scanning the area around them before they dared to take a step, ter-rified of the ghetto fighters. Despite the ŻOB's efforts, however, the Nazis were still able to capture about 3,000 Jews.

Later that night, the SS and their Lithuanian and Latvian collaborators left the ghetto. Other ŻOB fighters reported that the Germans, for whatever reason, did not use the Jewish ghetto police during this action. Despite the loss of a fighter, the atmosphere in the bunker was jubilant. For the first time, the ghetto Jews had resisted the Nazi army with firearms and met with some success.

We were all proud of our bunker mates' bravery against the overwhelming odds.

I pestered Sojnek about getting me involved in the battle, somehow, but he wouldn't give me an assignment. At the same time, Mother began to hound me about Father and Mietek. Where did I think they were? Had they tried to return to Warsaw? I kept telling her that they must have heard about the deportations from Warsaw, and Father would not risk such a trip. Though we faced death daily, she never let the questions go, she never stopped thinking about them. I still couldn't bring myself to tell her the truth, because I knew it would break her heart. She was a brave woman who could take daily tragedies in stride, as long as she thought Father was alive. Every now and then she would hug me tight, and I could feel her trembling body. At least we were together.

That night, little sleep was to be had. Sojnek and the other fighters left in the middle of the night for a rendezvous at ŻOB headquarters. Mother and I hadn't slept more than three hours when a courier woke us to say the Nazis were back, pouring in through all the ghetto gates, spreading out to capture the Jews. The ghetto streets were deserted, everyone left was in hiding, and the Germans, afraid of encountering resistance fighters, were not entering apartment buildings but were surrounding and entering the Schultz and Többens workshops.

The atmosphere in the bunker was tense. We were told to talk in whispers, because the SS troops were using listening devices to find Jews in hiding. Still, being in the bunker made us feel somewhat safe from the Germans, and I was hoping Sojnek would take me to fight the Nazis. But the waiting was interminable.

Finally, long after dark, Sojnek returned to the bunker alone. He told us the SS left after capturing 2,000 Jews, mostly from the shops. ŻOB fighters in the shops, buildings, and alleys fought the Germans and killed and wounded several. Unfortunately many of the resisters lost their lives because they had only handheld pistols and grenades against German machine guns and flamethrowers. Sojnek said the fighters could have taken a greater toll but were short on weapons and ammunition and could not arm the hundreds of volunteers who wanted to fight. There was very little help from the AK, and only a few additional arms had been captured.

The Nazi *Aktion* continued for two more days. We were told later that on the last day the Germans went on a murderous campaign, killing about a thousand Jews on the streets. All together, during the four-day action, the Germans and their cohorts captured and killed almost 5,000 Jews. Everyone attributed the low number of captives to the armed resistance of the ŻOB. We considered it the victory of a small group of ghetto fighters against the powerful Nazi army.

On the fifth day, the SS did not return. Many people hidden in bunkers, including us, left their hiding places and went out on the streets. Some people expressed pride in the ŻOB revolt and said if the fighters had been organized before the first deportations, the Germans might not have been so successful. Others feared the Germans would not leave the ghetto alone, and sooner or later, would destroy us all. Still, almost everyone agreed that the ŻOB fighters had stopped the latest *Aktion*.

The following day Mother and I returned to Niska Street, but we needed to find food. Mother took a few remaining pieces of her jewelry and sold them to smugglers, mostly young Jewish kids, 12 to 16 years old, who were nimble enough to crawl over the wall or through holes in it. If the Germans caught them, they were shot on sight. They bought food and other necessities on the Polish side with the money they earned selling goods from inside the ghetto, then they sold food and other outside items inside the walls.

When Sojnek showed up in our room a few days later, I insisted he intervene with the powers-that-be at the ŻOB and get them to allow me to join their ranks. He again promised to do so, and said he'd let me know as soon as he got an answer. At that time, the ŻOB assumed total control of the ghetto. They posted placards that announced the indictment and death sentences of Jewish collaborators.

We heard that the German command, with the cooperation of Többens and Schultz, the German owners of the factories and workshops, wanted to transfer their Jewish workers and their machines from the ghetto to Trawniki and Poniatowa, camps near Lublin. The ŻOB strongly opposed this, and in leaflets and placards distributed throughout the ghetto ordered workers not to volunteer and to oppose the move by any means. As a result of the ŻOB appeal, very few workers left. Later we heard that the ŻOB set fire to one of the factories to prevent its transfer. Neither Mother nor I worked for the Germans any more. Mother gave the ŻOB her last two pieces of jewelry, her engagement and wedding rings, the last material links to our former family.

In mid-February 1943, Sojnek came to tell me I was now a courier for the ŻOB. My assignment was to maintain contact between different fighting cells and, with other couriers, act as a lookout. Furious activity was going on under and over the buildings in the ghetto. Secure bunkers were being built, as were tunnels that connected bunkers between buildings and even streets. The ŻOB set fire to the big Werterfassung warehouse, where the Germans stored their loot before it was shipped. The fighters also tried to purchase guns from the outside.

Those who had to survive on their wits, like us, were called "wilds" and were not entitled to food rations. What little food we had was mostly gotten from Sojnek or by dealing with the smugglers.

Between February and the April revolt, my job, and that of the other couriers, was to learn safe passages between buildings and streets and find the best observation points for watching the Germans approach the ghetto gates. I was assigned to watch the Leszno Street gate and report any unusual action. More news from Treblinka arrived via ŻOB secret agents sent to scout around the camp's vicinity, and to top it all off, our food was running out. All we had left were a few beets, some cabbage, and about half a kilo of stale dark bread.

Everyone we loved—Mother's family, Father's family—with few exceptions had been wiped out. We had no one but Sojnek to turn to. Other people had worries and problems of their own and were unable to offer any help. We felt isolated and forgotten by the rest of the world, left without hope to face certain death.

Then in March, Sojnek told us the ŻOB got money after Mordecai Anielewicz, leader of the ŻOB, appealed to the citizens of the ghetto to donate whatever valuables they still had for the purchase of arms. In the end, he said, the Germans would get it all, anyway. In the midst of this chaos, I learned that Itzek and Halinka had survived the January deportations and were hiding in different bunkers. We managed to meet in Halinka's bunker to compare our stories.

Halinka's body and face were taut and drawn, her dress hung loose on her frame. Her bunker was overcrowded, and they had run out of food. She ate only one slice of stale bread with a bit of cheese each day, and in the last two days of the January action, hadn't eaten at all. I offered to bring her my food ration, but she refused it and said she wasn't hungry. Itzek and I were concerned about her well-being and made her promise she would let us know when she needed help.

Itzek was dejected. More of his family members had been killed, and the Germans had taken shots at him when he tried to cross a street. This get-together was nothing like our little New Year's party just eight weeks earlier. I tried to cheer them up by telling stories about the bravery of the ŻOB fighters and how the cowardly SS were taking cover wherever they could. I told them how proud everyone was of our little David against the Nazi Goliath.

Itzek wanted to escape the ghetto and join the partisans in the forest. He asked us both to join him, but I told him that I could not desert my mother. Halinka wanted to escape the cursed ghetto, too, but would not leave her mother, either. We wished Itzek success, and each of us promised again that if we survived we would meet again and celebrate. With some luck, Itzek might survive. Did I dare admit to myself that, in his absence, I was pleased I would have Halinka to myself?

In the beginning of April 1943, we could sense a pending deportation. The tension was palpable. Himmler had made his threatened visit. We hastily brought some of our personal belongings, provisions, and water to the bunker and conducted tests to ensure that all important items were functioning and that the entrance was well camouflaged. A couple of the older men in the bunker had hand pistols and ammunition they got from the smugglers, in case we were discovered by the Germans.

Michal, another courier, and I were assigned to a row of buildings on Ogrodowa Street, to patrol the rooftops and report any suspicious movements on the other side of the wall to the nearest fighting cell.

I was thrilled to be a courier but afraid to leave Mother alone. When I tried to discuss it with her, she admitted that she was afraid for me but that she was proud I would have the chance to avenge the deaths of our people. I no longer had the chance to see Halinka, because Michal and I lay on the peaked metal roofs of the old apartment houses from dawn to dusk and observed what was happening on the Aryan side of the wall.

Pedestrians strolled back and forth; well-dressed mothers walked with their children or pushed baby carriages. There were horse-drawn wagons on the streets and an occasional German military car or trolley would be seen. Nothing unusual was happening, and that astonished us. It was so normal we felt we were in another dimension, in a different world, just on the other side of a wall.

At night, Michal and I returned to our rooms, while a group of older lookouts took our places. In the first two weeks, there was hardly anything of interest to report. But we continued to keep a sharp eye on the streets and heard the war news that came to us via hidden radios and relayed by word of mouth. When it was reported that the Germans were defeated in Stalingrad and in Africa, we hoped the

Nazis would be too preoccupied to deal with the ghetto Jews. We grabbed at the news as a drowning man grabs at a lifeline.

Relentlessly, the days passed and Passover rapidly approached. Though there was no food, people tried to obtain matzo and other items for the celebration of freedom from slavery. Religious women were busy koshering their dishes and utensils, but we were all on edge. We knew the Germans always keyed their actions to the holidays and worried that Passover would begin with another deportation and more killings.

Sojnek had been busy with the smugglers. He came to our apartment with three matzos, some chopped liver, and a small bottle of wine. Together with the soup Mother was preparing, we had our Passover seder ready and were looking forward to it.

ABOVE: Street scene from the early Warsaw ghetto. Warsaw, Poland, c. 1940. *Bundesarchiv, Koblenz, Germany*

BELOW LEFT: Adam Boren six months after liberation. Hamburg, Germany, November 1945

BELOW RIGHT: Adam Boren's sister, Mina, ca. 1938–39

RIGHT: Adam Boren's father, Israel
Borenstejn, 1939

BELOW (PHOTO MONTAGE): Adam
Boren's paternal family: *back row, from left:*
Aunt Rena Borenstejn, Cousin Adam
Holtekener (Tofila's son), Aunt Tofila
Holtekener, Grandmother Pesha
Borenstejn, Grandfather Godel
Borenstejn; *front row, from left:* Uncle
Fredek Borenstejn, Cousin Adam
Borenstejn (Uncle Sojnek's son),
Uncle Sojnek's wife, Uncle Sojnek
Borenstejn, Uncle Trusterman,
Aunt Adela Trusterman. Except for
the Trustermans, who emigrated
to the United States before the war,
all were killed in the Warsaw ghetto
and Treblinka.

CHAPTER 13

On April 18, 1943, Sojnek reported that the Germans were massing on the Aryan side of the wall, signaling the next *Aktion*. But Mother refused to let that stop her from having her seder. She covered one of the crates with a white bedsheet and two Haggadoth she had managed to save. Sojnek conducted the service, while two other young boys from our house and I asked the *Ma Nishtana,* the Four Questions. We sipped the prescribed four glasses of wine and ate our "festive" dinner. Though we didn't have much, it felt good to bring back the tradition and talk about freedom.

When we were done, we headed for bed, but at about three o'clock in the morning of April 19, couriers from ŻOB woke us and ordered us to dress and get to the bunker, fast. Observers on night duty reported the Nazis and their cohorts were massed around the walls to prevent any Jews from escaping, a sure sign of a dragnet and deportation. Hurriedly, I helped Mother to the bunker. As soon as we got there, Sojnek ordered me to go to my post on the roof and report any German activity in the area.

At about 5 o'clock, before I could see anything in the darkness, I heard explosions, rifles, and automatic gunfire from the direction of the Zamenhofa Street gate. Several minutes later, huge flames lit the sky. We later learned the ŻOB fighters had exploded a German tank with one of their Molotov cocktails. The streets echoed with the sounds of war. The streets below were totally empty, not a soul was seen.

The Jewish remnants were hiding in bunkers, cellars, attics—wherever they could find a place to hide.

There was nothing to report from my area that morning, but as the hours passed, I saw the enemy draw a cordon around the periphery. Farther out of range, a group of civilians, probably Poles on the way to work, stopped to see what was happening. Other men and women continued on their way as if nothing important was happening.

In the early afternoon, a heavy pillar of smoke and fire rose from the intersection of Zamenhofa and Gesia Streets. It looked like the buildings were burning, and the sound of guns and bombs continued unabated. In late afternoon, I was relieved by another lookout and returned to the bunker.

There were at least 20 people in the bunker, most of them women with children and the elderly. As soon as I came in they wanted to know what was happening outside. I told them the truth, that there was another *Aktion* and that the ŻOB was fighting back. Mother was very calm as she hugged me, whispering that we were finally taking revenge, and that she was proud I was part of the resistance.

Sojnek came in later and told us the Germans had gone outside the walls but would be back in the morning. In the meantime he told us to relax, and we heaved a collective sigh of relief. Someone boiled water for tea on a Primus burner. Mother brought out some cookies she had saved, and we all sat on beds and crates and waited for Sojnek to describe what was happening. Despite the hopelessness of our situation, he said, we should be proud of the bravery and sacrifice of the ghetto fighters.

The *Aktion* began when the Germans and Latvians entered the ghetto through the gate at the corner of Mila and Zamenhofa Streets, and at the Nalewki Street gate. Several SS battalions of close to a thousand men, fully armed and followed by armed vehicles and tanks, entered the ghetto, marched down the middle of the street, singing, as if nothing could stand in their way. They were met by a fusillade of bullets, bombs, and grenades from the buildings lining the streets, causing panic in the German ranks. Two tanks following the SS battalions were hit by Molotov cocktails and burst into flames.

The Germans quickly retreated and left behind several wounded and dead. Later they came back—and this time they weren't singing as they marched—using the buildings for cover as the fighting continued. The ŻOB fighters had the advantage of using the buildings and rooftops as vantage points, whereas the Nazis were exposed in the streets below. Unfortunately, this advantage didn't last long. The Germans returned with firebombs and flamethrowers and soon set fire to the buildings held by the ghetto fighters. Our people went from roof to roof and continued their battle. Sojnek told us that this was happening all over the ghetto, that whenever the SS were met with a Jewish firefight, they retreated. Our casualties were low that day, only one fighter was killed and few were wounded. The Germans suffered greater losses than we did. Several were killed and many were wounded.

When Sojnek finished his description of the fighting, we all gave him a standing ovation for the bravery of our ŻOB fighters who fought against the mighty German military machine. To us, it seemed a miracle that we had, temporarily at least, beaten the unbeatable "Supermen."

On April 20, the ŻOB fought its main battle near Landau's brush factory. Sojnek told us the ŻOB set up mines and set them off when German troops tried to enter the workshop, causing casualties and panic among them. There was also fierce fighting on Muranowska Square, where the Germans sustained casualties, and we suffered even more losses than they did. In the main ghetto section, where we were hidden, the day was reasonably quiet, shattered only by echoes of the explosions and shots from the fighting. From my observation post, I saw smoke and fire from burning buildings in several parts of the ghetto.

Sojnek returned to the bunker that night and told us about the different battles that had taken place that day. Many of our heroic fighters had fallen, and the Nazis had captured several hundred Jews for deportation. Our voices sank to a whisper, and our conversations dealt mostly with the chances of our survival. Those of us who had seen the enemy and their formidable armaments knew those chances were next to nil; sooner or later, our fighters and we would be overpowered and we would be deported and killed.

Though Mother had already lost her daughter and did not know that Father and Mietek were gone, she was still somewhat optimistic and said that if it was God's will, we would both survive. That night we ate a couple of slices of dried-out bread with marmalade and shared a glass of tea heated on the Primus burner. Exhausted from the nervous tension, we all tried to sleep.

April 21, on the third day of the resistance, I left the bunker before daylight and went to my observation post on the rooftop. Most of the burning, I could tell, came from the area of the brush factory. Through the dense black night, I searched for any movement of the Germans, but nothing stirred on the streets below me. It was cold up there on that metal roof, and I was shivering. As day broke, two German armored cars raced through the street without stopping. Several shots rang out from a lower floor in the building, but the Germans escaped unharmed. They were torching the houses around us, and most of them were burning fiercely. People, including mothers with their babies in their arms, who were hiding in the attics of buildings now on fire, jumped to their deaths below to avoid being burned alive.

The sound of a carousel's music, the same melody, over and over again, carried over to us from the Aryan side of the wall, like some insane movie soundtrack. It was also Easter Week, which usually coincided with our Jewish Passover. From my perch on the roof, I could see Żelazna Street, where mothers, dressed in their finest, held their children by the hand and celebrated Easter as our Jewish tragedy unfolded, out of sight, just a hundred meters away.

That night Sojnek didn't return to the bunker. No one knew what happened to him, only that he had taken part in a large surprise attack on an SS unit. Without his information about what happened on the outside, we felt isolated and worried.

Early on the morning of April 22, we heard explosions directly above us. No one dared investigate. We sat in the bunker in total darkness and silence. Mother and I sat unmoving on the bed, holding hands. I felt her grip tighten on one hand, while another trembling woman grabbed the other. It seemed like we stayed that way for hours. Later we learned the SS had blown out a bunker in the other side of the building and had killed or captured those hiding there.

We knew it was a matter of time before they found us and killed us. One of the fighters told me and another courier, Kazik, to go to a building on Leszno Street and report back any German action. Kazik and I sneaked through the basement passages and alleys and climbed to the roof. Everywhere around us buildings were burning. We saw a German commando shoot people who were trying to escape the flames by sliding down ropes made of bedsheets or other materials. It was like watching a scene in a shooting gallery, only the Germans weren't shooting at metal targets. They were shooting at Jewish men, women, and children and enjoying it. It was horrible for us young boys to watch the slaughter. Kazik ran down to the bunker to pass on the grisly news.

A couple of hours later Kazik returned. His face was chalky white and he was sobbing. When I asked him what was wrong, what had happened, he could not look at me. Finally, in a shaking whisper he stammered out the truth. "Our bunker was discovered by the Germans," he sobbed. "They blew it up with everybody in it and set it on fire. No one in the bunker survived; they are all dead."

I wanted to scream, *"My mother!"* But Kazik clamped his hand over my mouth. I fell to my knees, sobbing. "I am going to the bunker!" I cried. "I want to see for myself if my mother is among the dead."

"You can't go there," he said. "The bunker is totally covered in rubble from the explosion, and there is a raging fire. The SS are still roaming around that area, and I almost fell into their hands."

I didn't care. I said, "I am going. I want to see for myself." But as I stood up to leave, Kazik grabbed me and begged me not to go, not to leave him. "We are the only ones left," he pleaded. "Let's stay together. There is nothing else we can do except look for revenge before we get killed."

I was in total despair. My mother—my wonderful, loving, suffering mother— was gone. First Father and Mietek, then Mina, and now Mother—my whole family was dead, murdered. Where was God? What had we done to deserve such horrors? I cursed Him. Kazik and I lay on the roof silently sobbing. We had both lost all we had. "Your mother and all the others in the bunker died instantly from the bomb explosion," Kazik said, trying to ease my pain.

When darkness fell, we left the roof. Fires raged all around us. The sky was blood red and we choked on the smoke. Where could we hide? We looked for bunkers but couldn't find any. As we ran farther along the street, we hugged the buildings in fear, and in the courtyard of one building found a young man hiding in a niche. He told us to go away, but when he heard our story, what our assignment was, and what had happened to our bunker, he took us to a well-camouflaged bunker. It was large, built below the cellar of the building, and seemed well equipped.

Three young men already there told us they had found the bunker empty, just two days earlier, and that, most likely, the Germans had deported or killed the in-habitants. We realized that whatever had happened there happened suddenly. A sizable store of food had been left behind, and everyone helped themselves to the find except me. Though I hadn't eaten a thing all day, I was too devastated by the death of my mother to eat. When they finished, we assigned each other four-hour watches and took our shifts.

In the morning we heard shots and grenade explosions responding to automatic weapons fire. It meant our fighters were still taunting the Nazis. I could not help but wonder what had happened to Sojnek. Was he still alive? There was no way to find out. Perhaps the next day I might find someone who knew him.

On April 24 and 25 the fighting continued, and we heard gunfire and sporadic explosions coming from different parts of the ghetto. The Germans, unable to get the Jews out of their hiding places and afraid to enter the buildings, used their flame-throwers and bombs to flush them out.

The light in the bunker fizzled out. One of the boys had a flashlight, so we were able to find a box of candles and matches. The weak, flickering light gave us some consolation in the gloom, where we huddled, terrified, lest the Nazis with their listening devices and their dogs find us.

That night one of the boys left the bunker to scout the area. He returned to tell us the streets were desolate. Not a soul, German or Jewish, was to be seen, and the entire ghetto was on fire, including the house we were hiding under. The top floors were burning fiercely, and the building next door was entirely aflame. We realized we had to get out before the bunker collapsed on us. The four older guys left and took the whole box of candles with them, leaving Kazik and me alone. What were we going to do?

We stood there in the center of the bunker, petrified. Because we hadn't heard from Sojnek, we had no idea what was happening outside and how we could save ourselves. The candle flickered one last time and went out. In total darkness we sat on the cot and cursed our situation, with nowhere to go and no one to ask for advice. We sat in the darkness unable and unwilling to sleep, waiting. What would happen to the burning house above us? Would it collapse on us? We could feel the heat rising in the bunker as the room slowly filled with smoke from the fire above.

CHAPTER 14

In the morning we left the bunker to find that the top floors of the building above us had collapsed and were smoldering on the lower floors. We decided it was safe, for the moment, to stay in the bunker, but later that morning, we heard someone trying to get in and we froze. We were certain the Germans were coming and, at any moment, expected bombs or grenades to be thrown into our space. After what seemed like hours later, we heard a soft voice in Polish and then in Yiddish say, "I am Shmulek from the ŻOB. Don't be frightened."

We knew Germans had tortured and forced some of the Jews they had captured to reveal hiding places and induced them to tell bunker occupants, in Yiddish and Polish, that all was safe, to come out. We didn't answer Shmulek. The voice again implored us to let him in. He said he was alone and not a spy, and to please let him in. We discussed it and decided it couldn't be a German trick, because the SS could simply have blown us apart, so we guided the fellow in. Shmulek crawled into the bunker with a flashlight in his hand. He saw us, but we couldn't see him because we were blinded by his beam of light.

"Don't you have a light?" he asked.

"No," I replied, "but maybe they left us some candles." We turned on his flashlight and looked everywhere without luck, until Kazik whispered, "I think I found some, throw the light here."

Fortunately, he found a full box of Shabes candles. We lit one and stood there looking at each other. Shmulek was about 165 centimeters tall, about 20 years old, dressed in an old Polish army jacket and wearing a hat, with a large pistol sticking out of his pants belt. "I was with a small group of fighters," he said, "and we were surprised by a commando of heavily armed SS. We killed two of them and wounded several more, but they succeeded in killing everyone in our group, except me. I was lucky—I fell behind some rubble, and they missed me."

We told him we had been hidden in the bunker in total darkness. Were the ŻOB still fighting the Nazis? Were there any Jews still left in the ghetto? Had he heard any news of what was happening on the war fronts in the Soviet Union and in Africa?

"We are still fighting," he said, "not with direct attacks against the Germans. We couldn't openly face them because we hardly have enough to stand against them. We have resorted to guerrilla tactics, hitting them in the back when they least expect it. But they retaliate by burning and shelling whole blocks of houses. We have lost a lot of firefights, men, and women, but we are not giving in. We'll fight them to the last fighter.

"Despite the SS listening devices, the dogs, and even captured Jews who reveal hidden bunkers," he told us, "there are still a thousand of us hidden in bunkers, sewers, and other hiding places in the ghetto. The Germans have captured only several hundred of our people each day. Still," he said, "if they continue the *Aktion* in the ghetto, they will, in the end, destroy us all.

"The German army," he told us, "is retreating on all fronts." The war news came from the BBC, from a radio on the other side of the wall, but even if the war news was good, the Nazis were persistent and intended to kill every Jew in Europe, especially those of us left in the Warsaw ghetto. Shmulek told us to try not to get captured, to hide if we could, and, if at all possible, to escape and join the partisans. We shared our food and water with him. He wished us survival and then he left.

When he was gone, Kazik and I closed and concealed the entrance to the bunker. What Shmulek had described was disastrous. We had two choices, survive or die. If we tried to get to the other side, our dirty and torn clothing would make us stand out among the reasonably well-dressed Polish population. We didn't have papers that would allow us to pass for Polish Catholics, and we were sure we would end up being denounced by some Polish hooligans. We decided to see if we could escape. Meanwhile, we would stay in the bunker as long as we could.

That same night we woke up when we choked on smoke that was seeping into the bunker. When we slid out of the entrance, we saw that the floor above us was burning and could collapse into the bunker momentarily. Quickly we went back in, grabbed the dried-out bread, candles, and a large bottle of water and left. Half an hour later, as we crouched behind a burned-out building, we watched the burning floor collapse into our bunker. We were lucky. If the smoke hadn't seeped in, we would have been buried and burned alive.

It was still dark and we had to find a new hiding place. But where? Even at night it was dangerous to move around. The Germans had night patrols that would shoot us on sight. Because most of the ghetto was burning, there was light everywhere. We crawled across the street to a burned-out building and tried to find a way in, but it was useless. What might have been a bunker was covered with rubble. Another building down the block had upper floors that were still smoldering, but the ground floor was still intact. We crawled over to it and, after searching the basement, found an entrance to an abandoned bunker.

When we entered it, the smell of smoke hit us hard, but it was not the smell of a burning building. We thought the Germans must have tossed a smoke bomb through a vent to flush out the Jews in hiding. We lit one of our candles and looked around. The bunker was not very large and may have held, at most, 15 people. The floor was covered with clothing that had been hastily searched and old bedding. Two decks of narrow beds stood against the walls, and under one of them, we found a box of dry noodles and kasha. We were so hungry, we ate them raw. Then we covered the bunker entrance as best we could and hoped the Germans would not return. We lay down on the bunks, exhausted, and fell asleep.

A huge explosion woke us and the bunker swirled with dust that filled our eyes and throats. We quickly crawled out and discovered the air outside was also filled with masonry dust. When it settled, we saw that the upper floors had collapsed. Though the bunker was still standing, it would be just a matter of time before it was crushed by the weight above it. Already covered in rubble, we decided the bunker, despite the danger, was a safe hiding place, and stayed.

When we heard sporadic gunfire, grenade explosions, and short bursts of machine-gun fire, we knew the war between the Germans and the ŻOB was still going on. We hadn't spoken to any fighters in a while and knew only that the ghetto was burning. The smoke everywhere irritated our throats and stung our eyes.

We returned to the abandoned bunker, lit a candle, and proceeded to straighten

out the mess. We found water, some dry biscuits, hard cheese, and a jar of marmalade, which we turned into a wonderful feast. We put out the candle and in the
darkness, in whispers, discussed the idea of escaping through the city sewers. First,
we had to find out where the manhole covers were. We hoped to meet Sojnek again,
because we knew he would help us.

We spent the next three days in the bunker, sitting in the darkness, lighting the
candle only to eat or relieve ourselves. At night we would sneak out to see what
was going on. The fires still raged, and we could feel the heat radiating from them.
There were no people anywhere. We thought we alone had survived.

On our fourth night in the bunker, a loud rumbling sound came from the outside.
We waited and hoped it would subside, but it became louder and more threatening.
Hurriedly we lit a candle, packed our food and a bottle of water, and got out of
there. A few moments later we watched as the first floor collapsed and destroyed
the bunker below it. Once again, my luck had held. We had not been buried alive.

But now we had no cover and needed to find a hiding place before the Nazi patrols came back inside the ghetto. We crawled our way across Ogrodowa Street one
at a time, and, by picking our way over burned-out buildings, finally made it to
Leszno Street. Before the war, Leszno Street had been an upscale boulevard lined
with beautiful old buildings and elegant shops. At one end stood the large modern
building that housed the city courts. I knew the neighborhood well because I had
gone to grade school there. Now the buildings were skeletons of their former selves
and tongues of flame licked them deeper into destruction.

The courthouse buildings were untouched by the gunfire or the blazes. Their
backs faced the ghetto, and several buildings that stood back-to-back with them had
so far been spared. The ghetto walls, about 4.5 meters high, had been built by Jewish
slave labor, using bricks from bombed-out and burned-out houses. The wall ran from
building to building, across streets and empty squares, and totally encircled the
ghetto. I remembered that it was topped with shattered glass embedded in concrete.

We moved toward the court buildings, crawling and hugging the walls around
us. As we got closer, we observed that the buildings behind them, inside the ghetto
walls, were heavily patrolled by Polish policemen and firemen to prevent them from
being consumed by fire. We realized we could never make it out and needed to take
cover quickly. The building nearest us was partially destroyed by fire and the lower
floors were still smoldering, but we had to take the risk and sought a hideout there.

As we searched the basement, we were happy to hear muffled voices coming from one corner. When we got closer to the voices, we found a pile of broken furniture that hid the entrance to the bunker. Speaking softly we announced that we were two Jewish boys who wanted to enter. For a second or two the sound from the bunker stopped, then, in Yiddish, a man's voice asked if we were alone. I answered that if there were Germans around, those in the bunker would already have been dead, and that we were alone. After a moment, the broken furniture covering the entrance began to move. We crawled in.

There were two young men, 18 to 20 years old, inside. After greeting us in Hebrew, they told us that they found the bunker two days earlier after they escaped from a burning bunker. We warned them that their voices could be heard in the basement and that from then on, we must speak only in quiet whispers.

We shared our food and stories with our new bunker mates. They told us how they fought the SS and how the Germans had torched the building they were using for their ambush. They ran from the flames, but didn't know what happened to the rest of their group. They had dispersed over the rooftops and were trying to find their fellow fighters in order to regroup. When they did, they would find out if we could join them.

The following morning, April 29, the smoldering fire on the floors above us burst into intense flames. We worried that we would be caught in the inevitable collapse, but it was still too dangerous to leave and look for another hiding place. We decided to stay, hoping we could hold out. Suddenly, about midday, part of the bunker roof collapsed and smoke and burning cinders fell into the bunker, blinding us. As I tried to make it to the exit, I tripped over something. My left hand and left foot dug into the burning cinders on the floor. The sudden searing pain was unbearable, and I screamed.

One of the fellows pulled me off the floor and clamped his hand over my mouth to silence me. As they ran out of the bunker, they dragged me with them. In the daylight I could see the skin of my hand hanging from my palm, with the open flesh covered with embedded soot. The pain in my hand and foot was unbearable. I showed my left foot to the fellows. They carefully took off the shoe and sock to reveal a coal that had burned through the sock and into my flesh.

One of them took off his shirt, tore it into strips, and bandaged my hand and foot. Though the pain was excruciating, I realized I had to keep silent in order not to endanger the others. I bit my lip until it bled. Kazik and the two other guys left me and went to look for another bunker, promising to come back and get me. I lay on the ground, in horrible pain. I didn't care what happened next. I just wanted the nightmare to end.

It didn't take long before Kazik returned and said that they had found a bunker in the cellar next door. It was primitive and empty. The Germans must have discovered it earlier and taken away the Jews hiding there. Kazik lifted me off the ground and helped me hobble to the new bunker. Once we got there, one of the fighters pulled a small bottle of alcohol out of his pocket and handed it to me. "Drink as much as you can," he said, "it will ease your pain." With my shaking right hand I held the bottle to my mouth and took a couple of gulps. Though it burned my throat, I drank some more, then handed the bottle back to him. After a while my head started to spin, and the pain subsided somewhat. Lying on the floor of the bunker, I fell asleep.

The next morning, April 30, the two young men told us that they would be leaving us to look for their group. They left me the bottle of vodka. We wished each other luck and survival.

Though the pain in my palm and foot had eased somewhat, I now had pulsating pains in my underarm and groin. By candlelight, I looked at my injured palm and saw that an infection had set in, that pus covered the open wound. There was nothing I could do. In the evening the injured hand and foot throbbed, and I developed a fever. That night I didn't sleep at all. Kazik found a jar full of water and forced it between my parched lips.

The next day, May 1, around noon, we heard loud German voices close to the bunker. Tear gas, a smoke bomb, or some sort of incapacitating chemicals were thrown into the cellar as booming, rasping, voices screamed, *"Alles raus, raus, ihr verfluchte Juden! Wer nicht rauskommt werd erschossen!"* (Get out! Out you damned Jews! Whoever does not come out will be shot!)

The stink began to permeate the bunker. We could do nothing but surrender. Slowly, with Kazik's help, I hobbled out of the bunker as I choked on the fumes. A full squadron of SS men stood there pointing their guns at us. *"Hände hoch!"* (Hands up!) they screamed. When we lifted our arms, a young SS man in gloved hands frisked us. Except for their commanding officer, none of them could have been more than 18 years old.

They stood there, with their legs in a wide stance, looking at us with contempt, pointing their weapons at us, daring us to provoke them into killing us on the spot. I stood there holding my bandaged hand up in the air with the other. I was dirty, my whole body and face were covered with ashes, but one young SS man walked over to me and stuck a cigarette in my mouth. He took out a lighter and moved his hand to light it for me, when another SS man standing nearby suddenly hit me in the head with his rifle butt and knocked me to the ground while he screamed at the SS man who offered me the cigarette. Kazik helped me up, and now my head was bleeding, too.

The SS continued to search the ruins of the building. They didn't find any more Jews and so moved us out to the street. Kazik held me up as we "marched" to the Umschlagplatz. The ghetto looked as if it had been hit by a massive tornado. The streets were strewn with the rubble of collapsed buildings. The Nazis murdered the Jews of Warsaw and destroyed the homes and shops they built. Jewish Warsaw was finished. As they herded us through the streets, I realized that the city of my youth was gone forever. All that remained were the gaping skeletons of her roofless buildings.

The SS kept yelling at us, "Faster, faster!" as if we were in a rush to go someplace. We joined another group of Jews being marched to the Umschlagplatz, the eastern Warsaw railroad siding. As we marched, other groups of captured Jews were forced to join us. By the time we reached the Umschlagplatz, more than 100 of us were in a column closely guarded by lines of SS men on either side, their guns pointing right at us. At the Umschlagplatz, they rushed us into a large room on the first floor of a building. The room was already full of captives who were lying on the floor, guarded by armed Ukrainians in black uniforms.

In broken Polish they ordered us to immediately lie down on the floor. All around me men, women, and children, some in pain, wounded and bleeding, were moaning softly. Next to me lay a young girl who was curled up in pain and vomiting a green substance. In horror, I asked a woman lying close to me what had happened to her.

"She was poisoned," she replied, "by a poison bomb thrown into her bunker by the Germans. The poor girl won't last long. There was nothing we could do to help her, not even get her a sip of water."

I asked her how long she had been in the Umschlagplatz building. "Two days already," she said. "No food or water, and no place to relieve ourselves. It's like a pigsty," she said. "They are waiting to assemble a large transport. This is our end."

In the misery around me I forgot about my own wounds and pain. I was in a hall of horrors. People, many of them children, were dying all around me, and some of them were already dead. The stink in the hall hung over us and made it hard to breathe. The constant moans of the sick and wounded penetrated my brain like a knife. Only the Ukrainian guards, screaming for silence, brought me back to reality.

I was alone. Kazik, who had always been at my side, had disappeared. Maybe he'd been pushed into another part of the hall or into another building, but there was no way for me to find out. The Ukrainian guards warned they would shoot anyone who stood up. Later that day, the Nazis drove more people into the hall. The mass of suffering humanity was packed tightly together and seemed to weave back and forth.

Nighttime was agonizing. The stench, the incessant moaning and pleas for water, the whimpering of children, and the crying pleas of the wounded or dying made me wish I were dead. I no longer had a reason to survive.

Early on the morning of May 2, the double doors of the building were opened and two SS men, their guns at the ready, stood in the doorway and screamed at us: "Everybody out fast!" The Ukrainians, in their black uniforms, stepped in with whips and swung at those unable to stand up. Panic spread. People trying to avoid the Ukrainian whips pushed against others, and some fell and were trampled by the crazed masses. The Umschlagplatz itself was surrounded by armed Ukrainians, Lithuanians, and Germans. Some of them were holding large dogs.

A train of covered freight cars, the kind used for cattle, sat on a railroad siding with its doors open. The Germans and Ukrainians herded us into the freight cars, hit those of us who moved too slowly, and tossed children into the wagons as if they were so much baggage. The sun peeped through the clouds, as if it were laughing at our misery.

Someone behind me helped push me into the wagon, and I sat curled up in one corner, near the one small, barred opening. In minutes the wagon was full, and with a loud bang, the Germans slid the wagon door shut. That's when the pain from my injured hand and foot, and my fever, returned with a vengeance.

For more than an hour, the train stood on the siding, then it started to move with a sudden jerk. Inside the dark wagon, a few men and women talked about escaping from the train. There were only two possibilities, they said. They could remove some boards from the freight car floor and slide under the train, or somehow remove the bars covering the opening in the wall.

The leaders of the planned escape moved the tightly packed people to one side of the car and examined the floorboards, looking for a loose one. Every board they examined was tightly nailed or bolted, and without tools it would be impossible to remove them. Then one man, who stood on the shoulders of another, attempted to examine the iron bars blocking the small opening. First he said the bars could not be removed, but when he looked again he thought perhaps they could be bent by a strong man.

There was one fellow who was two meters tall, with broad shoulders, standing against one of the walls. "Can you try?" someone asked him. He squeezed toward the opening and asked two men to lift him onto their shoulders. He grabbed two bars in his hands, and with all his strength tried to pull them apart. They hardly moved, but he tried again, without much success. After he took stock of the situation, he thought that if they held him so that his shoulders were pressing against the wall, he could get better leverage and push against the bars with his feet.

Several men pushed forward in the crowd and lifted him up in a horizontal position until his feet reached the bars and his back and shoulders were braced against the opposite wall of the wagon. With all his strength, he pushed his feet against one bar. Perspiration appeared on his face and his legs began to shake, but he continued to press. We all watched him give it his utmost effort, when suddenly one bar popped out of the opening. The man almost fell out of the hands of the men who held him aloft, but they caught him. After he rested a while, he set himself back in position to push out the next bar. After intense strain, he popped out the second bar. The opening created was then about 30 centimeters wide, wide enough for some thin people to pass through, but not wide enough for him or others who wanted to escape. He tried to push a third bar out, but that bar held. He was lowered down to the floor, and another man was lifted up to report on the outside. He told us we were moving through a forest.

"Let's wait till the train slows down at a curve and then jump out," he said. "That will give us a greater chance of escaping unharmed. Who wants to try?"

People began to argue. Some people were against any escape attempts because they felt the SS men we saw standing at the end of the train would shoot to kill any escapees. In fact, we'd already heard several rifle shots as the train moved along and assumed that was indeed the case. Other men and women argued that they'd rather die trying to escape than be murdered later.

The leader ordered those who wanted to jump to line up and remove any loose clothing, to make sure that nothing would catch in the opening. He asked them to lie flat on the embankment after they jumped and to stay there, not moving, until the train passed, so they wouldn't become targets for the guards. Because of the pain and infection in my hand and my foot, there was no way I would try to climb through the opening. My will to survive was gone. The sooner I died, the better.

The man who watched the opening said we were nearing a curve and that it was time to jump. The first to go was a young skinny man who was lifted up to the opening. He thrust himself out, feet first, then pushed himself away from the wagon. The rest of us froze in silence as we listened for the rifle shot that never came, and the train moved on. One after another, men and women jumped out of the train, and no shots were fired. We hoped those who took the risk weren't injured when they fell. The train came out of a wide curve into a straightaway, and the leader told the others they would have to wait until we came to another curve.

It seemed to take an hour before the "spy" told us another curve was approaching. The few remaining men and women who wanted to escape lined up and prepared themselves. One after another they were lifted to the opening and jumped out. Each time we held our breaths and listened for the sound of gunfire. We never heard any.

After I watched the able-bodied men and women successfully escape from the transport, I hated myself for not being able to follow them. The train moved on toward our unknown destination. No one else in our wagon tried to escape, and the big fellow who made it possible for the others stayed with us, because he couldn't fit. Those who stayed behind with him stood or lay on the floor in total silence and waited for the unknown.

CHAPTER 15

After several hours the train came to a stop. Again we heard bone-chilling German voices screaming orders and the wild barking of their dogs. The wagon door slid open, and an armed SS man shrilly shouted at us, "Out! Fast!" We jumped from the train to a raised platform and were immediately surrounded by SS men. Several men in striped prison uniforms with numbers sewn on their jackets stood next to our group. "Where are we?" we asked in Polish and Yiddish.

"Majdanek," one of them replied in a whisper, and added, "God be with you."

After the train was unloaded, the several thousand men, women, and children marched from the unloading platform to the camp, which was surrounded by several rows of barbed wire. At each corner of the compound, and equidistant along the walls, stood tall wooden watchtowers with mounted machine guns and gunners. When we came through the gate, row after row of long wooden barracks that looked like stables sat there in front of us. We were standing in front of a very large structure where they separated men from women and formed us into single rows. One by one, the men were ordered to enter the building, and then it was my turn.

I walked into a long, narrow hall. On one side, there was a row of benches where several prisoners sat with clippers and shaved the heads and pubic areas of the naked men standing in front of them. An SS officer with a leather whip in his hand stood facing the column of naked men as they approached, and with a twitch of his whip to the left or the right, indicated which door behind him the stripped and shaved inmate must enter, the door on the left or the door on the right.

When I entered, a man in prison garb told me to undress completely, put my clothing on a bench and then proceed to the barber. The prisoner-barber I stood in front of looked at my hand and foot, wrapped in the torn shirt, and asked me in Polish what was wrong. He told me to show him my wounds. I unwrapped my pus-covered hand and told him what had happened to me in the ghetto revolt.

"Stay with me here, until I tell you to move," he whispered.

Hundreds of the new captives moved out in front of the other barbers, while I stood silently in front of mine. When the SS officer stepped outside the building to see how many men were still outside, the barber pointed to the door on the right and whispered, "Walk through that door." Quickly, I followed his directions and entered the door on the right, to find myself in a corridor that led to a large shower room. Later I learned that the door to the left led to the gas chambers.

If the kind barber had not intervened and had me stay with him, I would have moved forward toward the SS officer and would certainly have been sent to my death because of the infections. I would thank him today, but I never did find out who he was. There were many naked men in the shower room; some stood under the shower heads, rubbing their wet bodies with shreds of fabric, trying to get the dirt off without any soap. I and others just stood there, waiting to get under the running water.

A few minutes later, another prisoner entered the room and ordered those under the showers to get out. As I held my injured hand high in the air, I got under a showerhead. The water was lukewarm and dripped down without pressure. I took a rag dropped by someone else and started rubbing my soot covered body with my good hand, but succeeded only in getting at the surface dirt by the time we were ordered to leave. I squeezed what I could out of the rag and wiped some of the water off my body, but while we were still wet, we were rushed into another room, where other prisoners handed us uniforms and shoes.

We got blue-striped pants and jackets. A prisoner behind the bench looked at me, and handed me some clothing, including a cap and wooden clogs like those worn by Dutch farmers. We weren't given underwear or socks.

Still wet from the shower, I tried to put the clothes on and found that they were too big and long in the pants and the sleeves. I looked around and asked others if they had gotten clothing that was too small for them. One man's pants and jacket were too small for him, but his clogs fit. We exchanged uniforms, but my wooden clogs were too big. When I tried them on, my foot was rubbed against the top of the clog. It was torture to walk in them. Fortunately, another man had clogs that were too small on him and made the exchange with me.

Dressed in our prison uniforms, we were marched to another section of the camp and given two narrow strips of cloth with Stars of David and numbers printed on them. We were told to sew the bands onto the left breasts of our jackets and on the upper left side of our pants. From then on, the numbers became our names, and we were to respond if we were called. The Star of David identified us as Jews. After that, we were each issued a metal soup bowl and spoon. We were warned by a prisoner not to lose them or let them be stolen or we would starve. We would not get replacements. We were also told to guard our clogs with our lives.

Then we were marched to "Field Four," an area with several rows of barracks and a large tent, all surrounded by a barbed-wire fence. We were led, running, to the tent, which was furnished with several rows of triple-decker bunks. The *Kapo,* the block foreman, assigned a single bunk to each set of two new prisoners. A straw-filled burlap bag served as a mattress. We had to share one thin blanket made of a nondescript material between us. My bedmate was Shmuel, and we were assigned to the upper bunk. Soon we were sitting on the bunk, sewing our identification tags to our uniforms.

The tent we were in was a quarantine barrack. All new arrivals spent two weeks in the tent before being transferred to wooden barracks. They told us we needed to be isolated in case we were carrying typhus or other infectious diseases. Prisoners from another barrack later told me that if a contagious disease broke out in the tent, everyone there was sent to the gas chambers.

It wasn't long before a gong sounded loudly and we were ordered by the tent leader to run to the *Appellplatz* (the roll call area) and assemble in rows of five deep across the yard. We were joined by inmates from other barracks and someone barked out an order, in German, "Attention, caps off." The columns of prisoners snapped to attention, and with our right hands, we rapidly removed our striped caps and held them tight to our sides.

In addition to the watchtowers, the barbed-wire fences around us were hung with signs that warned in German and Polish, "Attention! High Voltage." In the middle of the field, close to the entrance, was the *Appellplatz*, with a six-by-six-meter concrete pool full of water alongside it—water that was used in case there was a fire. On the other side, there was a raised platform that held the gallows. Every time I looked at them—and I couldn't avert my sight—I envisioned the gallows in Krzemieniec and remembered Father's and Mietek's executions. The two long sides of the *Appellplatz* were lined with wooden barracks. At one end of the field, surrounded by another barbed-wire fence, was a vegetable garden and chicken coops that were there for the benefit of the SS camp staff.

A group of SS men came into the plaza and spread among the prisoners' columns. "Two hundred forty-four prisoners; count checks," barked the tent leader in German to the SS. An SS man who held a long leather whip walked past each column, whipping the first prisoner in each row as he counted them.

We all stood at attention with our caps in hand for more than an hour. Finally the SS men finished counting and marched off the field. "Caps on!" yelled the tent leader. "Disperse to the tent!" When we ran back to our tent, we noticed that the prisoners from other barracks were standing in front of big kettles and held their bowls in their hands as soup was ladled out to them. We, however, were given nothing to eat that day.

I looked, but I couldn't find Kazik among the prisoners in our tent. I hoped he'd been transferred to another field or barrack and had not been sent to the gas chamber. Maybe I would find him later. Exhausted and depressed by the day's happenings, I lay down next to Shmuel, my bunkmate, a 32-year-old from Warsaw who had also lost his entire family. Remembering the warning we were given, I put my soup bowl, spoon, and clogs under the straw mattress and fell asleep.

I woke up, seemingly only a couple of hours later, to the loud gong. *"Aufstehen! Aufstehen!"* (Get up! Get up!) screamed the tent leader. "Make your bunks up straight and smooth or you'll be sorry!" he barked in German. Shmuel translated for me, and we proceeded to make up the bunk by standing on the edge of the bunk below us. My injured hand and foot were throbbing with pain. I couldn't stand it any more and went to the block foreman.

"Look," I said to him as I uncovered the pus-covered hand, "I need help; I can't stand the pain any more."

He looked at the hand and covered his nose because of the smell. "After the roll call," he said, "I will take you to the infirmary. I know a Polish doctor there and maybe he'll help you. Otherwise, it's not a good idea to go to the infirmary," he said, "unless you are ready to die. Most of the sick ones are shipped from there to the crematorium, but maybe you will be safe."

Just then an SS man stepped into the tent. *"Achtung!"* barked the block leader. All the prisoners jumped to attention and the SS man stepped to the row of bunks, looked at them, and in a loud voice, with a grimace on his face, spit out: "You'd better make your bunks up perfectly or you will wish you were dead. I'll be back to check."

We tightened the blankets covering our bunks, to make sure they were perfectly flat and straight. "Make sure that all the blankets covering the bunks are in one line, none sticking above or below the others," the tent leader advised. "The SS man sometimes shoots his pistol across the line of bunks, and God help those whose blankets get hit by his bullet." Again we checked the line of blankets, and they looked straight to us.

Four of our prisoners were sent, on the run, to the camp kitchen. They returned with two large kettles. The block leader ordered everybody to form a line in front of the kettles and started distributing the contents. The kettles contained a brown, hot liquid we called ersatz coffee, which was ladled into our soup bowls. We were told to drink it quickly, before the sound of the gong would force us to spill out whatever was left to run to roll call in the *Appellplatz*.

The gong rang. Everyone dumped what was left in their bowls and ran to roll call. A light rain was falling as we lined up in our thin clothing. We were soaked and shivering. We were ordered to remove our caps and stood there, cold and bare-headed, in the rain. The SS man was dressed in rain gear and moved slowly as he counted us. Suddenly he stopped. He took his whip and slashed it across the face of a prisoner who stood in the second row. He screamed, in German, that the prisoner wasn't standing at proper attention. The poor prisoner fell bleeding to the ground, but was quickly lifted by the men standing on either side of him.

When he finished the count, the SS officer said we would all be punished for not standing at attention properly by standing in the rain until he decided we had had enough. An hour later, shivering, we were permitted to return to the tent. Once we got back, the prisoner who had been whipped by the SS man was again beaten, this time by the block leader. The block leader told us all that if we allowed this to happen again, the punishment would be more severe.

When things settled down, the block leader brought me to the infirmary, located in a barrack at the end of the field. A long line of prisoners were outside, waiting to get in. The leader walked me to the front of the line, pushed away a sick prisoner who blocked the door, and brought me inside, where several prisoners waited for treatment. He walked over to a prisoner in a white apron, spoke to him, and pointed to me. Then the man in the apron walked over to me and said in Polish, "I am a doctor, show me your wounds."

The Polish doctor took me into a small cubicle and unwound the rags from my hand and foot and examined my wounds.

"You have some infection," he said. "How did it happen?"

I told him what had happened to me during the Warsaw ghetto uprising. They did not know that anyone had fought against the Nazis in the ghetto. None of them had heard anything about the destruction of the ghetto and how the ŻOB had killed as many Nazis as they could.

After he heard my story, the doctor took me over to a sink in one corner and took a bottle of fluid from a shelf. He slowly poured it over my hand and the liquid foamed over the infection. "This is hydrogen peroxide," he said. "It will clear off the pus." Then he dried off my hand and poured more liquid over my foot. After he dried me off, he bandaged my wounds with crepe paper.

"We have nothing here for the pain," he said, "but I will give you a disinfectant, blue crystals, called *Cali Hypermanganicum* (hypermangan of potash)." He told me, "Dissolve a spoonful of the crystals in your bowl, and bathe your hand and foot in it every day until a scab forms over the wound."

I thanked him for his care and kindness and expressed my gratitude to the block leader for bringing me to the infirmary. I felt they had saved my life. When we got back to the tent, none of the prisoners were there. Out on the field, *Kapos* were separating prisoners into work commandos. The block leader told me to wait in the tent while he fetched a broom. "Sweep up the tent and the barracks," he said, "but keep out of sight. This is your assigned work detail." I thanked him again.

As I swept the tent, prisoners in the work commandos were running back and forth with their arms full of rocks, as they were constantly screamed at and beaten. Whenever a Nazi or *Kapo* came by, I hid behind a wall and hoped they didn't see me. That was how I spent that day.

At the sounding of the midday gong, we lined up to receive a ladle of watery beet soup with nothing much solid in it. The "lunch" break lasted half an hour. If you were at the end of the soup line, you learned to drink your soup quickly, or you would have to dump it when the gong rang to get back to work.

It was dark before the gong that ended the workday sounded, and once again, we tired and beaten prisoners had to gather in the *Appellplatz* for another roll call. Again the orders to remove our caps and stand at attention rang out. We stood there, waiting for the SS officer to take the count. This time, to our relief, there were no incidents and we were soon dismissed to the tent.

When we came in, the block leader told us to wash up before we were issued our last meal of the day, soup and some bread. Many of the men were just too tired and beaten to do that. They just fell onto their bunks and refused to go. I took my bowl and went. The washroom was located in another barrack and was essentially a long trough with open spigots of ice cold running water. We didn't have any soap or towels, but soaked what small rags we had in the water and rubbed them over our faces and hands. I filled my soup bowl with water and mixed in a spoonful of the blue crystals the doctor had given me. I unwound the paper bandage and immersed my hand in the bowl. Then I removed the bandage from my foot and applied a soaked piece of the bandage to my foot. Then I washed out my bowl as best I could. Already my wounds looked better and the pus and the smell were gone. I rebandaged my wounds and went back to the tent.

There was already a line in front of the kettle, and the tent leader was distributing our food. Each prisoner was given a ladle of soup in his bowl, and 100 grams of black bread. The soup was a watery liquid with one or two cabbage leaves floating in it, and the bread tasted as if it was made of sawdust. Because we were so hungry, we quickly gulped down whatever we could.

Before the war began, Shmuel had been an engineering student in France and had returned to Warsaw on summer recess to visit his parents. When the war started, he was trapped. He tried to tell me more about himself, but I was too tired to talk. I climbed onto our bunk and fell asleep.

The next morning the gong woke us up, and we meticulously made up our bunks. We stood there, terrified, as we waited for the SS man, but he never came. Then the block leader doled out our ersatz tea, the gong rang again, and we all ran to roll call, following the usual commands. When the men were separated into working groups, I returned to the barracks to sweep.

Because we were sent to the washroom daily, I was able to soak my wound. Soon enough the infection and pain disappeared. A thin scab formed over my wounds, and I was able to move my fingers. I kept both my hand and foot bandaged to pretend I still had the infection, an excuse that kept me out of rock-carrying commandos.

After a week of sweeping the barracks and tent, the block leader assigned me to washing the pots used for our food. After morning roll call and the soup distribution, another prisoner and I carried the soup kettles to the water storage pool and wash them there. Luckily there was also some soup that clung to the bottom and the sides of the kettle. We would use our spoons to scrape up what we could and eat it before we started our work cleaning them. Those four or five spoonfuls of soup could mean the difference between life and death.

On my third day of kettle washing, I was leaning over the rim of the pool to scoop up water in my bowl and toss it into the kettle. An SS man who happened to stroll by kicked me into the pool. I fell below the surface and swallowed water. I didn't know how to swim. When I surfaced, I was choking and tried to reach for the rim of the pool, but the SS man laughed and pushed my hands back into the water and kicked me back into the pool. I would have drowned if someone had not called him away, and two prisoners nearby came and pulled me out of the pool.

Scared and shivering wet I ran back to the tent, where I undressed, and wrung out my wet clothes. With nothing else to wear, I had to put my wet clothes back on. I couldn't hang them up to dry on the bunk post until after the night gong rang and we went to sleep.

The next morning I told the block leader I was too scared to wash the soup kettles near the pool again. He told me that nothing like that had ever happened before, and that I was stupid for not wanting to do such easy work. I insisted that I couldn't do it, that I would rather go hungry than be constantly afraid of drowning.

It took four weeks before we were transferred to a wooden barrack, one that was also lined with triple-decker bunks. At one end of the barrack, behind a partition, the block leader, the *Blockälteste,* and his assistant, the *Stubendienst,* had their quarters. The block leader in this barrack was a former teamster from Warsaw, a Jew nicknamed "Moyshe Gazel" (Moyshe the criminal), and his *Stubendienst* was Sowa.

Moyshe and Sowa were pitiless, sadistic criminals. Under any pretext, one or both of them would beat prisoners into unconsciousness and steal bread rations.

We feared them more than we did the marauding SS. Often these two would wake us up in the middle of the night and order us to scrub the rough floors with our own rags, or they would order us to make up our bunks before they would let us go back to sleep. The SS knowingly selected such sadists to torture and wear down the prisoners.

In my new barrack I was assigned to share a bottom bunk with Heniek, a young boy from Warsaw. We were both assigned to a construction commando that was working on a two-story building. We would be taken to the work site every morning after roll call. They ordered us to carry 18- to 23-kilogram sacks of cement up to the second floor. I found the heavy work was almost beyond my strength. The cement sacks leaked, and the dust mixed with our sweat and hardened on our backs. It felt like needles cutting into our skin. Once a prisoner tripped on the stairs and spilled some cement. He was beaten and ordered to clean it up with his hands. What made it unendurable was the constant screaming of the *Kapos* and the SS, who yelled at us to work faster, faster, faster.

When the 12-hour workday ended, I could hardly walk back to the barrack. But before we could get our meager rations, we still had to go to the washroom to soak off the hardened cement from our bodies. Soon, I was beyond exhausted. Life became more unbearable than ever.

Every moment I expected to be beaten by the SS, the *Kapo*, or the block leader. If not, I would die of starvation. Everywhere I looked, prisoners were as thin as skeletons, their skin was gray, their eyes blank. They stared into nowhere, their prison clothing hung on them or they were grotesquely swollen by hunger, just this side of death. We called them *Muselmänner.* Where that name came from, I didn't know, but it meant they were near death. Would I become one of them?

The camp commandant of Majdanek was SS *Obersturmführer* Anton Thumann. I think Thumann must have been selected for his post for his lack of humanity and his sadism. He would strut through the camp in his pressed uniform, polished riding boots, and gloved hands holding a leather horsewhip, like an arrogant beast.

Once, during his daily walk, he noticed, among a commando of prisoners smoothing out little stones between the barbed-wire fences, a prisoner who had either fainted or fallen asleep. Furious, he ordered everyone working between the wire fences into the field, immediately. They came running out, dragging the unconscious prisoner between them. The crazed *Obersturmführer* kept hitting the prisoners, who cringed before him, and called for the *Lagerälteste,* the highest-ranking prisoner in the camp, to come forward. Everybody and everything stopped.

The "camp elder" stood at attention in front of Thumann, who screamed, "Twenty-five lashes to every dog in that commando."

A roll call was ordered and then four prisoners were brought to a wooden platform in the middle of the *Appellplatz.* The bottom was flat and had a board attached to it at a 45-degree angle. Six prisoners stood to one side of the platform, and the seventh lay on the ground. Two huge *Kapos* stood on either side of the platform, and they each held huge leather whips.

The first prisoner was ordered to drop his pants and lay down on the platform. His hands and feet were tied down with straps and his buttocks were prominently exposed.

On the order of an SS man, the two *Kapos* raised their whips and ordered the tied-down prisoner to count the strokes. With full force they whipped him, alternating the count strokes, one, two; one, two. The prisoner kept count, screaming in pain. After ten strokes he passed out. One of the *Kapos* poured a bucket of water on him. His buttocks were like raw meat. When he started moaning, the *Kapos* ordered him to keep count again, and continued to whip him. When he passed out again, they poured water over him and started again.

The prisoner could no longer scream, he could only moan. I stood at attention in my column, crying softly, my body shaking. Finally the *Kapos* threw the bleeding body to the ground, and others dragged him off. This same torture was carried out on all the other prisoners. They screamed until they could only whimper. Then they were dragged off, bleeding. They finally put the last prisoner, who was unconscious, on the platform. Though they poured water on him, he didn't stir. No sounds came from him, but the *Kapos* pulled down his pants and after binding his hands and feet, whipped him mercilessly. His body jerked with each lash, until they hit him 25 times. When they finally untied him and dropped his body to the ground, he was dead.

Several days later, after a roll call, the SS dragged a prisoner to the gallows. A *Kapo* bound the inmate's hands behind him and placed the noose around his neck. We stood there waiting for the inevitable, and I was frozen in the past, in a scene remarkably like the one in front of me. Though I stood at attention, I could not look at the condemned man because the execution in Krzemieniec kept flashing before my eyes.

SS *Obersturmführer* Thumann accused the prisoner of trying to escape, and informed him that the penalty for that offense was hanging. When the prisoner heard his sentence, he spit in Thumann's direction and cried out in Polish, "Long live Poland." Thumann bellowed out the order: "Hang him!"

I didn't look, but I heard the loud cracking noise of the trapdoor snapping open under the sentenced man and his last moan. The SS let his body hang there for two days. It was something we had to look at during every roll call. For those two nights, I could not sleep.

Every day at roll call we also counted up the dead. There were those who were beaten and starved, and there were those who committed suicide. The gong marked our days and nights relentlessly. The cold and rain chilled our bodies. When I found pieces of paper, I put them underneath my thin jacket, trying to keep the rain and wind from my body. I hoped that Moyshe Gazel would not find out or he would beat me.

Because we were allowed to shower only once a week and because we had no soap, we were all infested with lice. In the evening, after we ate our rations, we stripped off our shirts to look for lice. It was a wretched scene; we sat on the edge of our bunks, killing lice with our thumbnails, our bodies covered in red scratches.

The days repeated themselves in their hopelessness. My attention was devoted to avoiding Moyshe and Sowa, and watching out for the SS. Sometimes in the evenings, before lights out, Heniek and I would talk in whispers about our lost families and the uprising in the Warsaw ghetto. I told Heniek how my Father and brother were murdered, how my mother and Mina died, how I had managed to survive.

Heniek told me how his family was killed in the uprising, and that as far as he knew, he was the only one in the family who had survived. We were both so starved we would fantasize about the foods we used to eat before the war. I told Heniek that my favorite dish was noodles with pot cheese, sprinkled with cinnamon and sugar. If I survived the war, I wanted a room of my own with books, and noodles with cheese, sugar, and cinnamon.

Late in June 1943, we heard the SS was looking for electricians. Though my knowledge of electronics was limited to what I had learned in school, and the best

I knew how to do was wire a bell to a battery, I ran to register. I told the prisoner clerk that my grandfather and father were electricians and that I had been my father's helper doing all types of electrical work. Without asking me anything about electricity, the clerk wrote down my number, the number of my barrack, and told me to go back and wait.

Several weeks later, on July 7, the block leader called me and told me to go to the registration block to be transported. When I asked him where I was going, he said he didn't know but it had to be better than Majdanek, because everyone on the transport was a mechanic. When we arrived at the transport barrack, we were given slivers of soap and thin, small pieces of torn shirt to use as towels and ordered to take showers.

It felt wonderful to wash my body with soap and to dry it. After the shower we were given fresh prison clothing and wooden shoes and assigned a bunk. Even though the bunks still had straw-filled sacks as mattresses, they felt like real beds. After roll call, we were given a bowl of a watery beet soup and a larger piece of bread than we were used to. I felt that whatever happened next could not possibly be worse than Majdanek. If I stayed there, I would be dead in a month.

July 8, early in the morning, about 800 of us were marched to a railroad siding. Thirty of us were loaded into one cattle car, but we were not locked in until an armed SS man climbed into the wagon carrying a folding chair. He ordered us to sit on the floor, and after the door was slid shut, he sat down on his chair in one corner and held his automatic gun on his lap, with its muzzle facing us. Two hours later, the train began to roll.

CHAPTER 16

Later that same afternoon, the train stopped at a railroad siding. We were ordered to disembark. Several SS men, some of them holding large dogs, and a group of prisoners in striped uniforms were there to greet us.

Once again, the SS barked orders at us to form columns of five. We were guarded on both sides by the SS and the prisoners, as we were marched toward a compound of large, red-brick buildings. We passed through a gate, and I noticed three words wrought in the iron arch above me: *Arbeit Macht Frei* (Work Makes Free). A prisoner walking next to me whispered, "This is Auschwitz."

We entered the camp and we were stopped in a wide opening between buildings, where an SS officer ordered us to strip and form a single column in front of him. Naked, we approached him. He was dressed in a well-pressed uniform, his riding boots were highly polished, and he held a leather whip. It was like repeating the nightmare of Majdanek. I stood naked before him as he looked me up and down and ordered me to turn and walk a few steps. He looked into my eyes and directed me, with a flick of his whip, to the left. Other prisoners, he directed to the right. Later I learned that I lived through a selection by the notorious Dr. Josef Mengele. The prisoners who were sent to the right went directly to the gas chambers.

We were allowed to dress and then we were ordered to form a single line. A prisoner handed each of us a piece of paper with a number written on it. Mine was 127956. Moments later another prisoner approached us with a long tool that had a needle on its end. After he read the number on my piece of paper, he took his needle and tattooed it on my left forearm. From then on I was known as Prisoner 127956. (Later I learned that, of 800 male prisoners from Majdanek, only 424 were transferred to Buna. The rest of them were sent to the gas chambers.)

When they finished putting tattoos on us, we were marched to a square and loaded into waiting trucks. The convoy was guarded by several motorcycle-mounted SS officers who led us out of the camp. Less than half an hour later, we arrived in a camp closed in by a double barbed-wire fence and guarded by watchtowers. When the trucks came to a stop, we were ordered to get out.

We were in a camp called Buna, officially known as Auschwitz-Monowitz. Buna was originally built as part of Auschwitz by the German chemical combine I.G. Farben as a synthetic rubber and gasoline factory. Farben built the factory near the camp so it would have a steady supply of slave labor. Like Majdanek, Buna consisted of several rows of wooden barracks and an *Appellplatz*. I found out later that the interior barbed-wire fence was electrified.

When they finished counting us, we were sent, on the run, to a shower block, where we were ordered to strip and leave our clothing and wooden clogs on a bench. We stood in a large shower room for more than half an hour waiting for water to come out of the showerheads. Then, suddenly hot, almost boiling, water was spraying over us. Without soap I rubbed hot water all over my body. Then a door opened, two prisoners in striped clothing ran in and screamed at us in German to get out.

We were still wet when we were herded into another room, where a prisoner gave us each a bundle of prison clothing and a pair of old, torn shoes. The technique they used to frustrate us was identical to the ruse they used in Majdanek. We furiously attempted to exchange pants, jackets, and shoes to find sizes that would fit, at least marginally. I was lucky to find that the old shoes fit, more or less, but the pants and jacket were much too small. After trading with smaller prisoners, I found clothing that sort of fit, and wet as I was, tried to climb into them. I was now a prisoner in Auschwitz. I was a numbered slave.

After we dressed, we were assigned our blocks. Inside each block were several rows of triple-decker bunks. The barrack I was assigned to was empty, except for the block leader and his helper, who assigned us two to a bunk. I was the last. He looked at me and pointed to a bottom bunk that I would have to myself.

The bunks were covered with thin blankets, and as in Majdanek, used straw-filled sacks as mattresses. Two narrow aisles ran the length of the block, which was divided in two. The smaller section, which housed the block leader and his assistant, had a table, a few benches, and several narrow lockers. The larger section of the barrack housed the prisoners. At one end of the aisle stood a couple of metal buckets that were to be used as urinals during the night. The block leader's assistant gave each of us a metal soup bowl and spoon, and, like his predecessor in Majdanek, warned us to guard them with our lives. No replacements would be issued, even if the items were stolen. Then he handed each of us two short, narrow strips of white cotton, imprinted with our numbers and a star formed by overlapping yellow and red triangles to identify us as Jews.

A green triangle was assigned to criminals, a red one to political prisoners; pink triangles were issued to homosexuals, and black ones to the antisocial. Temporary civilian prisoners wore the letter E for *Erziehungshäftling,* reeducation, and were mostly Polish and other nationals who committed minor crimes, like being late for work, trading on the black market, or smuggling. For smuggling, for example, the penalty was 30 or more days in Auschwitz.

Most of those in privileged positions, such as *Lagerälteste* (camp leader), *Blockälteste* (block leader), *Kapos* (work leaders), and kitchen staff, wore green triangles and were brought to Buna because they were known for their cruelty. The intent was to use them to help run the camp.

We were ordered to sew the strips with our numbers and stars on our uniforms, one on the upper right leg of our pants, the other on the left breast of our striped jackets. While I sat on the bunk and waited to get a needle and thread, I spoke to the people sitting near me. All of them were from the Warsaw ghetto and had been captured during the uprising. Later we realized that prisoners with numbers that were in the 127000 series were mostly, if not all, taken from the Warsaw ghetto during and after the revolt. All of them, like me, lost their entire families.

I was surprised when I discovered that in addition to the standard blue-striped pants and jacket, I was also given a shirt. Now I had a shirt, leather shoes, and a bunk all to myself! After Majdanek, it was like a miracle.

As soon as I finished sewing the numbers onto my uniform, I heard loud German martial music coming from a prisoners' orchestra playing near the main gate. I ran to the door to see what was going on and discovered that the working commandos were returning to camp after their day's work, forced to strut in uniform to the marching music. As soon as they were out of SS range, they stopped marching and dragged themselves, drained, to the *Appellplatz*. When all the commandos were back, the orchestra stopped, a gong announced the roll call, and we mustered quickly for the count.

In Buna, the *Appellplatz* was in the center of the camp, a large space able to hold as many as 10,000 prisoners. On one side, there was a square of green grass where a gallows stood on a platform. More than 60 wooden barracks surrounded the plaza. It was where the prisoners were housed and where latrines, showers, the kitchen, and special barracks for the privileged were located. The privileged were the camp leaders, the *Kapos*, and other prominent criminals. Separated from the main part of the camp were eight barracks that housed the notorious infirmary, surrounded by a fence of its own.

The roll call drill was identical to the one in Majdanek. We stood at attention with our caps clutched to our sides. Thankfully, the counting in Buna didn't take as long as it did in Majdanek, and after we were ordered to put our caps back on, we went back to the barrack for our evening meal.

I noticed that some prisoners would maneuver themselves in line so as to get best advantage of the thickest soup in the pot. Whenever my turn came, the block leader would mix the soup vigorously and pour a full ladle into my bowl. The soup was similar to the one served in Majdanek—*steckrüben,* cattle beet soup—mostly yellow water with a few leaves floating in it. Hungry and thirsty as I was, it disappeared into my stomach in a hurry.

After we got our soup and bread, we sat on our bunks and tried somehow to repair our torn clothes, sew on buttons, or fix our falling-apart shoes with pieces of wire. Or we would try to deal with our latest physical injuries. I and other new-comers pumped the old-timers for information about the camp. We wanted to know what we needed to be aware of, what and who to avoid, and anything else that might help us survive. Some of the old-timers were so despondent they avoided talking with us, saying at most that we would find out for ourselves, soon enough.

A few others, who perhaps had some pity on us, warned us about several dangers: "Don't let your shoes, clothes, soup bowl, or spoon out of your sight day or night, or they'll be stolen, and you won't get replacements. No matter what an SS officer or *Kapo* says to you, answer *'Jawohl'* (Yes, sir) and stand at attention. Be careful of prisoners who will try to talk you out of your soup, bread ration, or anything you own, and keep yourself clean and your clothing in good order to avoid beatings. Most of all, learn to conserve your energy; you'll last longer."

Our barrack was full and all the bunks had double occupancy, except for a very few. All together there were 200 prisoners. I was very lucky to have a bunk to myself. Before I went to sleep, I would go to the latrine and get back before lights out. The prisoners lay on their bunks like sardines in a can, head to toe, covered with the same blanket. Only one bulb in the room was lit—the one over the urine buckets.

Before I would lie down, I would roll my shoes, cap, soup bowl, and spoon into my striped jacket and place it under my straw sack to make sure it wouldn't be stolen during the night. We were ordered to sleep with our pants on. That first night I couldn't fall asleep.

I wondered what would happen to me next. Would I be able to absorb and survive all those horrors? Would I turn into one of those shuffling *Muselmänner*? Something inside me wanted to fight the depression. Frankly, Buna was better than Majdanek, at least at first glance, and maybe with a little more luck, I could hold on. In the darkened barrack, the night sounds included the soft moans and groans of the other prisoners, and, from time to time, a stream of urine hitting a metal bucket.

When the morning gong sounded, it was still dark outside, and the block leader's helper was screaming. We knew we had to rush and had to make up our bunks properly or we would be whipped. As it got lighter outside, we ran to the latrine and stood in line to relieve ourselves, went to wash without soap in cold water, and then ran back to our block.

By the time we got back, there were prisoners already in line in front of the kettle. As in Majdanek, if you weren't finished "eating" before the gong sounded, you had to dump your food and run to roll call.

Though it was July, the early mornings were cold and windy. During roll call we stood at attention with our caps at one side and our bowls on the other, shivering for the hour it took until roll call was over. The old-timers went into different commandos and were marched to the Buna plant, while we newcomers were ordered to wait. Then two *Kapos* came over to our column and began to select prisoners. One of them looked me over from head to toe and spit out: "Get over there, fast!"

I quickly joined his commando.

We were marched out, in rows of five, through the gate. Fifteen minutes later, we entered the Buna works. The large industrial complex was surrounded by barbed-wire fence and SS guards. There were several large buildings, some with tall smoke-stacks and some still under construction, surrounded by cranes.

We were led to a wooden shed and handed pickaxes and spades. Then the *Kapo* pointed to a ditch next to the shed and ordered us to form teams of two, one with a pickax and the other with a spade, get into the ditch and start digging. The ditch was 60 centimeters wide and about 90 centimeters deep, marked by string lines. Those of us who didn't understand his orders turned to the others for explanation.

The bottom of the ditch was soft mud and standing water that filled my shoes. I shivered as I shoveled mud out of the ditch as the other prisoner loosened it with the pickax. Because there was so much water, the mud was heavy and slid from the shovel onto me. It didn't take long before my partner and I were both completely covered with mud. When I saw the other prisoners, they too were covered with mud, and looked like creatures from another planet.

The *Kapo* spent most of his time inside a toolshed, where he was probably sleeping. He came out a few times to scream at us, "Faster, faster you Jew pigs!" By the time he blew the whistle for the noon break, I could hardly lift the spade anymore. Worn out, I tried to climb out of the ditch, but I needed the help of another prisoner and then collapsed on the ground.

Every muscle in my body ached from the unaccustomed heavy work. The skin on my freshly healed left palm was blistered and broken from rubbing against the dirty, muddy shaft of the spade, and there was blood oozing from the wound, but there was nothing I could do. There was no clean water anywhere near us.

A few minutes later a wagon came around and dropped off our kettle of soup. The *Kapo* blew his whistle again, to make us stand in the line, and I noticed that the inside of my soup bowl was splattered with mud. Using the inside corner of my jacket, I tried to clean it out as best as I could. Unlike the other *Kapos,* he didn't stir the soup with the ladle, so we got a very thin watery mix with one or two leaves of vegetation floating in it, and he got the thick, more nutritious soup that sat at the bottom.

The rest of the day was torture for me because holding the spade was excruciatingly painful. I switched hands, but digging was awkward, and more mud would land on me than on the shovel. Finally the *Kapo* blew the whistle at the end of the workday. We all crawled out of our ditches, our faces and clothing covered with mud. Bent and worn out, we formed columns of five and marched back to the camp.

Just before we got there, the *Kapo* stopped the column and ordered us to stand at attention and then march properly through the gate to the martial music. The SS man counted our returning column. From the gate, we dragged ourselves to the *Appellplatz*. This time it took almost two hours before we were allowed to go to our blocks.

Before I went to the block, I went to the washroom, stripped off my muddy pants and jacket, and rinsed them in cold water several times until I was able to get most of the mud off. I used what strength I had left to wring them out, then tried to rinse the mud out of my shoes. I washed my face, head, neck, and injured palm. Because I had no choice, I put my wet clothing and shoes back on and went back to the barrack. Several other prisoners washed themselves, but others, too worn out, stood against a wall or lay on the floor, still covered in mud. The threatening voice of the block leader's *Stubendienst* chased them to the washroom.

After they gave us our soup, I stripped off my wet clothing and hung it on the wall side of my bunk, where I hoped it would dry before morning. Then I put my wet shoes under the straw sack for safety.

Later, when I talked to an old-timer, I found out that the ditch we were digging was for electrical cable. When I told him how awful the job was, especially in mud and rain, he assured me that was not the worst work I could be doing in Buna. The worst was in the cable commando that laid the thick, heavy electric cable, pulling it on their shoulders, as they stood in the wet and muddy ditch. He said that those working in the cable commando never lasted more than two months. He said all newcomers began in the ditch, either digging or pulling, but if I survived those, I would be transferred to an electrical commando where life would be tolerable. He advised me not to despair and to hold on.

My left palm quickly became infected, and I could feel the gland throbbing in my armpit. As I lay on the bunk, I wondered how long I would be able to tolerate the deplorable conditions, the cold and starvation. Would I turn into a *Muselmann* and be gone in the next selection? Or would I last long enough to be transferred to the electrical commando? Finally, holding my injured palm up in the air, I fell asleep.

The predawn gong sounded. My left hand was pulsating with pain. I dressed in my still-wet clothing and shoes, made up my bunk with one hand, and stood in line for the ersatz tea and the bread portion. I ate and drank the tea quickly, and showed the block leader my swollen palm. "How will I be able to work in the ditch with this hand?" I asked him. "Can I go to the infirmary to have it bandaged?"

"Not now," he said. "In the evening, after roll call you can go. Show your hand to your *Kapo,* maybe he'll give you lighter work."

The roll call took place in the rain, and my already damp clothing was soaked. We stood there shaking with the cold until we were marched out of the camp to the upbeat marching band, an ironic reminder of our slavery. Once we were at the job site, I showed my swollen palm to the *Kapo* and pleaded with him to let me stay out of the ditch. "You can hold the spade in your right hand, so don't try to fool me. Get into the ditch and start working, fast!" he screamed at me.

The mud came up to my ankles, and for every step I took, I had to slowly lift my feet, or I would lose my shoes. Each shovelful was a torture. The pain in my palm and under my arm became unbearable. In agony, I finally pushed my spade into the mud and stood there with my head and shoulders bowed, crying.

"What the hell do you think you're doing, just standing there?" screamed the *Kapo.* "Get back to work or I'll beat the life out of you."

"You can kill me," I retorted. "I don't care any more. I can't work with this hand."

"Get out of the ditch, and come here, fast!" he ordered. As I got closer to him, he punched me in the face, and I fell into the mud. "Get up and into the toolshed. I'll deal with you later," he spat at me.

Once I was in the toolshed, where it was warmer and drier, I didn't care about what would happen. I crouched in a corner on the floor and waited. A few minutes later, the *Kapo* walked in, looked at me, and in a normal voice said: "Don't make a move or a sound, and I'll let you stay here." He pulled a crate over to the other side of the shed, sat down, took out and lit a cigarette. I continued to crouch silently in my corner, shivering. Before he finished the cigarette, without a word, he threw the butt at me. I grabbed the still burning butt, rubbed the smoldering tobacco between my fingers, and hid what was left in my shirt pocket. It was worth at least a quarter of a bread portion to me if I found a smoker in the camp.

When the midday break came, the *Kapo* ordered me outside to get my soup. Right after I ate, as I stood in the rain with the other prisoners, he passed by me and pointed to the shed, "Get in there! Fast." he ordered. Everyone looked on in amazement because it seemed he still had a bit of humanity left in him. I spent the rest of the day crouched in my corner, while the *Kapo* dozed on a crate on the other side of the shed. When the klaxon rang at the end of the day, the commando was lined up and marched, tired and soaking wet, to the *Appellplatz* in Buna.

As soon as the misery of roll call was over, I ran to the infirmary, where there were already two dozen prisoners waiting. We were ordered to undress. There we were outside the door, naked, holding our clothing, shoes, and soup bowls in the pouring rain.

A doctor, who was a prisoner and wore a white coat over his striped clothing, took my hand and poked at the wound. I screamed in pain. "We'll have to cut to let the pus out," he said. "Go over to the surgery room and they'll do it."

The surgery room was a cubicle where another male prisoner in a white coat was waiting. The man put my hand, palm-side up on the table next to him. He took a small piece of cotton and some alcohol and ordered the prisoner nurse to hold my hand tightly against the table. With a swift move of his scalpel he sliced my palm open. The pain was horrendous, but I didn't scream.

The doctor squeezed the pus out, wiped the palm again with alcohol, and bandaged it with that crepelike paper bandage. "Come back in two weeks, for me to look at it. I am giving you a pass *(Blockschonung)* to stay in the camp, and you will not be sent out to work."

The *Blockschonung* saved my life. I didn't have to go back to the trenches. Because I was in the camp during working hours, I could "organize" (steal) extra food from the camp kitchen, and maybe even find an extra shirt. I thanked the doctor for his care, got dressed, and returned to the block. The block leader's assistant had already distributed the evening soup, but he had saved my bread portion and handed it to me. As hungry as I was, I didn't care that I had missed the soup because I knew that the next day I would have the opportunity to organize more food. Slowly, making sure that not a crumb was lost, I ate my bread.

The prisoner on the next bunk noticed my bandaged hand and asked me what had happened. I told him about the surgery in the infirmary and that the doctor had granted me a *Blockschonung*. He said that I was lucky and that it may have saved my life. He also advised me to make the *Blockschonung* last as long as possible, even if I had to prevent the wound from healing.

"How?" I asked him. "Maybe by smearing some dirt on the wound to cause an infection," he said. "Even if it hurts, it's better than digging ditches."

"I have the *Blockschonung* for two weeks," I told him, "and I'll be watching the wound to make sure to stretch the *Blockschonung* time."

After hiding my soup bowl, spoon, and shoes under the straw sack, I went to sleep. The next morning after roll call, the commandos left for work, and I returned to the block. The block leader ordered me and another *Blockschonung* prisoner to return the morning teakettles to the camp kitchen. We threaded two heavy wooden sticks through the kettle handles to carry them to the kitchen block. Before we handed them over to the prisoner at the gate, we had to wash them out with water standing in some nearby drums.

While we slowly washed the kettles, I looked for an opportunity to steal some food. Through the open kitchen door I could see a group of prisoners cutting potatoes and turnips. When the prisoner guarding the entrance turned to talk to somebody, I pointed to my mouth and the potatoes and then to one of the prisoners cutting potatoes, so that when the guard moved away from the door, he threw four potatoes to us.

I hid the potatoes in my jacket by tying its ends and forming a pocket. We were happy with our newfound prize, but we had to figure out how to cook them. To the best of our knowledge there was no way to do it in the block. Perhaps the block leader and his assistant could help us and we would share the potatoes with them, but they had nothing to cook with. I suggested that the block leader lend me his metal bucket. Then I could rig up a contraption that might get the potatoes cooked using electrolysis; it was a trick I had learned from my cousin Salek Gold, when we were little. By inserting two alternating-current electrical wires into water with salt in it, an electrolytic reaction occurs, and the water boils.

I explained the process and he agreed to let me try. His assistant gave me a metal bucket and a piece of wire about 122 centimeters long. Using the light-switch box in the block leader's room, I stood on a dry wooden plank and, with a knife, carefully separated the two wires in the electrical line and exposed a bit of bare wire. I asked the other prisoner to fill the bucket with enough water to just cover the potatoes. Then I placed the bucket on the wooden plank and connected one wire to the bucket handle and threaded the other wire through a small piece of wood that I placed on top of the bucket, so that it was immersed in the water.

Wearing dry gloves the block leader gave me, I connected the two wires from the bucket to the electrical wires. I told everyone not to touch the bucket or test the water or they'd get an electric shock. As we watched the water, nothing happened. "Hey," I said, "we forgot the salt and it won't work otherwise."

The assistant brought out a spoonful of salt, which I poured into the bucket. Within minutes the water in the bucket slowly bubbled, and after maybe ten minutes, started boiling. The block leader and his assistant stood there stupefied. Half an hour later I disconnected the bucket and took out a potato to see if it was cooked. It was.

The block leader brought out a piece of margarine; we sat down at the table in his private area and ate our hot potatoes with gusto. He asked if I could build him an electrolytic gadget to use for boiling water and I promised that as soon as I had the chance I would. Then, on the side, he told me he would take good care of me. All in all, it was a great day. I had gotten out of the trench-digging commando, eaten a freshly boiled potato with margarine, and made a friend of the block leader.

The next day, I was sent to the kitchen to fetch the noon soup. After I ate my portion, the block leader called me back to the kettle and poured me a second portion. The rest of the day I spent sweeping the inside of the block. In the evening, when the workers returned from Buna and assembled for roll call, I looked at their mud-covered and exhausted bodies with sorrow and pity. Yet I felt glad that my fortunes had turned and I wasn't working there anymore.

The next morning, I was ordered to sweep out the barrack again. The day was drier, the mud had gone, and the work was light. There were no *Kapos* nearby to order me around or threaten me. But as I came out of the block, I heard moaning coming from behind the next barrack. When I went to see what happened, I saw Sowa, the murderer from Majdanek, being beaten and kicked by two political prisoners. I was told Sowa had been put on the transport from Majdanek to Auschwitz against his will and was transferred to Buna. A prisoner from Majdanek had reported him to the prisoners' secret political committee and, after a kangaroo court, they had sentenced Sowa to a slow death by beating. The SS did not care if one prisoner killed another and did not interfere. I stood there and watched, glad that the bastard was being paid back for his murderous actions in Majdanek.

Around noon, the sun came out and the air cleared. I could see the Carpathian Mountains in the distance, their peaks covered in snow. In this place of horror where everything and everybody looked gray, where we were without hope, where no flower grew or bird flew, the pristine, snow-covered mountains meant that there still was another world out there.

The pain in my hand and the swelling had subsided over the last few days, and the wound was healing. I had to do something to stop or slow down the healing, or I would be back on the ditch-digging commando. Behind the barracks, I unwound the paper bandage. The flesh around the cut was still red and swollen, but the cut was almost closed. I picked up some dirt from the floor and, as the old prisoner had advised me, rubbed it into the cut. I rebandaged the palm, hoping that the dirt would cause an infection and prolong the healing.

Whenever no SS men or *Kapos* were around, I sneaked around the camp trying to learn about it. On one side of the camp stood Barrack 29. It was surrounded by a barbed-wire fence with a closed gate. When I asked, I learned it was the camp's brothel and was used by German and Polish prisoners who could come up with two "camp" marks. The girls in the brothel were Polish prisoners forced into prostitution.

Auschwitz coupons worth two to four marks were distributed weekly to prominent German and Polish prisoners, which they used in the brothel or in the prison canteen, where they could purchase cheap loose tobacco or toilet paper. The brothel and the canteen were both off-limits to Russian and Jewish prisoners.

When I heard music coming from a barrack, I discovered it was the prisoners' orchestra in rehearsal for the once-a-week classical and jazz performances they gave in a tent to entertain the camp VIPs. I was told the SS men sat in the first rows, behind them sat the prostitutes, then the criminals, then the camp leaders, the block leaders, and the *Kapos,* as if it was the opposite of real life. The rest of us were forbidden to listen.

In the few days that my palm was allowed to heal, I wandered around the camp listening and learning. I was told to watch out for a Gestapo man from the main Auschwitz camp named Kaduk. Kaduk was a sadistic murderer who derived pleasure from tormenting and killing prisoners. One of his tricks was to toss aside a cigarette butt as he walked around the camp. If an unsuspecting newcomer ran to pick it up, he would find himself the monster's target.

"Are you a smoker?" Kaduk would ask in a polite voice. *"Jawohl,"* the prisoner would answer. Kaduk would give the prisoner a whole cigarette and ask him if he wanted to light it. When the prisoner would say yes, Kaduk would reach into his pocket as if to take out a cigarette lighter, pull out a small pistol, point it at the prisoner's face, and with a smile, say, "Here, have a light." Then he would shoot the prisoner in the face, pocket the small pistol, and walk away, smiling.

I was also warned not to get close to *Kapos* with green triangles, because they were murderers, or to go near the electrified fence (unless I wanted to commit suicide), because the guards shot anyone who went near it.

The old-timers also told me about the Auschwitz killing-machine and how transports of thousands of Jewish men, women, and children were brought in cattle trains from all parts of Europe. They told me how a small minority of able-bodied men and women would be selected for work. Meanwhile, thousands upon thousands of unsuspecting people would be marched to a barrack to undress and be herded into the gas chambers, which the SS pretended were normal showers. The bodies were turned to ash in giant crematoria. Some days, when the wind blew toward our camp from Birkenau, we could smell burnt hair and flesh.

One of the most terrifying experiences I was warned about were the "in-camp" selections that would take place when the camp became crowded with new deportees and the SS wanted to thin out the ranks. Prisoners were ordered to stay in their barracks with the doors locked, and the block leader would give each prisoner his identification card.

Then we stripped and stood naked in a single line in front of the SS man, who would take our ID cards from our hands and check us over. When he was done he would give our cards to either the block leader, on the right, or his assistant, who stood on the left. Most of the men whose cards were handed to the assistant on the left were already *Muselmänner;* older, sick prisoners; or people the SS man simply didn't like.

In the meantime, I hadn't forgotten my promise to the block leader, and after scrounging around the camp, managed to find a piece of Bakelite and some wire to make his electrolytic water-boiling gadget. After I tested it and gave it to him, he gave me a whole portion of bread.

In my meanderings around the camp, I met a man named Kovo who was newly arrived in Buna and came from the Greek city of Salonika. He had been a law student at Salonika University and spoke fluent German, French, Italian, Greek, Arabic, and Hebrew. A few months after he arrived in Auschwitz, he had learned a "passing" Polish. We would meet often after roll call and trade tips on how to survive.

Kovo told me that when he and the others from Greece had arrived at the main Auschwitz camp, Dr. Mengele had taken 100 young men from the Greek transport, among them some of Kovo's friends, to do experiments on sterilization. According to Kovo, their genitalia were repeatedly exposed to high doses of x-radiation, and they were later castrated so Mengele could examine the results. Later, many of them sickened and died from radiation poisoning. Luckily, Kovo had not been selected for the experiment.

CHAPTER 17

Two days before the end of my *Blockschonung,* a young *Kapo* wearing a Jewish star on his Auschwitz number came to my barrack to look for me. He told me he was Leo Ziegler, of Electrical Commando 141, and that I would be working for him inside the Buna electrical power station. He also said that I would be transferred to Block 21, where all the prisoners in his commando were housed.

Knowing I was going to work indoors, even though I didn't know what I would be doing, gave me some hope, and the young Jewish *Kapo* seemed friendly. He was from Hamburg and had been captured three years earlier and deported to several concentration camps. His entire family had been murdered.

I took my few possessions, soup bowl, and spoon, and said good-bye to my old block leader and the *Kapo.* I went to Block 21, which looked exactly like the old one. The only difference was that the prisoners looked less starved and they and their clothing looked cleaner.

The *Kapo* took me to the block leader's cubicle and told him I would be working in Commando 141, that I was assigned to his block, and handed him my identification card. The block leader looked to be in his 50s, and his number was marked with a Jewish star. I learned later that he was from Berlin, that the Gestapo had arrested him on *Kristallnacht,* and that he had lost all of his family. He had a kind face and spoke softly to me.

I was assigned a top bunk already occupied by Moniek. Moniek was just 18 and a very nice person. He was from Łódź and told me about life in the Łódź ghetto—

the starvation, the constant fear, and the loss of all hope. I told him that the same conditions prevailed in the Warsaw ghetto until we revolted.

Being assigned to the top bunk was a letdown. The slanted roof of the barrack was no more than 46 centimeters above us, which meant we couldn't sit on our beds. Ours had to be the first bunk made so that the others below us could make theirs.

I had little to complain about. I was now assigned to indoors work, my bunk-mate seemed nice, and the *Kapo* and block leader seemed like decent people. That night the rekindled hope for survival was so strong, I couldn't sleep. But the next morning began like all the others. We made up our bunks, tried to wash, and ran to the *Appellplatz* for roll call in the rain. But this time, I wasn't so bothered. I was looking forward to my new working conditions.

After we were counted, Ziegler assembled the commando, and we marched toward the Buna works. As we went through the gate in time to the music, I heard the *Kapo* report to the SS: "Commando 141 with 35 prisoners, count correct." As we entered Buna, I saw my former comrades about to start digging ditches in the rain. I felt terrible for them, knowing that most of them would not survive.

We entered the large concrete building that housed the Buna power-generating station. Three aluminum rails were suspended from the ceiling of a large hall, and the *Kapo* told us that they carried high-voltage current. He warned us that we needed to be careful when we carried metal pipes so that they wouldn't make contact with the rails, because if they did, we would be electrocuted.

We were brought into a long, narrow room where a German civilian told us that he was Herr Müller, the master mechanic. He asked if any of us knew how to read electrical drawings. Several of us raised our hands, but the truth was that the only experience I had reading electrical drawings was before the war, when Salek and I wired two crystal radios from drawings. Still, I felt confident that I would learn fast. Herr Müller led me to an electrical control cell on one wall of the room, where a prisoner was wiring electrical components together.

"This prisoner will be your helper; teach him how to work the cell," he said and turned to me. "After you learn, I'll assign you to a new cell."

"*Jawohl,*" I answered.

The room was warm and clean. On two opposite walls there were several switching cells, each about two meters by two meters. Each cell contained varied electrical controls, relays, and switches that were interconnected with insulated wire. This cell already had the controls mounted on it, and we had to wire them according to the drawing that stood on an easel next to the cell.

The *Kapo* warned us that any mistakes we made would be considered sabotage and we would be shot, so we would be much better off if we didn't make any errors. He also told us to take orders pertaining to our work only from Herr Müller and that, because of the important and delicate work we did, the SS guards were to leave us alone. In fact, I could hear him tell the SS that our work was important and that we could not be disturbed.

Karel, a political prisoner (he wore a red triangle), was the name of the man I was assisting. Later he told me that he was from Prague. He was arrested by the Gestapo and sent to Auschwitz for being a member of the Czech resistance movement. He spoke fluent German, passable Polish, and was friendly. He showed me how to wire the controls.

First we looked at the drawing to determine which control had to be connected to the central terminal. Then we bent the wire in precise 90-degree angles around other components and connected them to the selected control. The completed connection was checked against the drawing at least twice to ensure that no errors were made. I watched Karel wiring the cell for the rest of the day and helped him stretch the wire to straighten it before he used it.

I noticed several workers in clean civilian clothing, men and women, who walked by and spoke to each other in Polish. I asked Karel who they were. They were Polish, Czech, and German civilians who worked for the private German companies building the power station. He quietly warned me not to talk to any of them when the SS were around.

In the back of my mind, I was figuring out a way to make contact with them, especially the Poles, so that we could set up some kind of a trading system. I decided to keep my eyes open and pay close attention to what was going on for the next few days. The blessing was that the SS stayed away from us. To me, this was a miraculous transformation of circumstance. We had a minuscule connection to the outside world, and the news passed secretly by the civilian workers was that the German army was retreating from the eastern front. Maybe, just maybe, I might survive.

Herr Müller, after observing my work for two weeks, assigned me to an adjoining cell to wire controls by myself. The cell contained the easel, the drawing, and a step stool so that I could reach the upper part of the panel. Sometimes I'd sit on the stool when I wired the lower section of the panel. The work was easy and also interesting. I learned how the various relays and switches worked by reading the drawings. No one, not the *Kapo* or Herr Müller or the SS, ordered me to work faster. Their only demand was that I not make mistakes or it would be, literally, the death of me.

After several weeks working in the cell, I made eye contact and exchanged a few words with the passing Polish civilian girls, making sure that the patrolling SS man either was out of the room or had his back turned to me. The Polish girls were at first a revelation. In the camp there were only the bedraggled, starving women prisoners with their shaven heads, who dragged their tired bodies around, trying to survive. These Polish girls were young, healthy, well-fed, and nicely dressed civilians. I asked one of them, in a whisper, if she could bring me some bread in exchange for clothing or other items I could bring from the camp. The next day, while the SS man was out of the room, she came by the cell, dropped a small bundle wrapped in paper on the floor and kicked it toward me.

I pretended to pick up a tool and quickly retrieved the bundle, hiding it under my jacket. Later, when I made sure no one could see me, I opened it and found a piece of black bread that weighed almost half a kilo. With the sharpened handle of my soup spoon, I cut the bread into three pieces and hid them behind the string holding up my pants. After I closed my jacket, I made sure that nothing was visible. Then I worried about getting into camp without getting caught. The SS guard at the camp gate routinely scanned the entering prisoners for any signs of smuggling. When they spotted a suspicious prisoner, they'd stop the column and search everyone.

The penalty for smuggling was 25 lashes, or worse, interrogation and torture by the camp Gestapo to obtain the names of collaborators among the civilian workers. If you gave the Gestapo the names, the people were arrested and sent to the "reeducation camp" in Auschwitz. I made sure to be on the far side of column from the SS guard, and that day we made it through the gate without being stopped.

After roll call, I ran to the clothing warehouse barrack and offered a prisoner working there a portion of the bread in exchange for a shirt in good condition. The prisoner examined the bread, went inside, and brought out a shirt I accepted after examination. I handed him the bread and ran to my block for the soup and bread break. I just made it. The block leader asked me why I was so late and I lied and told him I was in the latrine because of my stomach. Later, in my bunk, I shared a portion of the bread with Moniek. The other I saved for the next day. To make sure that no one could steal the shirt from me, I wrapped it around my waist, and for the first time in a long time, I went to sleep without being tortured by pangs of hunger.

In the morning, Moniek helped me tie the shirt around myself and under my pants to make sure it didn't show. The punishment for stealing clothing in camp was more severe than that for smuggling stuff in, even though the SS had stolen those items from Jews before murdering them.

But that morning roll call lasted longer than any previous one. I was very nervous and scared. What if they decided to search us? I calmed myself down, because this Polish girl was probably going to supply me with bread and keep me alive. Finally roll call ended, but my anxiety attack didn't end until we passed through the gate without being searched.

When we got to the power plant, I ducked into an empty cell, removed the shirt and dropped it into an empty box. Later, when the opportunity presented itself, I whispered to the Polish girl where it was hidden. She said she might bring me something the next day.

I was good at my job. Herr Müller noticed and said that if I continued that way, no harm would come to me while working. He seemed a decent person, and we all trusted him. Another mechanic working under Herr Müller was a *Volksdeutsche* (ethnic German), who always tried to be more German than Germans, sang Nazi songs, and greeted other Germans with his right arm stretched out in a "Heil Hitler" salute. We did not trust him and stayed out of his way.

Haim, another member of our commando, worked in the cell next to mine. He was a very short fellow who liked to sing Polish and Yiddish songs and always had a smile on his face. I came to like him and we became good friends. (I learned many of the Polish and Yiddish songs I still sing today from Haim.) I told Haim we'd be partners in my smuggling operation, because I felt he would be inconspicuous because of his height.

When we returned to camp that night, the roll call took hours. The SS man kept repeating the count over and over, while we stood at attention with our caps off. In the block, after the distribution of the watery evening soup, some of the prisoners sat on their bunks trying to fix their torn clothing and shoes. Others just lay down on their bunks, too tired or depressed to care about their appearance or well-being.

I took a chance and went to see the block leader to tell him about the electrolytic water heater I built for the block leader in my old barrack. If I made one for him, and it worked, he said he would make me the *Kesselwascher* (washer of the soup kettles). As there was always a film of soup clinging to the kettle's inner walls after soup distribution, I could scrape at it with my spoon before I washed them and I could get an additional four to six spoonfuls to eat. Returning the washed kettles to the kitchen barrack also gave me the opportunity to organize a few potatoes or beets. It would be a good deal. The few extra spoonfuls of soup and the smuggled-in bread might save me from starvation. Maybe I would survive.

The next day, while working at the cell, another Polish girl passed by and whispered she had hidden a paper bag with a piece of kielbasa and bread in the empty cell behind me, and that she would like to get some women's clothing for it. Just the thought of kielbasa and bread made my saliva run. I whispered I would try to bring something the next day, but I worried that the first girl had told this one about our transactions and that might become very dangerous for me. I warned her to be very careful and not to tell anyone or I might be killed.

I asked Haim if he would be willing to help me smuggle in the bread and kielbasa. I told him that Moniek, my bunkmate, and the two of us would share in half of the kielbasa and bread, and the other half would be for barter. Haim accepted and assured me that he had no fear of being searched. We agreed he would smuggle the bread, and I, the kielbasa.

I was nervous that Haim might betray us if any fear showed in his face, but when I looked, his face was perfectly calm. We marched through the gate, our *Kapo* barking out the usual report, "Commando 141, 35 prisoners returning to camp, count correct." The SS counted the entering rows of our commando and stared at our faces, but didn't stop us or search anyone. I heaved a sigh of relief.

In the barrack, Moniek, Haim, and I decided to wait after roll call and soup distribution before we divided the bread and kielbasa. Lying on the bunk, I wrapped the kielbasa tightly to make sure the aroma didn't waft around. The three of us, like three musketeers, happily anticipated the forthcoming feast.

As if to torture us, the roll call dragged on and on. Later we found out that a prisoner was missing from another block. After two hours of searching, he was found dead in his bunk. The men in that block had to drag the dead body out and lay it alongside the column so the counting could proceed. Worn out from standing at attention for more two hours, we all dragged ourselves to the barrack for soup.

After we scraped the last of the soup from our bowls, Moniek, Haim, and I left the barrack supposedly to wash our soup bowls. We found a quiet spot behind the wash barrack, and making sure no one noticed us, we unwrapped the kielbasa and bread, split it in half and put half away. We divided the rest into three portions, one for each of us. Sitting on the ground with my back against the barrack wall I slowly chewed the bread and kielbasa with relish. No words could describe the pure pleasure we felt at that moment, but it was too late for me to run to the clothing barrack to make a trade for the rest of the bread and kielbasa. I would try again the next day.

The next day at Buna, I explained to the Polish girl why I hadn't brought her clothing, but that I would try again later that day and bring it tomorrow. It was important that she believe me and maintain contact for future trades.

Some days, when we couldn't organize extra food and the hunger pains were especially strong, we discussed the foods we would eat after liberation. Haim's preference was a thick Hungarian goulash with a lot of potatoes. He would elaborate how he loved to dip pieces of bread in the spicy, papriky gravy. I still preferred the dish of flat noodles with pot cheese, sugar, and a sprinkle of cinnamon on top, like my mother used to make. Just the thought made my saliva run. It was an exercise in masochism and self-torture, but it took our minds off our problems.

At one end of the power plant were benches that contained hand drills, files, and other tools. During the midday soup break, I worked at the bench to assemble an electrolytic heater from discarded parts. In the waste box I found broken carbon rods and flat pieces of Bakelite. I drilled two holes in the Bakelite and inserted the carbon rods, then attached insulated electrical wire to the rods. It looked good, but would it work? After I smuggled it back to camp, we would have to test it.

That night I showed the heater to the block leader and told him we needed to test it. If it worked, I would become a *Kesselwascher*. After soup distribution, I got a bucket from his assistant and filled it with water. I sprinkled a pinch of salt into it, placed the heater on the bucket and connected the wires to the previously scraped electrical line. We stood around the bucket and waited. After a few minutes bubbles started to appear.

"It works," I said. "It will start boiling in a few more minutes."

The assistant leaned toward the bucket and was about to stick his finger into the water.

"Don't touch it," I shouted, "you'll get electrocuted!"

Soon the bubbles in the water got bigger and the water started to boil. After disconnecting the heater, I showed them how to handle the apparatus without getting an electric shock. The next day I became the *Kesselwascher* for the evening "soup" and knew that, at least for a while, I would be eating a little better because I might be able to steal some potatoes and beets from the kitchen. Though I thought about going into the business of building water heaters for block leaders, I decided not to make them any more, because the risk was too great. It would be better for me to concentrate on my dealings with the Polish girls.

In October and November 1943 it rained almost every day. I saw the desperate, hopeless look in the eyes of the prisoners standing next to me during *Appell*. My commando worked in a closed building, which would help me dry out, but the others who were forced to work outside in the cold and rain already looked like walking skeletons.

The extra few spoons of soup, the occasional extra piece of bread, the easy work inside the power plant, meant that my body and spirit were sustained. Even with tragedy all around me, I didn't lose hope. Only in my dreams did images of my murdered family return. It was as if my mind tried to protect me from going insane by suppressing my memories during waking hours.

The prisoners in the block I was in were of all the nationalities in Europe. Often it would sound like the Tower of Babel with everyone speaking in varied languages: Polish, Yiddish, French, Czech, Greek, Russian, Dutch, and others I didn't even recognize.

Some prisoners—Czechs and Poles, not Jews or Russians—received food packages from home. The Czechs always shared some of their packages with other prisoners, but the Poles never did. They sat on their bunks and ate their kielbasa, white bread, and cakes without offering even a crumb to the others. They received many packages that were stored in the *Blockälteste*'s cupboard. There was so much, some of it turned moldy and had to be thrown out. I could understand selfish Poles not wanting to share with the Jews, whom they hated. But they refused to share their packages with anyone, even those who were seriously starved and non-Jews.

In this, they treated anyone who was not Polish equally badly and made me ashamed of my countrymen.

One day in November, we were locked into our barrack, handed our ID cards, and told to strip for another selection. Prisoners whispered advice to each other: walk straight, with steady steps; rub your cheeks to bring out some color; keep your head up. The block leader opened the door and an SS man stiffly marched in. We were assembled in one half of the barrack and proceeded to walk in a single row toward him. As before, the SS man took the card from the approaching prisoner and, glancing at him, passed the card to the right to the block leader, or to the left to the assistant.

Silently, the prisoners watched the SS man's hand. Like a god, he made instant decisions of who would live and who would die. After he finished, without even glancing back, he marched out. My card and Moniek's went to the block leader, as did those of the rest of the people in my commando. We would live at least a little while longer. But 20 percent of the prisoners in our barrack were sentenced to die that day. The 45 condemned prisoners traded their shirts, their spoons, and anything they had of value for a portion of bread or soup so that, at least, they wouldn't have to die hungry.

Winter approached. Fierce, freezing winds carrying rain or snow inundated us whenever we went to roll call. We stood at attention, sometimes for hours, with bare heads and caps held to our sides while the warmly dressed SS took their time, as if purposely exposing us to the merciless elements in order for us to die sooner. Without protective clothing or layers of fat to insulate us from the cold, we stood there forlorn, shivering, our teeth chattering. I cursed God. Only the news from the front gave me the will to hold on. As the war news became worse for the Germans, the atmosphere toward us in the power plant changed for the better. Even the Nazi *Volksdeutsche* foreman must have heard the news, because he stopped mistreating prisoners working under him.

Then, in early December 1943, I woke up in the middle of the night feeling sick. I was burning with a high fever and shivering. Moniek woke up and asked me what was wrong. I told him I was sick and didn't know why, because the night before I felt fine. But though I hoped the fever would go down by morning, after wake-up call, I could hardly get off the bunk. I still had a fever and knew that I could not go to the infirmary because it meant certain death. I went to roll call instead, and

Moniek helped me up. When I finally got to the power plant, I told Herr Müller I was sick. He took me to an empty cell and opened the door.

"Lie down there and rest," he said. "Nobody will bother you there; I'll check on you later," he said, and closed the door. I noticed the sign on the door: a skull and cross bones and bold letters in German that said, ATTENTION, HIGH VOLTAGE, DO NOT ENTER. The high-voltage rails in the cell were about 122 centimeters off the ground, and lying down on the floor didn't affect me, so I fell asleep.

At noon, the door to the cell opened and Herr Müller said, "Crawl out, and get your midday soup. If you still feel sick, I'll let you get back in the cell." I thanked him for his kindness and, wobbly, I walked to the soup distribution.

Kapo Ziegler asked me where I had been that morning because he hadn't seen me. I told him Herr Müller put me to work in the high-voltage cell, and after the soup break, I returned there and was locked in until our shift was over. The fever broke late that afternoon. I felt better but I was still weak and wobbly. Moniek held me up as we marched back to camp.

Standing, shivering, on the *Appellplatz* in the cold rain, I suddenly remembered the time when as a child I sat on a windowsill and watched raindrops hitting the panes, listening to the sound of the drops as if they were a magic drum. How different that was from the *Appellplatz,* where every drop of rain was torture.

Back in the block, I had just enough strength to stay in the line for soup. Swallowing the hot liquid brought some warmth into my body, but I quickly stripped off my wet clothing and climbed up to the bunk, totally exhausted, and fell deeply asleep. Later, nothing could wake me, not even the call for lights out or Moniek climbing into the bunk.

In the early morning, I felt much better, and before roll call, ran to the clothing block and bargained with the foreman to take the bread and kielbasa in exchange for some piece of women's clothing. After a short while he brought out a flowered cotton skirt. The skirt belonged most likely to a young Jewish girl or woman murdered in the Auschwitz gas chamber. It was clean and in good shape, so I accepted the trade. Quickly I wrapped the skirt around my waist, under my pants, and ran back to the block.

In the power station I hid the skirt under some crates in an empty cell. Later, after I made sure that the SS man was out and nobody was watching, I whispered the hidden location to the passing Polish girl. Before the end of the day, she thanked me for the skirt and promised to bring something for me the next day. She probably never thought that she'd be wearing a murdered Jewish girl's skirt. I was not about to tell her where it came from.

The Polish winter arrived in a chorus of snow flurries cut by icy winds. The situation of the prisoners working outdoors was unbearable. In thin prison garb and with bare feet in old shoes, the still-living skeletons walked in columns, snow and mud freezing to their feet, causing them to wobble like drunken sailors. Looking at them, I knew most would die in the dirty, churned-up snow. They would be replaced by others.

Most evenings in the barrack, prisoners passed the time by telling each other their life stories. Among us were a university professor, teachers, doctors, rabbis, writers, musicians, other professionals, and tradesmen. Each had a tragic story about parents, wives, children, sisters, brothers, and extended-family members who perished in some murderous way. I heard hundreds of stories, each different, yet all the same. I wondered, if some of us did manage to survive the war, how we would live with those memories.

Fiercer than ever that year, Old Man Winter collaborated with the Nazis in their attempt to annihilate us. He hardly allowed us a glimpse of the blue-white, hope-inspiring peaks of the Carpathians in the distance. The sun itself went into hiding, as if ashamed to witness the scenes below it. As we stood in the *Appellplatz*, buffeted by icy sleet, half-naked, we shivered out our unheard prayers for a quick death.

The work at the power station became routine for me. Herr Müller gave me an assignment to train a new prisoner. The fellow learned fast and soon was doing the work for me. I spent some time with Haim, in the cell next to mine, to talk about our lives before Auschwitz, sing songs, and compete in our homegrown poetry recitals.

Before the war, Haim taught Polish literature at a Hebrew school in Warsaw. He had a terrific memory and could recite two or more poems by Adam Mickiewicz, Maria Konopnicka, Julian Tuwim, and others, to each one of mine. We became good friends and fellow smugglers. The little bit of food we managed to organize saved Moniek and us from starvation.

During that cruel winter, people tried to escape. Some succeeded. Most of those who tried were Poles or Czechs whose borders lay only a few kilometers from Buna. The problem was that every time there was an escape attempt, all the prisoners were kept standing at attention on the *Appellplatz* for hours. Misery reached its peak when the SS captured escapees. After they were interrogated and tortured by the camp Gestapo (to see if they had collaborators), they were dragged to the *Appellplatz* during an evening roll call and hanged in front of all of us. It was especially hard for me to take.

The news that drifted in about the German defeat on the eastern front continued to be good for us. It always brought me a bit of hope and great satisfaction that those supposed *Übermenschen* (supermen) were being beaten. But there was a question haunting the dark alleys of my mind. Would they kill us rather than allow us to be liberated?

Moniek, Haim, and I agreed that we'd stick together and help each other. We knew that alone we had no chance of survival. Luckily all of us worked indoors on the electrical commando, so we were in touch both at work and in the barrack. *Kapo* Ziegler knew of our bond and treated us with respect. He never raised his voice or hit anyone on our commando. We knew we were lucky to have him. Herr Müller became increasingly helpful to us. Even the civilian Polish girls, who hated the Russians, smiled as they passed by our workstation and whispered the latest news from the eastern front to us.

The winter also haunted my sleep with nightmares of my parents. I dreamt I was playing with Mina or Mother and would waken with a muffled scream. Night after night I relived the execution, or, once again, the burning ceiling fell on me in the Warsaw ghetto bunker. When I couldn't fall back asleep, I would listen to the never-ending procession of the prisoners headed to the urine bucket and the sound of the stream hitting the bucket wall.

At last winter's curse ended. For the first time in a long time, a clear sun showed its face and wrapped us in a hint of warmth. Those of us who were still alive acquired new strength from its rays. Our thoughts centered on how to prevent starvation. When a "fresh" Hungarian transport arrived in the camp, those selected to live looked well fed, and I could not help but wonder how long it would take before the camp system ground them down to *Muselmänner*.

They were "lucky" to arrive in Auschwitz at the end of winter, to be spared the misery of cold, mud, and wind. Many of them spoke Yiddish or German or both. They told us that the German army was in retreat on a wide front, and that the Red Army was close to Hungary's borders, not that far away from us.

Hope, hope, hope. Even with starvation, one could survive on hope, especially in spring and summer. Then new transports arrived from Hungary, and from Łódź and Poznań in Poland, crowding the already overcrowded camp. It looked like the Germans were capturing and shipping Jews to Auschwitz from territories threatened by advancing Soviet troops. Everyone was saying that the SS would reduce the crowding by selection.

By October 1944 the crowding became more intense, and the talk of a forthcoming selection intensified. Panicky individuals showed their naked bodies to others, hoping to hear that they looked good, that they did not yet look like *Muselmänner*. Still others knew that they would not make it and accepted the fact calmly.

I remember it was a Sunday. We worked only to midday, then returned to camp for roll call and soup. Suddenly the gong went off. It meant *Blocksperre*—lockdown. We were locked in our barrack for selection. The *Blockälteste* locked the doors, handed each prisoner his identification card, and ordered us to undress. As old-timers, the new people asked our advice. What should they do? We tried to calm them down, tried to assure them that they looked good.

Everyone was ordered to the back of our section, when the door opened and the SS man stepped in. The selection took less than half an hour, and more than 20 percent of our barrack was sentenced to death. Later the *Kapo* told me that more than 3,000 prisoners were selected to be gassed and cremated in Birkenau on that one day.

We understood that Death was our companion, part of our being. For us it was not a question of *if*, it was a question of *when* death would reach for us. At work, Haim, Moniek, and I looked at each other constantly as if to assure each other we were still alive.

The Americans and British made several bombing runs at the Buna works in October and November 1944, destroying and damaging several buildings. Luckily no prisoners were killed, but they were forced to rebuild the damage. Conditions were deplorable because the roads and the open grounds at Buna works were covered with deep mud and rubble, up to the prisoners' knees. Though the work was murderously difficult, the prisoners I managed to speak to did derive some satisfaction from the destruction wrought by the Allies. Luckily, for the time being the power plant escaped any damage. Our commando continued our work as if the camp hadn't been bombed.

The front was getting closer, and soon it was winter again, but the transports of Jews continued to arrive in Auschwitz. We heard artillery explosions coming from the nearby battlefields. Yet the Germans still ordered us to keep wiring the control panels, and it saved our lives.

Christmas was coming, and the Polish girls talked to each other about their plans to travel home for the holiday, about the food they would be preparing and the pleasure they would feel to be with their families and boyfriends. We couldn't imagine what that could be like.

In late December 1944, the power plant was hit during an Allied bombardment. All work inside stopped. Fortunately it took place at night, after we returned to camp, so no prisoners were wounded or killed. We saw wave after wave of Allied planes fly over Buna and discharge flares and bombs. The blasts tore at my eardrums, and the earth shook. As I lay on the ground, worried I would be killed, I watched the destruction with glee.

The next morning, Ziegler told us we would not be working in the power plant that day; we would be working in the camp under the direction of our *Blockälteste* and the *Stubendienst*. Most of the day was spent cleaning the inside of the barrack. Outside, we moved rocks in the snow from one place to another. That evening I stood at *Appell*, shivering for a long time, waiting for the SS to come out and do the count. Perhaps, I thought, the aerial bombing and the sound of artillery had put fear in their corrupted souls, and they were at a loss as to what to do with us.

We heard about the invasion in Normandy, the collapse of the German army, the retreat from all fronts, and the attempt on Hitler's life by his generals. We didn't know whether to be excited or afraid. Prisoners who joined us from Majdanek told us how the SS was killing everyone. Before retreating westward, they herded the prisoners into barracks and set them afire. Prisoners trying to escape from the burning barracks were killed with the machine guns set up on the four corners of the camp. No one survived. I realized I was lucky to have been transferred from Majdanek to Auschwitz-Buna. Luck was a key factor in my survival.

Late in December there were rumors circulating that gassing of selected prisoners in Auschwitz-Birkenau had stopped, but I did not believe those stories. In my mind I believed that the SS was spreading the rumors to avoid a possible prisoners' revolt. Prisoners had already blown up a crematorium in Birkenau. We had to watch as one of the prisoners who participated was hanged on the gallows at the *Appellplatz*.

Until the first week in January 1945, our electrical commando kept working in the part of the power plant not damaged by the bombing. Herr Müller hardly ever came over to inspect the work we were doing. When he did come over, he would just stand and look, without saying a word.

The *Volksdeutsche* foreman was still going around mouthing the propaganda posters *Wir siegen* (We are winning), and the Polish civilians whispered their fears of the Soviet army to us. They hated the Soviets more than the Germans. As Jewish prisoners, we prayed for the victory of the Allies and our early liberation by the Red Army.

At the end of that same week, all work in the power plant stopped. We heard bursts of distant artillery getting closer. Rumors flew: the SS had plans to evacuate the Auschwitz complex, including Buna. Our fears intensified. Would they kill us all as they had in Majdanek? Would they evacuate us? Where to? Who knew?

CHAPTER 18

On January 18, 1945, after the roll call and distribution of bread, the *Block-älteste* informed us that the camp would be completely evacuated that night. We would be given another portion of bread and allowed to take our blankets. We were to prepare ourselves as best as we could for a long march.

Everyone tried to get extra shirts and blankets, to repair their torn shoes and clothing, and to get rags to wrap around their feet. Moniek, Haim, and I had hidden the extra portions of bread we got from the Poles. We also had a couple of shirts and underwear I got from the Polish girls. We divided the bread and the shirts among us and cut the underwear into foot-rags.

That evening we were served our daily watery soup and the extra portion of bread. When we were done, we were told by the *Blockälteste* to run to the roll call with our blankets, and that after the count we would be marched out of the camp. When everyone asked him where we would be going, he claimed that he didn't know. Perhaps he knew but wouldn't tell us.

It was getting dark and roll call took no time at all. We were formed into columns of five, and block after block was marched out of the camp. Our block was marched out toward the end. More than 10,000 prisoners formed a long column into the night. On both sides of our column were the SS guards—on foot, on bicycles, on motorcycles, and in trucks—they screamed at us, *"Schneller, schneller, laüft schneller!"* (Faster, faster, run faster!), hitting us with their whips if we fell behind. Soon the weaker prisoners were unable to move fast enough and fell out of the column. I heard the inevitable rifle shots and looked behind me to see the bodies of killed prisoners being dragged into the roadside ditch. Night fell. Except for the occasional shine of SS flashlights, we were in total darkness.

All I could hear was the knocking of thousands of wooden clogs against the pavement and the constant screaming of the SS guards. Hours later, the rifle shots rang out constantly as more and more weakened prisoners fell behind. I didn't know where we were, or where they were taking us, but I was getting tired, and the marching became harder. Moniek, Haim, and I promised to support and even carry each other if one of us couldn't walk anymore.

A rumor that we were headed for a camp in Gleivitz passed through the column. Gleivitz was a concentration camp 50 kilometers from Auschwitz-Buna. How many of us would be able to march that far? After the first four hours, the pavement we marched on turned to muddy snow that clung to the bottoms of the wooden clogs, making it impossible for prisoners wearing clogs to walk. More prisoners weakened and fell to the ground. As our column passed them by I heard more shots. Luckily, Moniek, Haim, and I wore leather shoes that were issued to the electrical workers in Commando 141.

The SS flashlight beams revealed a never-ending column of prisoners, bent in pain against the cold as they shuffled on, heads and shoulders wrapped in scrawny blankets, their clogs crackling the snow under their feet. When first light broke on the horizon, the column finally reached Gleivitz and the SS called a halt. We collapsed to the ground like one giant organism, a mass of prisoners. Lying on the edge of the column, I scraped handfuls of snow to my mouth and slowly let it melt to slake my thirst.

Moniek, Haim, and I huddled together on the wet ground, covered with our blankets, trying to keep warm. We took out our last portion of bread and chewed it slowly. No words were exchanged. Depressed and shivering, we just stared at each other. On the ground around us lay thousands of prisoners from other camps, a huge, shivering mass of humanity.

Later that morning the SS ordered us to march to a railroad siding occupied by a long row of open freight wagons. Screaming and whipping us as usual, the SS forced us into the wagons. Those wagons were marked in Polish "6 horses or 30 people." The SS packed 100 of us into each wagon, so that there was hardly enough room to stand. Moniek and I were the last to be forced into our car. We stood packed against the wall of the wagon. Haim was forced into another wagon, and we never saw him again.

The train stood on the siding, fully loaded with prisoners, for several hours. Toward evening it finally started moving slowly. With all the misery, packed in like sardines, the open wagons kept us alive, at least for some time. If the SS had packed us into closed wagons, we would have suffocated for certain.

In every second or third wagon, there was a booth above the car where an armed SS man stood and scanned the train with a searchlight. We stayed on our feet all night, shifting occasionally from foot to foot. Some of the prisoners, those injured or sick, were quietly moaning. Otherwise silence prevailed, except for the clickety-clack of the train.

When morning broke, we found two prisoners, dead, standing up in the packed mass. We stacked the stiffened and frozen bodies against one wall of the wagon and several prisoners had to sit on those bodies for lack of space.

The train moved past small Polish railroad stations, occasionally stopping. Polish railroad workers stood and stared at us, doing nothing despite our pleas to have them throw snowballs over the wagon walls so we could wet our lips. Not one snowball was tossed to us. Mostly, the Poles turned their backs on us and walked away.

The lack of water created a terrible thirst. Moniek had a small metal cup to which we attached a string and lowered it to the roadbed to collect some snow as the train moved. We gathered just enough to wet our lips and pass on some to others.

Days and nights went by. It became unbearable to stand. To alleviate the pain, the entire wagonload of prisoners would switch from foot to foot, swaying, almost dancelike. But the thirst was most unbearable. Lips and tongues dried out, felt like wood. Words came out of our throat as rasping sounds. Daily, prisoners died and their bodies were piled up against the walls. Some prisoners lost their minds from thirst, hunger, and cold, and jumped out of the moving train to be instantly shot by the SS.

Then, as if by some command, every wagon began throwing out their dead, near or just past towns as the train went by. After that happened once, the train was stopped in an open field and an SS officer (later we were told it was Dr. Mengele), brandishing an automatic rifle, warned the prisoners that he would kill us all if one more dead body were thrown out without his order. But from then on, the train made periodic stops at open fields and the SS would order us to throw out the dead.

Except for the few spoonfuls of snow Moniek was able to gather with the metal cup, no water or food was given to us. I was getting delirious, and if not for Moniek shaking and talking to me, I would have collapsed. Sometimes I couldn't differentiate between day and night, as crazy dreams and nightmares devoured my mind.

Then the train crossed into Czechoslovakia. Suddenly on every bridge and trestle we rode under, there stood Czech people who threw large balls of snow and loaves of bread into our passing wagons. The SS were shooting at them, but still they threw us the snow and bread. Several large snowballs and bread loaves fell into our wagon. One snowball fell on my head. Crazily Moniek, others, and I grabbed fistfuls of the snow and shoved them into our mouths. The cold snow numbed my mouth, but it was water, if only a spoonful. Some of the snow fell to the floor. Like an animal, I licked it off.

Tragically, several starving prisoners jumped on the falling loaves. The ones on the bottom were suffocated by the pressure of several bodies on top of them, all trying to reach the bread. Moniek and I were able to rip a chunk of the falling bread and hold on to it under our jackets. Much later I heard that the Czech underground found out about our train and spread the information to the Czech people. Even though many prisoners on our death train died, many of us were given a chance to live by their heroic actions.

That night the train stopped at a small Czech town. The SS jumped off their watch stations and surrounded the train. Suddenly a large group of Czech civilians entered the station carrying buckets of water and baskets of cut-up bread. At first, as we watched, the SS tried to stop the Czechs from nearing the wagons, but after some negotiation they came over. In Czech, a language similar to Polish, they told us that they were permitted to distribute water and bread to all of us.

Next to our wagon, facing me, a Czech woman lifted a metal cup of water in one hand and a chunk of bread in the other. "Pass it down," she softly said, "we have enough for all." I passed the bread and water to Moniek and looked at her as she handed me the next portion of bread and water. She was crying openly.

The SS warned the Czechs not to talk to the prisoners, or they would stop the water and bread distribution. Still our looks spoke to them, and their eyes spoke to us. The crying Czech woman was replaced by a tall young man, who kept handing me water and bread. At first I passed several cups of water and pieces of bread to Moniek to pass on to others, but I finally couldn't hold out any longer and stopped to have a drink and a bite of the bread myself before resuming the distribution to others.

During the distribution, the SS closely watched the prisoner wagons, not permitting Czechs, except those distributing the food, to come close to the train. Suddenly an SS officer yelled "Stop!" and ordered the Czechs off the train platform.

Only about half of the prisoners in our wagon got water and bread. The Czech, hearing the SS order, lifted the whole water bucket toward us. Moniek, another prisoner, and I leaned over the wagon wall and lifted the water bucket inside. The Czech then pushed a burlap bag full of cut bread at us. Moniek and a couple of other prisoners surrounded the water bucket and bread to keep other prisoners from trying to grab it. I thanked the Czech in Polish and German and hoped God would repay all of them for their heroism.

Moniek asked prisoners who had not received bread and water to raise their hands and keep them up. He also warned that anyone who had already received and tried to get another portion of bread before bread and water was distributed to all would be thrown out of the wagon. Then Moniek and two other prisoners passed bread and water to the prisoners holding up their hands. I stood there watching so that no one received portions twice. There were several chunks of bread left, so we decided to break each chunk in half, and gave them to the most starved-looking prisoners.

It's hard to describe the feeling of drinking that half-cup of water. When I got my share, I just held the cup for a moment, tipped it to my parched lips, before very slowly, in small sips, drinking it. I waited a while, hoping not to lose the sensation of the water passing through my throat, before I took a bite of the bread.

The train stayed at the station for several hours before it started moving. We all realized that by crossing into Czechoslovakia, the train was taking us south of Gleivitz, but to where? During the night and the following day, the train was shuttled to the side and stopped for several hours to let other trains pass by. Later the train passed several railroad stations whose names were in German. That meant we were out of Czechoslovakia and in Austria. It was night when the train pulled onto a siding and finally stopped. The SS jumped off the train and surrounded it. We could see lights in the distance that came from watchtowers, so it could only be a concentration camp, but which one?

There were two camps in Austria everyone in the wagon had heard of: Maut-hausen and the Gusen KZ. Both of them were killer camps. The Gusen KZ was a rock quarry, and no prisoner lasted more than two or three months after breaking and lugging around huge stones. Mauthausen prisoners, we heard in Buna, worked in underground caves building plane and rocket parts. Few of those prisoners, ex-cept those transferred to Auschwitz, survived for long. Fear ran through us all. This would be the end of the line.

The train stood at the siding all night. No matter how weak and tired we were, no one slept. All of us dreaded the moment when the sliding gates on the wagons would open and the SS would order us to disembark. But late in the morning of the next day, the train suddenly lurched and slowly backed out of the siding, then started moving in earnest. With the sun in the east, we realized that we were headed north, but where were we going? We sighed with relief when we realized that it wasn't the two camps we were thinking of.

The train moved slowly, stopping sometimes for three or four hours to let other freight trains go by. During one stop in an open field, we were ordered to throw our dead prisoners out of our cars. The SS, to make sure none of the corpses were live prisoners trying to escape, riddled them with their automatic guns. It was horri-fying to see dead bodies jumping in the hail of bullets. Among the dead were at least 30 people from our wagon.

There was no relief for our thirst. The bits of snow Moniek scraped up with his cup melted to a spoonful of water, just enough to wet our lips. We tried to use the bucket the Czech had given us to gather snow, but the string holding the bucket broke, and we lost it.

I don't know how long we were on that train. All I remember were daily stops to throw out the corpses. Every day, two or more prisoners died in our wagon. One day we lost the metal cup. There would be no more drops of water to wet our lips. The thirst became unbearable. My mouth and lips were so cracked and dry, my throat so parched, I could not speak. The only sound I made was the raspy sound of breathing. A couple of times I lost consciousness. If Moniek hadn't shaken me back to life, I would have died.

Finally, the train stopped at a siding, the door of our wagon slid open, and the SS ordered us out. We could hardly stand or walk. Most, including me, fell on the platform. Several men in striped prison clothing, standing next to the SS men, ran toward us trying to help us stand up. *"Wasser, wasser,"* came the sound from our throats. But there was no water. The local prisoners ran to the side of the platform, gathered some snow in their hands and passed it to us. The SS just stood there looking but didn't interfere with their actions. A prisoner handed me a small ball of snow, which I shoved into my mouth. My mouth got numb from the cold, yet the bit of water that melted into my throat revived me. Moniek and I stood up holding each other. Around us groups of prisoners lay on the ground, unable to raise themselves. We just left several prisoners in the wagon; they were either dead or too weak to get up.

After maybe an hour, local prisoners pulled a wagon with buckets of water to the platform. They started pouring water into the metal soup bowls we always carried. Like a wild animal, I drank about half of the water in my bowl before I choked and threw up whatever water I had swallowed so rapidly.

After resting a little, I slowly sipped the remaining water in my bowl. The prisoner distributing the water, who must have seen me throw up, walked over and poured some more water into my soup bowl. I just sat on the ground and slowly sipped the liquid. The water-distributing prisoner asked me in whisper, "Where did you come from?"

"Auschwitz KZ," I replied. "Where are we now?" I asked him.

"Sachsenhausen KZ," he said.

In Buna we had heard about Sachsenhausen from old prisoners who were transferred from there to Auschwitz. They told us that Sachsenhausen was located on the outskirts of Berlin and was one of the first concentration camps set up by the Nazis. I remember the joke those old prisoners told us—in Berlin, silence was golden and speech meant Sachsenhausen.

After the water was distributed, the SS ordered everybody to get up and form into columns of five. Not all prisoners were able to get up; some just lay on the platform. Moniek and I joined the line, and after the SS counted us, they marched us toward the camp. We were a sad-looking sight, dragging our feet and draped in our ragged blankets. During the march, some prisoners fell to the ground; they were left there or pulled to the side while the columns continued on. We never did find out what happened to those left on the platform and those who fell by the wayside. Most likely they were killed. Later we heard from other prisoners that only about 20 percent of our transport arrived alive.

The barrack assigned to us was larger than the barrack in Buna. Inside was row after row of triple-decker bunks. Each two rows were joined to form six bunks. The *Stubendienst* assigned me to the top row with four other prisoners. Where only four prisoners would sleep in Buna, here one more person had to fit between the two bunks. The camp, an old prisoner told me, was overcrowded with new arrivals from other concentration camps.

Weak and tired, I could hardly lift myself to the top bunk. Once up, I lay down for the first time since we left Buna and fell asleep. I was awakened by a gong and the yelling of the *Stubendienst* to run to roll call, where I saw many more columns assembled than we had had in Buna. It looked to me like twice the number of prisoners.

After roll call we assembled in the barrack for soup and bread. The line was long. When I finally got to the kettle, the soup poured into my bowl was like brown colored water with nothing in it. The portion of the black bread was half the size of the portion we got in Buna, about 100 grams. When I saw the tiny portions they called meals, I asked Moniek how we could possibly survive on such rations.

There was no way we would be able to organize some food in this camp. I quickly swallowed the meager rations, crawled up to the bunk, and, too tired to wash up, fell asleep. In the morning, after a portion of ersatz tea and roll call, we were assigned to different working commandos. My commando of about 40 prisoners was marched to an armored, totally enclosed train car and loaded into it for a ride of 15 to 20 minutes. When we got out of the armored wagon, we were in a large industrial complex called the Heinkel Werke, where they manufactured German Luftwaffe fighter aircraft.

I was assigned to a riveting section, where I had to crawl into the aluminum fuselage of an airplane and hold an iron block against a rivet being pounded into it. There was no heating in the work hall, and it was extremely cold in the cramped space. The sound of the riveting reverberated inside the fuselage with the intensity of machine-gun fire, and I felt as if my brain would burst.

During the midday break, I tore off pieces of my shirt and stuffed them into my ears, which helped a bit. Two days later, the German foreman asked our commando if anyone knew how to read and follow engineering blueprints. I stepped forward and told the foreman that in Buna I worked from blueprints to wire complicated controls. He took me over to a small room in another hall, and turned me over to a civilian German sitting behind a desk. After the foreman left, the civilian asked me if I knew how to read blueprints. Where had I learned?

I lied and said that I had attended a technical school and told him of my work in Buna on the control cells. He got up from his desk and walked toward a blueprint pinned to a wall. I saw that one leg was off the floor and he was using crutches. Pointing to a section of a fuselage, he explained to me that our work would be to inspect rivets to see if they were set correctly. He emphasized that there were thousands of rivets in a fuselage, and we would check on every one. He asked me if I understood and I replied, *"Jawohl."*

After time in a noisy, cramped, and cold fuselage, the new assignment was a blessing. The German master whose name I have forgotten, but will call Herr Hans, was very pleasant. He explained that he was wounded while serving on the eastern front, and that for the rest of his life he would have to walk with crutches. We walked over to a finished fuselage, and starting from the top, we checked and counted the rivets against the drawings. Because of his injury, we walked and worked very slowly.

The work was very easy, but the hall was not heated and it was very cold. Because of the cold, Herr Hans's injured foot ached, so about every half-hour, we returned to his small office where there was a small coal-fired heater. We pretended to study drawings of the fuselage in case an SS man would walk in unexpectedly. Herr Hans seemed to be as much afraid of the SS as I was.

A few days later, as I felt more secure with Herr Hans, I showed him the small slice of my daily bread portion and told him that unless I could obtain some additional food, I would most likely starve. He knew how little food the prisoners were getting and promised to try to get some extra food for me. He also told me that he had a wife and a little daughter, but had lost total contact with them and didn't know if they were still alive. I told him I had lost my whole family.

"How?" he asked.

"I'd rather not talk about it," I told him.

He didn't ask again.

The next day, after making sure that no one was near, he took out a large boiled potato and handed it to me. "Sorry," he said, "that's the only food I could bring you. I don't have enough to eat either. It looks like the war will end soon, so let's hold on."

I thanked him and said that a potato would make the difference between life and death. He promised he'd try to bring one every day. Our coal for the heater was finished, so I promised Herr Hans I would steal some from the pile outside the hall every day.

Each day Herr Hans would hand me a boiled potato, and once he even gave me a piece of black bread and margarine. I ate only half of the bread and potatoes and saved the rest for Moniek, who was not doing well. His work commando worked outside in cold and snow, and he was losing strength every day. He also felt sick but was afraid to go to the infirmary. I was very afraid that he would not last long.

More prisoner transports arrived daily; the bread rations got smaller, the daily soup more watered down. Hunger became a minute-to-minute, constant physical pain. There were no ways to organize edible crumbs of any sort. Moniek became weaker each day and, unable to stand on his own two feet any longer, was taken to the infirmary. He was, by then, a living skeleton, a gray-skinned sack of bones. He looked at me without saying a word. As I hugged his skeletal body, I sobbed. I never saw Moniek again.

What kept me alive was working indoors, that and the occasional potato Herr Hans brought me. To overcome hunger cramps I began to chew tree bark and pine needles. Perhaps because of that, I broke out in red spots all over my body and had terrible stomach cramps that at times doubled me up in agony. I didn't go to the infirmary because I knew I would never get out of there alive. At work, Herr Hans allowed me to hide under his desk to rest and watched for the passing SS guard. The sickness lasted a week, and then the red spots faded.

At the end of February 1945 the Allied bombers, perhaps by error, dropped bombs on our camp. Several prisoners were killed and many were wounded, but our side of the camp escaped damage. That evening, after roll call and soup, the *Blockälteste* ordered the prisoners to form into groups of eight and gave each group a small loaf of black bread to distribute among themselves. Each group appointed a leader to cut the bread into equal pieces, or as close to that as possible, for distri-bution to his group. The cut bread was laid out on a bed with a numbered piece of paper on top. The same numbers were put in a prisoner's cap and each prisoner would then draw a number from the cap for his portion.

One evening in February, the group of seven prisoners elected me as the bread-cutting leader. Very carefully, with all the other prisoners intensely watching me, I cut the bread. First I cut it in half, then, I cut each half into quarters and each quarter into eighths. I was watched so that not a crumb was lost. After each person picked a number from the cap and took his portion of bread, I was left with two portions, one was mine but I didn't know who the other piece belonged to. I wrapped the extra portion in a rag and waited for some prisoner to claim it. After more than an hour, with nobody claiming it, I had a terrible time holding on to it. I waited maybe 15 minutes more, then walked outside the barrack and, hiding behind the wall, ate the extra portion.

Two hours later a prisoner came to our group and demanded to know who had his portion of bread. I stepped out and told him what happened and that I had eaten it. He made me go with him to the *Blockälteste* and told him that I ate his bread. The *Blockälteste* asked me if that is true, and I answered yes, and told him how it happened. The *Blockälteste* forced me to bend over a bench and had the *Stubendienst* whip me across the buttocks ten times with a leather whip. I felt too guilty even to cry out, though it pained me terribly. The *Blockälteste* ordered that my bread portion would be given to the other prisoner. In pain, and full of shame, I dragged myself to my bunk.

Next day, my buttocks swollen, I could hardly walk to roll call. Later, I told Herr Hans what had happened the night before, and how ashamed I was. The pain of my swollen buttocks stayed with me all day, and I felt that as severe as the penalty was, I deserved it.

It was late March 1945. Nightly, the Allies bombarded Berlin and we could hear the thumping echo in the dark. The camp's siren would wail, announcing the air attack. We prisoners were ordered to leave the barracks and lie down, rain or shine, on the ground. We heard the approaching sound of the airplanes, saw the criss-crossing beams of the searchlights, and heard the explosions from German anti-aircraft guns.

Then, like Christmas stars, brilliant multicolored markers dropped from Allied aircraft to mark their targets. The earth shook. Lying there on the ground, we looked up at a beautiful sound-and-light show presented to us by the Allies. I remembered the bombardment of Warsaw. This was the revenge. Several times during air raids, because I was unwilling to go out in the rain, I hid in the upper bunks, even though I could have been severely beaten if caught.

The situation in the camp deteriorated each day and with every arriving transport. The bombing of Berlin forced us from the barracks nightly and deprived us of what little rest we got. Though at first I enjoyed watching the destruction of Berlin, I began to curse the Allied air force for depriving me of much-needed sleep. I kept asking myself why the Allies didn't make daytime bombing runs.

The front was moving closer to us. Herr Hans told me that the Red Army was approaching Berlin and would be there before long. We heard the muffled sounds of artillery fire coming from the direction of the city. Still the work at the Heinkel Werke continued. Herr Hans and I continued to inspect the rivets on the same fuselage. According to my calculations, not one of the jet aircraft being built in our hall left the building completed.

Death was part of my hourly existence. I became inured to it, because every day the situation in camp got worse. Starvation and disease were rampant. Selections stopped, and there were no executions. Though liberation was at hand, more and more *Muselmänner* were created. They were sacks of starved skin and bones, who dragged their feet through the camp, looking for some food, their eyes blank, only days or just hours separating them from the liberation of their souls, liberation of another sort. The busiest commando in the camp was the death commando that loaded corpses on two-wheeled carts and brought the dead to the crematoria.

In March the weather grew warmer, which was a sort of blessing, except that with March came the rains. Being wet most of the time, day and night, robbed me of my strength and my will to live. How much longer would the war last? The sound of the approaching artillery kept my hope alive.

In the beginning of April 1945, we heard rumors that we would be evacuated. The railroad tracks to the Heinkel Werke were damaged by bombardment, and we didn't go out to work for a few days. Then, after a week, the track was repaired. We went back to work, but not for long. On that first day back, Herr Hans told me that because of shortages of parts and fuel, the work at Heinkel Werke would stop. He shook my hand and wished me luck and survival. He didn't know what would happen to him and whether he would ever find his family. He said he was terribly sorry for what his countrymen, the Germans, did to others and me.

Our Heinkel Werke commando was put to work cleaning the grounds around our barrack and others. They stopped hounding us to work faster and the screaming finally stopped. Except for the SS in the watchtowers, there were hardly any SS around. It seemed as if the camp were run by the *Kapos* and the *Blockälteste*. The only sounds that reassured me, that allowed me to hope for a future, were the sounds of Allied bombs and gunfire throughout the interminable days and nights.

CHAPTER 19

In mid-April 1945, the rumor came true and we were evacuated. One morning we were given an extra portion of bread and told to take our blankets and assemble on the *Appellplatz*. Only prisoners able to march were formed into columns; the others were ordered to remain in their blocks. The fear among the weak and sick prisoners was that those who remained behind would be killed by the SS. Some prisoners who could hardly walk left the barrack for assembly and hoped that somehow they'd be able to march with the columns.

Again, tens of thousands of prisoners were marched out of concentration camp in rows of five, heading west, away from Berlin. As far as the eye could see, we prisoners moved in our now familiar uniforms, bent against the wind, clomping along in wooden clogs, with our blankets thrown over our heads like prayer shawls. The SS guards on both sides of us were on foot, on bicycles, on motorcycles, and in cars that followed our moving columns. Those who fell behind were shot, their bodies dumped into the roadside ditches. We had seen all of this before on the march from Buna.

When darkness fell, we were directed into an open field and immediately surrounded by the SS, who ordered us to lie down. Tired and cold, I wrapped myself in my thin blanket, took out half of my bread, and slowly chewed each tiny bite. It was silent around us. We were too resigned and tired even to talk.

As the sun rose in the morning, so did the brutal SS voices. We again formed into rows of five and, weak and hungry as we were, moved back to the road. Looking back at the field we just left, I could see several prisoners on the ground, because either they were unable to continue marching or they were already dead. After a few minutes I heard gunshots coming from the rear. The SS were killing those who were unable to get up and march.

Our columns entered a main road, and we were pushed to the right shoulder by the SS. We continued our march as we allowed full German troop carriers, armored vehicles, field cannons pulled by horses, and other military vehicles in the center of the crowded road to move slowly past us, in the same direction, away from the advancing Red Army.

At midday, our column was ordered to stop and move into a ditch, which happened to have a narrow stream running alongside it. I, and others who could, ran to the brook with our soup bowls and scooped water from it. I was drinking when I was pushed into the water by a group of prisoners trying to get to the brook. Fortunately, the stream was shallow and someone helped me out of the water, but I was soaking wet. The SS guards ordered everyone away from the water and back to the ditch. I stripped off my wet clothing to wring out the water, and then put the wet clothing back on. The SS forced us back on the road.

We marched, or more accurately, dragged ourselves along, each day. We would stop at midday to rest for a while and then march until evening, when the SS would order us to sleep in open fields. The German Wehrmacht was in full retreat and crowded the roads. On the fourth night, the SS herded us into a large barn on a German farm. We were ordered to climb to the loft and sleep. The SS surrounded the barn, but inside we found bales of dry hay. We opened them up and spread the hay on the floor. The softness and smell of it brought back memories of the happy times at the Golds' farm so many lifetimes ago.

I woke up when it was still dark outside, and the cows were mooing below us. I remembered that the chute from the barn loft to the animals in Mr. Gold's barn ran along the wall, so I crawled along the wall to find the chute. I used my hands to feel my way across the floor until I found the trapdoor, and with soup bowl in hand, slid down to the barn, where the cows were ensconced in their stalls. I found a milking stool by feeling around with my hands, dragged it to the nearest cow, and started milking her into my soup bowl. First the stream of milk sprayed all over me, but then I managed to direct it into my bowl. The sound of milk streaming into my soup bowl woke a few prisoners, who slid down the chute and were groping their way around and disturbing the cows, who began mooing loudly. Afraid that the SS would hear and start investigating, I quickly drank the milk in my soup bowl and crawled back up the chute to the loft.

The fresh milk in my mouth tasted like heavenly nectar, but I wasn't prepared for the consequences. Just an hour later, as I lay in the fresh hay, my stomach cramped up and I just barely made it to an empty corner of the loft. I had a terrible case of the runs and if I had delayed a moment longer, I would have soiled myself. Apparently my starved stomach was not prepared to digest milk. But I must admit that the taste of that fresh, warm milk was worth every moment I suffered.

Morning found us back on the road, and from the position of the early sun, we realized we were still heading westward. The war was obviously coming to an end, but would that happen before or after I was dead?

Several times American fighter planes strafed the road, but they always shot ahead of our prisoner columns, as if they were aware of our presence on the road. Some German soldiers who ran to the roadside away from the hail of bullets tossed away their gas-mask metal canisters. Moving behind them, we found several canisters and I picked one up. Later in the day, as we rested in a ditch, I removed the mask and kept the can for some future use. It came in handy the very next day.

A farmer in a horse-drawn wagon loaded with beets approached us from the opposite direction. As the wagon moved by the prisoners, a hundred hands reached into the wagon, mine included, and grabbed beets. I stuffed two beets into the canister before the astonished German farmer whipped his horse into a gallop fast enough to salvage part of his crop. It happened so fast, the SS couldn't stop us. Fear ran through us when they ordered us to lie down in a field later that night. Would they shoot us now? I looked for a possible escape route, but there was none. We were surrounded by the SS. They screamed that anyone who got up or moved without permission would be instantly shot. The only light came from SS flashlights that pierced the darkness, and despite our fears, we soon fell asleep.

In the morning, the shouting SS woke us and marched us back to the road. All of us were chewing on the beets we pilfered from the farmer's wagon, the only food we'd had since the march began. When we marched downhill, I could see columns of prisoners marching in front of us. The middle of the road was occupied by the "invincible" German army traveling in both directions, seemingly in chaos. At midday, Allied fighter planes swooped down in front of us and strafed the Germans, who jumped off their vehicles and lay down in the ditches, next to us. The air raid lasted only a minute or two, but the Germans panicked and it was a pleasure to see it happen.

After several minutes, we were ordered to get up and march again. German vehicles sat burning in the roadway as the Germans carried their wounded and dead away on stretchers. Again, no prisoners were hit. As we marched farther down the road, we found Germans dragging dead horses into the ditches. The horses were pulling their wagons and cannons and had been killed in the air raid.

When we saw the dead horses, we grabbed our sharpened spoons and headed over to get fresh meat. I cut a few small pieces from the horse's belly and stuffed them into my salvaged canister. My hands and uniform were covered with blood, and I looked wounded. But back in the column, I chewed on the rough meat with great satisfaction. For the rest of the day, our column marched along as we chewed on the horse meat, our clothing splattered with blood, our heads and shoulders covered by our blankets, the living representatives of hell on earth. Aliens from some strange planet.

That evening the SS locked us in another barn. They had no idea that the barn contained storage bins full of potatoes and cattle beets. When they locked the doors, we stuffed our pockets. As I crawled along the floor, I stumbled across a pitchfork. If I could puncture some holes in my canister with the pitchfork, I could burn wood in it and bake the horse meat and potatoes. I placed the metal container on the floor and after a couple of tries I succeeded in punching holes in it. Several other prisoners who had canisters saw what I did and followed my example.

The next day, we lit small wooden branches that we found at the side of the road and put them inside our canisters and swung them to and fro as we marched along. In that way, I was able to successfully bake the few pieces of meat I had left with a couple of potatoes. It was incredible to see a column of hundreds of starving men swinging gas-mask canisters back and forth as they walked along in a cloud of smoke from the burning wood. The SS didn't interfere. They stopped shooting prisoners who lagged behind. They must have finally realized that the end was near.

Relentlessly, they continued our march to the west. Our column became smaller. Many had died. Some had escaped, but we never did find out if they were successful. Each evening, before dark, we were herded into a barn, where we could usually find something edible, such as potatoes, beets, or even once the slops a farmer fed to his pigs. That menu kept me and others alive and able to continue marching. We felt that the SS kept us alive and moving to save their own skins. After all, if they weren't guarding us, they would have been sent to the eastern front.

We were once stopped at a water pump when a German soldier standing nearby came over and handed me a cigar. Without saying a word, he turned around and walked away. What was I to do with it? I didn't smoke, and there were no civilians around who would trade it for food. I hid it in a pocket and hoped I would soon get a chance to use it for a worthwhile transaction. The German's behavior was unusual and reinforced my belief that the war was coming to an end.

During the second week of the march, another prisoner and I were asleep in a barn, completely covered by hay. When we woke up I realized we were the only two people in the barn. All the prisoners in our column and the SS had left while we were still asleep. We peeked through the barn gate and saw a group of soldiers in German uniforms sitting around a fire, baking potatoes. For some strange reason, they were speaking to each other in Russian, and from their Slavic faces we saw that, in fact, they were Russian. We decided we had nothing to lose and went out to ask them to share their potatoes.

At first they were startled to see us in our prison uniforms. In my fluent Russian, I explained we were Polish prisoners of the Germans, abandoned by the guards and other prisoners while we slept. They laughed and told us not to be afraid, to sit down and have some potatoes.

"Who are you?" I asked them. "How are you Russians in German uniforms? Are you a part of the German army?"

They explained they were prisoners of war captured on the eastern front and forced to join a division formed by former Soviet general Vlasov, who was also captured by the Germans. They told me they hated the Germans and hoped that the war would end soon so that they would be able to go home.

As we were sitting there eating the baked potatoes, an SS man, a guard from our column, suddenly appeared. A tremor ran up my spine. I was sure he would kill us as runaways. A Russian soldier, noting the fear in our faces, asked in Russian why were we terrified. We both stood at attention and did not reply. The SS man came closer, and in a pleasant, soft German asked us how come we were not with the column. I replied that we had overslept. He smiled and said he also overslept, and then asked the Russians in German if he could have a potato. He said he had salt and was willing to share it with us. It was a shock to hear an SS man speak that way, but I translated his offer to the Russians and they accepted and invited him to join us.

It was surreal. Eight Russians in German uniforms, two Jews in striped uniforms from a concentration camp, and an armed SS man sat around a fire together eating baked potatoes as Allied artillery "crumped" in the distance. It was beyond a wild dream—the SS man treated us as if we were human! When we finished, I put several of the baked potatoes into my gas-mask canister and waited to see what the SS man would do.

The Russian soldiers got up, wished us luck, and left the farm, while the SS man sat by the fire eating his potato. The two of us stood a few feet away and waited. When he got up, he thanked me for translating and advised us to go on the road with him and look for the column because it might be too dangerous for us otherwise. If we were caught by the wrong Nazis, we would be executed as escapees.

"*Jawohl!*" we replied, and marched out with him behind us. It was clear that the SS man was just as afraid of getting caught as we were, because I had seen German soldiers, most likely deserters, hanging from telegraph poles along the road. By escorting us, he would be covering himself, too.

At midday we found our column resting in a ditch. The columns of German soldiers that passed us by looked like broken men, heads down, their uniforms in disarray. At last they looked human, but they were still fully armed and posed a terror and danger to us, as did the continual strafing by Allied planes. We spent that night in a barn, where I managed to scrounge up a few potatoes.

The next day as we moved along, I cooked the potatoes in my canister. At least I was assured of some food, but the side of my left foot was blistered from rubbing against my shoe and finally burst. It made each step I took very painful. I hobbled along as best I could until we stopped to rest around noon.

I took off my muddy shoes and tied them together. Then I wrapped my feet in pieces of a shirt I had managed to organize before we left camp and hoped that I would be able to continue walking. Across the road, German soldiers were pumping water into their canteens in front of a farmhouse. We were told we would be permitted to get water when they were finished. When the soldiers were done, I ran over, pumped water into my bowl, and drank it down.

As I was about to refill my bowl, a German officer walked over to me and handed me a couple of pills. "Those are vitamins," he said. "Eat them, it will help you."

Realizing that I did not trust him, he took out two more of the same pills and swallowed them. I then swallowed mine and thanked him. With a grin on his face he turned around and walked away as the soldiers watched. When I got back to the column, I told the fellow standing next to me what had happened. But it was too late. The suddenly found compassion would not compensate for the horror the Germans had perpetrated on us.

The days dragged on toward the end of April as we still dragged ourselves, and each other, along the roadside. Each day, the artillery noise got louder and closer. Those of us who made it thus far became loyal comrades and supported each other, sharing food we managed to steal, and carrying each other, physically, when necessary. The blessing was that the days grew warmer, and it finally stopped raining.

On May 1, when the sun was directly overhead, a German on a motorcycle wove his way in between the soldiers and farmers packing the road. He was screaming that the American army was 5 kilometers in front of us. Moments later, another soldier on a motorcycle came at us from the opposite direction screaming that the Russians were 15 kilometers behind us.

The German troops abandoned their trucks and cars in the middle of the road and tossed away their knives and pistols. Officers tore the epaulettes off their uniforms, along with other rank insignia. They simply vanished. We, the prisoners, were the only people left on the road.

I stood in the ditch, totally bewildered. In front of me, weaving its way through the stalled vehicles came an American army Jeep with four American soldiers standing in it. A machine gun was mounted on its hood and a soldier was aiming it from side to side. A small, two-wheeled wagon covered with a tarpaulin was being pulled by the Jeep.

As the Jeep pulled alongside us, it stopped and the soldiers jumped off. They pulled the tarp off the trailer and filled their arms with small khaki-colored packages—K rations—and gave them to us. Others immediately opened their packages and started eating, but I stood holding my rations as if paralyzed.

It was exactly two years to the day that I had been captured by the SS during the Warsaw ghetto uprising. And now, on May 1, 1945, I was free. Hundreds of images ran through my mind: my mother, my father, Mina, and Mietek were all dead, gone forever. I was all alone. Tears ran down my face. Not because I was free, but because of the emptiness. As I stood there holding the K ration in my outstretched hands, one of the soldiers came over to me and said something softly, but I didn't under-stand. Then he suddenly embraced me and hugged me. My tears stopped, and I smiled at him. It gave me hope; I wasn't alone any more.

The Jeep moved away. Slowly and cautiously some of the prisoners from our column climbed on the abandoned trucks to look for food. A prisoner found a German army belt with a holstered Luger pistol and handed it to me. I don't know why, but I took it and strapped it around my waist. I pulled out the pistol and looked at it. How many lives did it take, I wondered, and I put it back in the holster. A couple of days later an American officer took it away from me.

Shots and sounds of explosions came from the woods around us. Later, we found out that Russian prisoners were shooting escaping SS and Wehrmacht sol-diers and blowing up farmhouses with *Panzerfaust* (bazookas).

It never occurred to me then to kill Germans. Maybe if I could have found those who killed my family or the murderous SS sadists in Majdanek and Auschwitz, I wouldn't have hesitated because they didn't deserve to live. But to kill people just because they were Germans was beyond my ability.

Two prisoners I knew from Warsaw, Stefan Szczupak and Sewek Dytman, and I decided to confiscate one of the horse wagons on the road and proceed to the next German town, Schwerin. When we got to the outskirts of the town, we had to decide what to do with the horse. We had no food for him, nor did we know where to leave him. We found a sack of dry potato flakes on the wagon and fed them to him, but the poor horse's mouth was almost glued shut from the mix of potato flakes and his saliva. Then we quickly brought the horse a bucket of water to help him unglue his mouth.

An American soldier approached and told us in halting German that prisoners were being housed in the former German army barrack, and that we should go there to get food and medical treatment. Inside the barrack, they set up army cots with bedsheets, pillows, and blankets. This was luxury! In a room next door, American army doctors examined the incoming prisoners. As I stood naked before one doctor, I flashed back. A selection! But of course it wasn't. The doctor was very polite and gentle; he looked in my throat, in my ears, turned me around, and in Yiddish an-nounced to me, that although I was highly undernourished, I looked healthy. He gave me some vitamin pills to take and told me to strengthen my skinny body by eating several times a day.

We were assigned bunks to sleep in and each of us was given a large Red Cross box. In it, I found goodies I hadn't seen or tasted since before the war: chocolate, tuna and salmon, powdered milk and powdered coffee, dry cereal, orange juice, and small packs of Chesterfield cigarettes.

I immediately attacked the food. Chocolate chip tuna fish, powdered coffee and salmon, yum, all those foods together. It didn't take very long before my stomach revolted. I had to drop everything and run to the toilet. I had bloody diarrhea and cramps, but in the camps I had learned that the best medication for diarrhea was charcoal. I crawled outside the barrack, found some pieces of wood that I burned into charcoal, and I chewed on it. Soon my diarrhea and cramps stopped, and I stopped eating from my Red Cross box.

Other, weaker prisoners who had voraciously eaten the contents of the Red Cross food box were not as lucky. Several had their weakened stomachs burst and they died. Others had to be hospitalized. Seeing the results of their generosity, the American army doctors quickly collected the remaining food boxes from the prisoners and fed us broth and crackers instead.

The next day Sewek, Stefan, and I decided to leave the former German army barrack and start out on our own. First thing in the morning, we took the horse and wagon to a nearby farmer and ordered him to take care of the horse. Because we were still dressed in our prison uniforms, we struck fear in the farmer's heart and he agreed to take care of the horse. Back on the streets, we followed a group of prisoners heading for the town's railroad station, where there were piles of uncollected and abandoned German luggage. We opened the luggage to look for food and clothing. I found several pairs of men's underwear and shirts that I packed into one bag and several jars of marmalade, which we promptly opened and ate with our fingers.

One of the valises I found was full of Reichsmark, the Nazi regime money. We threw the paper notes into the air and let them fall anywhere. We thought they were worthless. In the evening we returned to the barrack to wash and to sleep.

The next morning, with the Luger pistol still hanging at my side, we went looking for private rooms to stay in instead of the barrack. On the main street we saw a sign for a hotel and decided to try our luck. When he saw us in our uniforms and with my Luger at my side, the man behind the counter started shaking and stuttering in German and asked what he could do for us.

"We want a large room with three beds and a kitchen stove," I told him in German.

"We only have rooms with two beds," he replied.

"Then we must have two double bedrooms, and right away."

Without a word he handed me two keys and pointed up the staircase. We went up and found nice rooms with a small kitchen stove and sink. We left our newly acquired goods in the room and went out.

Stefan, Sewek, and I collected our horse and wagon from the farmer and went to get some food from other farms. On the way out, we picked up two more survivors in their camp uniforms. Several American soldiers on the town street looked at us with amazement as we galloped by. About an hour and 20 kilometers later, we entered a small village of maybe two dozen homes and barns. I saw a young teenaged girl standing in a doorway looking at us. "Where is the house of your village mayor?" I asked her.

She pointed to a house across the road. "What's his name?" I asked.

"Müller," she said.

We steered the wagon to the mayor's house, jumped out, and knocked at the door. A man in his 60s opened it and stood there looking at us, with fear in his eyes. "What do you want here?" he asked, as he took note of the Luger at my side.

"Are you Herr Müller, the mayor?" I asked.

"Ja," he replied.

"We want several large breads, five dozen eggs, large cheeses, five liters of milk, at least two kilos of butter, and a bag of fruits of whatever you'll find—apples, pears—and if you don't want anyone to get hurt, we want it all in less than half an hour. *Mach schnell,* hurry up!" I barked. We sat in the wagon laughing as we watched the mayor on the run. We were giving him just a tiny bit of what the Germans had given us.

Within half an hour the mayor and two elderly farmers came to us carrying two full baskets. "Are all the food items we ordered there?" I demanded. *"Jawohl!"* they all answered.

"Thank you, we will be back some other time," Sewek said, and we turned the wagon around and headed back to town. At the hotel we unloaded the food baskets, gave the other two fellows their share, and drove the wagon back to the farmer. We told the farmer to take good care of the horse.

In the hotel room we unloaded the basket and planned a feast. We broke a dozen eggs into a pot we found, put in a lot of butter and placed it on the stove to cook. The two large breads were homemade, still warm from the oven. We cut them up into long, thick slices and covered them with butter. On top we put thick slices of the farmer's cheese. When the scrambled eggs were ready, we sat down at the table, and clinking our milk-filled glasses to our future, we proceeded to eat. It was the realization of a dream we had all dreamed in the camp. Slowly, we chewed every bite thoroughly and sat there looking at each other and smiling.

We were free.

During our visit to the barrack that evening, an American Jewish officer told us that the area and the town of Schwerin would be turned over to the Red Army. After my experience in the USSR, I had no wish to live under the Soviets. He advised us to get out of Schwerin and go to either Lübeck or Hamburg in the British zone. We returned to our hotel room and made ourselves cheese sandwiches on that great farmer's bread. It tasted like the best cake to me. Then we packed the rest of the food away, and tired as we were from our day of escapades, we went to sleep on the nice clean sheets and pillows.

The next morning we woke up early, and each of us took a bath in the bathroom next to our room. It was heaven for me to lie in warm water with a real bar of soap and then dry myself with a thick, soft towel. After we made breakfast our plan was to take the horse and wagon to Lübeck. We asked the farmer for directions and persuaded him to give us enough oats and hay for the horse to manage the journey. Then, off we went.

In order not to tire our poor horse, we proceeded slowly, perhaps at five kilometers per hour. Several times we stopped to feed the horse, and by late afternoon, we found a small group of former prisoners sitting by the road, cooking a cow they had caught. Four of them were from Sachsenhausen, but were not part of our group. They invited us to join them if we would give them a lift to Lübeck. We gladly accepted their offer and joined them in the feast, but first we unhitched the horse from the wagon and tied him to a tree.

Toward nightfall, one of the men, who used to be a farmer, set up a smoker using a wooden beer barrel left on the road. He built a smoldering fire under the barrel and hung pieces of meat skewered on pieces of wood from the top, which he covered with a burlap bag we found in the wagon. The barrel soon filled with smoke from the fire and we took turns all night long to maintain the fire and smoke.

In the morning the meat was ready and the farmer assured us that the meat would stay fresh for at least a week. We divided the meat up among ourselves, and when I tried a piece, I discovered it was very tender and tasty. Then we hitched our horse to the wagon, fed him the oats and water, and started our journey to Lübeck. In order to save the horse's strength, half of us would ride in the wagon, and the others would walk alongside. We would take turns every couple of hours.

We were on a narrow country road and met very few people. But as we passed by the German farms we could see faces staring at us from behind windows or from doorways. We must have been quite a sight—a group of uniformed prisoners riding and walking alongside a skinny horse, headed to nowhere. We wondered what they might be thinking as they saw us wander down the road. Toward evening we could see Lübeck in the distance and decided to spend the night at a German farm along the road. When we approached a farmer, I had to calm him down and assure him that all we wanted to do was to sleep in his barn and leave in the morning.

I told him that if he wished, he could ride the next day with us to Lübeck and take the horse and the wagon back to his farm. When I said that, his face lit and he led us to the barn and showed us the way to the loft. We unhitched the horse and gave him to the farmer who led him to a stable. Before we climbed to the loft, the farmer's wife brought us a large loaf of bread and a container of fresh milk. We thanked her, and after eating it, went up to sleep. The deep hay in the loft felt soft and smelled of the farm life of years long gone.

We ate our leftovers for breakfast and hitched up the wagon, took the farmer, and headed into town. For two hours, he didn't say a word. We rode and walked in silence. When we entered the town I asked the farmer if he could direct us to a hotel. He nodded his head and took us to a hotel near the railroad station. I went inside and insisted that I speak to the manager. The clerk, looking somewhat frightened, ran off and soon returned with an older, serious-looking German. Before he could say a word, I informed him that we were seven former prisoners from German concentration camps and demanded three or four rooms for a week. Without any question, he nodded his head, said, *"Jawohl!"* and instructed the clerk to give us the keys to four rooms.

We took our meager belongings from the wagon, said goodbye to the farmer, and entered the hotel. Sewek, Stefan, and I took two rooms, and the other four split into two rooms. We pulled straws to see who would get the single room and I won. We had bread and smoked meat for dinner and, tired from our journey, we went to sleep. The next morning, three of us went out to scout the town. Except for American military vehicles passing through and some soldiers walking by, the streets were deserted. Only by midday did the streets begin to fill. We met some other prisoners and asked if there was a meeting place and a place to eat.

"The International Red Cross Office is where you could register your name, look for survivors, and get a food package," one replied. "It's on the next street, around the corner."

In the Red Cross office, a very polite German girl asked us if we would like to have our names registered so perhaps others could find us. Also, we could submit the names of people we would like to find. She told us that the information would be distributed internationally. I registered my name. Knowing that my immediate family was dead, I didn't put them on my list and submitted only the names of my uncles, aunts, and cousins. I hoped some had survived. We were each given a food package and 200 old Reichsmark. I looked through the list of registered survivors but didn't find anybody I knew.

It was May 5, and though we were in Allied-conquered German territory, the war to the east of us was still raging. We were told by an American that the German army was in full retreat on all fronts, and that the war could end any day now. A few days later, the sounds of honking car horns and whistles startled me out of an afternoon nap. It was May 8, 1945. The German army had capitulated, and the German command had surrendered. It was finally over. I was still alive.

CHAPTER 20

Now that the war in Europe was over, what were we to do? Where could we go? Sewek and Stefan suggested that we go to Hamburg to find out what was going on. We decided to leave by train the next day, if they were running. We went back to the hotel, opened our Red Cross packages and found cans of salmon, sardines, sliced cheese, crackers, chocolate, and milk powder. We were not about to repeat the eating orgy of the barrack in Schwerin. We ate only the canned salmon with some crackers and had a piece of chocolate for dessert. Then we went to sleep.

The next morning at the train station we were told that the train from Lübeck to Hamburg was running and would depart in two hours. That gave us enough time to pack our belongings and eat our sandwiches in the railroad restaurant. When we returned to the platform, the train for Hamburg was already there. We got our tickets and boarded the first-class wagon, which was almost empty. The rest of the train was packed. But this train, with its plush seats, was much more luxurious than the trains I had taken to Majdanek and from Majdanek to Auschwitz. Before the train started moving, two British army officers joined us in the cabin. After the train began to move, a conductor opened the door, looked at us in our prisoners' uniforms, saw the British officers, and closed the door without asking for tickets. We laughed, and the officers laughed with us, but we couldn't really communicate with them because of the language barrier.

During the trip we debated our futures. None of us wanted to return to Poland.

I said that under no circumstances would I live under a Communist regime, and certainly not in antisemitic Poland, especially after what I had experienced in Warsaw during the uprising, in the camps, and on the transports.

I said I wanted to go to Palestine, to the Yishuv, to get away from all those anti-semites and to be among Jews. I remembered the promise Itzek, Halinka, and I made to each other in the Warsaw ghetto that we would meet in Palestine. Both Sewek and Stefan said that they would go to Warsaw to search for those in their families who might have survived, but both said they wouldn't live in Poland either, for the same reasons. Stefan and Sewek dozed off. I sat near the wagon's window and looked out.

The train passed several small towns and villages, neat farmhouses with red-tiled roofs. Occasionally I could see people sitting outside, children playing, enjoying themselves, as if there never had been a war. Where was God's justice? Even though I came from a religiously traditional home, how could I go on believing? And yet, I couldn't renounce my Jewish heritage. If I did, it would be another victory for the Nazis. My family would then fall into oblivion. Still, when I looked at those apparently carefree, well-fed Germans, who was I to blame for our catastrophe?

We finally arrived in Hamburg, and across the railroad station square, we saw a sign for the Hansa Platz Hotel. "Let's go in there and see if we can get a couple of rooms," I said. The hotel was in a narrow building, only three stories high. Most buildings on both sides of the hotel were partially or totally destroyed by bombing, but the hotel building stood there, whole. Inside, a woman behind a small counter looked at our prisoners' uniforms, but before she spoke, I said in German that we must have at least two rooms for the three of us. Without saying a word she picked up a bunch of keys and led us down a corridor to the first room.

The room was large enough to hold two single beds against the wall, a night table with a lamp by each bed, and a table with two chairs. The one window looked at the Hansa Platz. I nodded to her that the room was acceptable, but we needed one or two more. The next room was a copy of the first one, also with two beds. She then showed us the bathroom and toilet between the two rooms. I told the woman that we would take the two rooms, and we agreed to her price.

Stefan and I shared one room; Sewek was in the other. After we washed up, we went exploring. Hamburg once had been a large port city; now it stood in ruins, bombed to bits by the American air force. A joke making the rounds said that Hamburg was once a warehouse city, now it was a were-house city—once there were houses here, once there were houses there. Some Germans told me that Hamburg was an international town and known for being anti-Nazi, but I didn't believe that. I never did meet a German after the war who was ever Nazi. I asked myself, where were all those Germans who screamed "Heil Hitler" in the newsreels I saw in Warsaw before the war?

We ran into a group of former prisoners who told us that the British army had established an office to handle concentration camp prisoners' affairs. They were issuing special passports and distributing clothing coupons and food. It was too late to go there that day, so we returned to the hotel to have a bite and went to sleep.

In the morning, I asked if there was a restaurant where we could have breakfast. There were no restaurants serving food in Hamburg, but the Bahnhof Cafe at the railroad station served ersatz coffee. We went there with our sandwiches and found it was packed. The cigarette smoke hung in the room like a dense fog. A table became available and we quickly sat down and ordered coffee. We unwrapped our cheese sandwiches and proceeded to enjoy our breakfast. Many of the others sitting at tables near ours looked on jealously while we slowly ate.

"The hell with them," I said, "let them suffer a bit, they deserve it."

As we sat at the table sipping our coffee, a soldier in a British army uniform came over, and in clear Polish, shouted: *"Jak się masz Adek?"* (How are you Adam?) I almost fell out of my chair. It was Kovo, my fellow prisoner in Auschwitz-Buna. We hugged and kissed each other and there were tears in my eyes. Several times after roll call in Buna, he and I would exchange tips on how to survive in Auschwitz. After the spring of 1944, Kovo disappeared and I assumed that he was either transferred to another camp or killed.

"What happened to you? Why are you in a British army uniform?" I wondered out loud. "Sit down, have a glass of tea and tell me all."

He sat. "It's a long story; sometimes I can't believe myself that it happened," he said with a smile. "In February 1944 in Buna, I was setting railroad rails. One day, late in the afternoon, a train bearing Italian army soldiers stopped next to our working commando, because of our work. When they saw us, some of the Italian soldiers threw us pieces of bread and sausage. I grabbed a sausage, hid it under my jacket, turned to the soldiers and in Italian said, *'Grazie, mille grazie.'*

"'Are you Italian?' one of them asked me in Italian.

"'Yes,' I lied.

"'Why are you a prisoner?' the soldier asked.

"'Because I am a Jew,' I quietly replied.

"The soldiers talked among themselves, then six of them jumped out of the standing train. Two of the soldiers approached the SS guard and talked to him in rapid Italian while the four others surrounded me, and in seconds had pushed and carried me onto the train. The engine whistle blew and the train started moving. The two soldiers talking to the SS man ran and jumped on the train as it started to pick up speed.

"Inside the wagon the soldiers were laughing at how they had fooled the *Tedeschi* (Germans). They took out a bottle of wine and started singing, dancing, and drinking to their victory and my salvation. 'I must get out of the prison clothing,' I told them. 'Do you have any civilian clothing I could wear?' I asked.

"'Sure,' they said. 'Let's see who's your size.'

"After a few minutes one of them came out with a pair of green overalls that could pass for a civilian's and a khaki sweater. Another soldier looked at my feet and came back with a pair of leather boots and woolen socks and told me to try those on. They fit fine and I thanked him. The only other thing I will need, I told them, was some kind of cap to hide my shaved head. One of the soldiers brought me a woolen ski cap. Seeing how hungry I looked, they brought out bread, cheese, and sausage, food I hadn't eaten or seen for over a year.

"They told me the next stop was Kraków. I told them that I must jump off the train before then, as I was sure the Gestapo would be searching the train for me. They all agreed. As the train neared Kraków it slowed down. I thanked the soldiers, embraced them, said goodbye, opened the wagon door, and jumped off.

"I walked and then rode in a passing Polish farmer's wagon to Kraków. In the city I approached a well-dressed man and a woman who were conversing in Polish. I introduced myself to them as a French Pole, and said that I needed to speak to someone from the Polish underground. At first they were suspicious and tried to leave, but I took the risk and showed them my tattooed Auschwitz number. The woman left and the man told me to follow him. He led me to a small cafe and told me to wait there. After about an hour, two men came in and asked me to follow them. We walked to an apartment house and went to an apartment on the third floor. Without introducing themselves, they began questioning me. How did I escape from Auschwitz? Where in France did I come from?

"Luckily I had visited Paris as a boy with my parents and remembered streets and places there. When they questioned me in French, I replied in French. Evidently they were satisfied. They led me to a small room with a bed and told me not to leave until they came back next morning.

"In the morning the two men returned with a tattoo expert. They explained to me that he would hide my Auschwitz tattoo. They asked me what I would like to have tattooed over my number, I told them a De Gaulle cross would do nicely. After breakfast they told me that Kraków was too close to Auschwitz and was swarming with Gestapo, SS, and German police, and that they were sending me to Warsaw. After the man tattooed over my number we left the apartment. They arranged new identification documents for me as a truck driver and brought me to a truck depot, where I was an assistant driver on a run to Warsaw.

"In Warsaw I was met by a man from the Polish Socialist Party Underground Army, who led me to a room on the outskirts of Warsaw. Again I was questioned by a couple of men and stayed in a suburb of Warsaw until the Polish uprising. I was captured by the German army and shipped to a prisoner of war camp in Germany.

"In March 1945, the Allied forces were getting close to camp, and we heard the artillery getting louder every day. One evening, while working outside the camp unloading trucks, I escaped. I walked all night toward the sound of the artillery, and the following night I crossed over to the side of the fighting British army.

"I told the British interrogator who I was and that I was fluent in German, Polish, French, Italian, and Greek. The next day an officer came over and asked me if I would like to join the British army as an interpreter in the intelligence corps. 'Yes,' I replied, 'it would be an honor to serve and fight the Germans.'

"That is the story of my escape," Kovo finished.

"Your story, Kovo, is like a movie," I told him. "You should write a book about it."

The next day we went to British army headquarters to register and obtain clothing coupons. The Former Concentration Prisoners Passport gave us special privileges: free transportation, medical care, food, and other services. The clothing coupon entitled us to one of each: suit, coat, shirt, underwear, and pair of shoes. We also received UNRRA [United Nations Relief and Rehabilitation Administration] food packages and medicine if we needed it.

We went back to the hotel, took our baths, and changed into our new clothes. I bundled up my prisoner's clothing and threw it into a garbage can. I wished that I could have thrown my memories of that life into the rubbish with it and forgotten about it.

Later that afternoon we walked around the railroad station area. Everywhere we looked, all we could see were the skeletons of bombed-out houses. German men and women were clearing the rubble from the streets, brick by brick, passing them one to another and into a dumpster wagon.

It reminded me of the work we did in Majdanek, except that no SS man stood over them with a whip. The bombed-out city was a depressing sight, yet I felt it was payback for what the Luftwaffe and SS did when they totally destroyed the Warsaw ghetto and Warsaw.

Several weeks passed during which we met other survivors and asked each other about families and friends. Sewek found out that his sister survived and was living in Warsaw. He went to Poland to bring her out. Stefan and I didn't find anyone. I went to the International Red Cross to inquire about a cousin of mine named Mietek Benderman, who immigrated to Melbourne, Australia, in 1938. He was my mother's sister's son, and we were very close before he left. I asked if they could find his address in Melbourne for me, and they promised to search and notify me.

In June we met another young survivor, Nina Rodzynek, a Jewish girl from Poland. Nina lost her whole family and was suffering from acute asthma, so we decided to take care of her, to become her substitute family. We brought her to a German doctor who told us Nina was undernourished and weak and that her asthma was severe. He suggested that she leave for a drier climate, so we moved her to the southern part of the country, to a resort area called Bad Nauheim. Sewek volunteered to escort her, and, the following week, after getting new clothing for Nina, they left by train for Bad Nauheim.

In the meantime, I worked on getting to Palestine. The following day I went to the office of the Jewish Agency and registered for Aliyah, immigration to the Yishuv. I was told that it might take several weeks, but the agency would keep in touch with me.

Two weeks later, when I returned to my hotel room, I was shocked to find my Aunt Cesia Iberkleid, my father's sister, sitting on my bed. With her were Sewek, Nina, and Stefan. After a lot of hugging, kissing, and happy tears, Sewek told me that he found my aunt, my Uncle Peter, and my cousins Lusia and Ruth after he and Nina arrived in Bad Nauheim. Sewek met several survivors on their way to a picnic to celebrate the Hebrew holiday of Lag b'Omer.

There, Sewek spoke to a girl named Lusia from Warsaw, who asked him what school he attended before the war began.

"Zgromadzenie Kupców," Sewek replied. Then Lusia told him her cousin, Adam Borensztejn, had gone to that same school. "Did you know him?" she asked.

"Adam is alive and well in Hamburg," he told her, and Lusia ran to tell her parents.

I decided to join my family in Bad Nauheim and asked Aunt Cesia to spend the night with us. The next day we would leave for Bad Nauheim. We spent the rest of the day buried in our memories. In the morning we went to the International Red Cross, where I was given the address of my cousin in Melbourne. His name had been changed to Mark Benderman, and I wanted to hurry and mail him a letter before we left for Bad Nauheim. It was already late morning and the trip would take at least six hours, so we postponed it again, for the following day. In fact, the trip took almost ten hours, and we passed through many German towns and villages that seemed untouched by the war. When I thought of the Jewish losses, the sense of injustice welled up inside me.

I had a tearful reunion with Uncle Peter, Lusia, and Ruth. Again, we each told our stories of survival. Uncle Peter was hidden in a Polish home for which he paid with the family valuables. Lusia was hidden in a Catholic convent as a Christian, and Aunt Cesia, who had forged papers that identified her as a Ukrainian, stayed with baby Ruth and worked as a nurse for the Germans. After the war, they all met in a previously arranged place in Poland. To me it was a miracle that their whole family had survived. In the days that followed, I told my aunt that I wanted to make Aliyah and settle on a kibbutz and that I had already registered with the Jewish Agency. Aunt Cesia begged me to stay with them, that they had registered for emigration to the United States and were waiting for their visas. They implored me to join them and I could not refuse. I agreed to go to the United States, though in the back of my mind, I knew I still wanted to go to the Yishuv.

A week later I went to the American consulate in Frankfurt to apply for a visa.

First I had to take a medical exam and prove that I was not a criminal by presenting a certificate from the local police. I was told that if everything checked out properly, I would be allowed to travel to America under the auspices of the United States Committee for the Care of European Orphan Children, but that it might take several months before departure because of the scarce availability of transportation.

Several days later I went back to Hamburg to collect my personal belongings and to say goodbye to Stefan, Sewek, and Nina. Unfortunately, Sewek went to Poland and took with him what little money Stefan and I left in his care. Nonetheless, we had a small going away party with Nina and the few friends we had made in Hamburg. We had such a great time drinking and singing, some German neighbors called the police to complain about our noise.

In the letter I wrote to Mark before I left for Bad Nauheim, I described the deportation from the Warsaw ghetto, and told him that all of his family—his parents and siblings—like mine, were annihilated by the Germans. In his response to me, which arrived a few weeks later, Mark wrote that he had read about the Warsaw ghetto and had anticipated the tragedy of our family. He was happy I had survived and offered to send me papers so that I could immigrate to Australia. He also included a description and address of a Jewish girl from Warsaw who was living in Melbourne and suggested that I correspond with her.

I wrote back and said that I really appreciated his offer, but that I would be emigrating with Aunt Cesia and her family to the United States. I promised to correspond with him, and would, maybe, visit with him in the future. I also promised to write to the girl in Polish, and hoped that, since she was from Warsaw, she'd be able to read my letter.

Weeks and then months passed, as I waited for the call from the U.S. consulate. In the meantime, I tried to learn some English by reading Jack London's *Call of the Wild* in English. I read it in Polish as a young boy and later in Russian, and then in German. I only had to understand two or three words in an English sentence to understand the meaning of the rest of the sentence. It was a torturous way to learn, but I slowly learned more words without constantly checking the dictionary. Several times I returned to Frankfurt to check with the International Red Cross to see if perhaps someone was looking for me, but no one was.

While in Frankfurt, I met survivors who came back from Poland and talked about the terrible antisemitic acts the Polish people were still perpetrating on the survivors. One told us about the pogroms in Częstochowa and other towns and villages where Polish hooligans murdered Jewish survivors returning to their villages to look for their families. The Poles feared the returning Jews would attempt to re-possess their homes. The Polish authorities and the Catholic church did not even try to stop those pogroms.

No wonder the Nazis set up the extermination camps in Poland! As precise as the Germans were known to be, they must have done their research to find the most fertile killing grounds. Fortunately for me, my brain's defense system put my experiences behind a stone wall. I took my life in Bad Nauheim one day at a time, without thinking of the past and my lost family. I lived with my aunt and uncle and spent most of my time reading books in German that I found in the house library and the books from Hamburg that I used to learn English.

I made a few young friends among the local survivors, and we used to wander along the countryside and appreciate its beauty. The area around Bad Nauheim that fall was beautiful. The leaves on the trees were turning red, the sky was a crisp, bright blue, the clouds were uncommonly white, and the fields were like a painting, full of many-colored wildflowers. The sight made me forget I was in Germany.

Then sometime in September 1946, I received the letter from the American consulate that requested a meeting with the consul. I got a haircut, put on my best clothing, and armed with the medical and police certificate that testified to my good character, I took the train to Frankfurt. The consul, a pleasant person, glanced at the medical and police certificates then asked me if I spoke English.

"No," I answered in German. "I can speak German, Polish, and Russian, not English, not yet. But I am trying to learn it."

He asked me about the schools I attended before the war, and in which camps I had been incarcerated. He got up from his desk, walked over to me and handed me a document.

"This is your visa to the United States," he said. "You shall report as soon as possible to the Emigrant Staging Area in Bremerhaven (port of Bremen) and wait there for the ship to New York. Good luck."

He shook my hand and left the room. I stood there, frozen, wondering how my life would change with yet another trip into the unknown. I got back to Bad Nauheim as quickly as I could to tell everybody the news and learned that the Iberkleids had also been asked to proceed to the Emigrant Staging Area in Bremerhaven. We made plans to leave the following week.

The staging area in Bremerhaven was in a former German military barrack. I was assigned to a room with three other single boys, and the Iberkleids were sent to a family barrack. We were surrounded by a barbed-wire fence and the main entrance gate was guarded by Ukrainian guards in black uniforms. For a moment it looked as if we were back in a concentration camp. Later I learned the British army had set up the guards to prevent outsiders from entering the area. Upon request we could obtain passes to leave the camp and return, so it wasn't a concentration camp after all.

In the barrack I became friends with two Polish boys, Henry (Heniek) Uffner from Częstochowa and Adam Kawalek from Kraków. Heniek and his brother Adam and his sister Irka, my cousin Lusia, and I formed a group. We met in the common dining room, outside on the field. Whenever we could, we would get away from the mass of people in the camp to talk and discuss our future, the books we read, politics, and anything else that interested us.

After we spent more than two months waiting for berths on ships to America, we were told that there was a maritime strike in New York City and that it would take additional time, perhaps months, before we would be able to leave.

To pass the time I read books, studied English, played cards, corresponded with Mark and the Polish girl in Melbourne, and dragged myself around the towns of Bremen and Bremerhaven. In his letters, Mark tried to persuade me to move to Australia and perhaps marry the girl I was writing. Although the letters I received from the girl (I forgot her name) were interesting, I had no desire to move to Australia or marry anyone. I let Mark know my feelings, but with good humor, he persisted.

The maritime strike in New York ended in November and we boys were scheduled to leave on the first available ship. Aunt Cesia and her family were leaving on the next one. On the day of departure, we were taken by bus to the port, where a large ship, the *Marine Fletcher*, waited for us. We were asked to form a single line and hand our boarding passes to the attendants on our way up the gangplank.

Like the good ex-prisoners we were, well trained by the SS, we lined up and marched on board. The ship was a U.S. Army troop carrier and was not excessively comfortable in any way. The cabin I was assigned to was a very large room under the deck, filled with two-tier-high wooden bunks that held some 300 people. I chose a top bunk next to a wall. The thin mattress was covered with a white sheet, a blanket, and a pillow. Between my bunk and the next, a small rotating fan was mounted on the bulkhead to offer some relief from the heat in the crowded cabin. Unfortunately, my neighbors in the next bunk tied the fan to blow only in their direction, and no amount of pleading could force them to share the air.

Once the ship was under way, we all went on deck. As the shores of Europe slowly faded, I wished that I had never lived on that cursed land. I looked eagerly toward the day I would land in America, the land of the fantasies of my youth: the land of cowboys and Indians, mountains and prairies, and as we were told over and over, the land of unlimited opportunities.

It was impossible to sleep in the hot, stifling cabin, so some of us took our blankets and pillows and went up on deck for the night. The star-covered sky sparkled above us, and there were no sounds except for the rhythmic thump of the ship's engine and the waves foaming against the sides of the ship. After three calm days at sea, we were hit with heavy winds and a rainstorm. We knew we were headed for rough seas when the dishes slid off the table and water sloshed around the inside of the water pitcher as we ate our dinner. Even before the storm hit, people were running to the rails as seasickness hit them, hard. Some didn't make it to starboard or port. Down in the cabin, people vomited, moaned, and groaned in their bunks. But some of us, like me, were lucky. We didn't suffer from the dreaded ailment, and for a few days, until the storm subsided, had the dining hall almost to ourselves and could eat all we desired. At night we lay on deck, face to the stars, and sang old Polish, Yiddish, and Russian songs, accompanied by Adam Kawalek on the mouth harmonica. I hardly ever stepped into the smelly cabin, except to run in and out as I held my nose while I changed my underwear and shirts.

After a week came that moment of magic, when the ship dropped anchor in the Port of New York, in the middle of the Hudson River, and the throbbing engines stopped. The passengers who could, stood at the railing, gazing at the American shore. To our left stood the mighty Statue of Liberty, with her lighted torch in her outstretched hand, a marvelous sight. When I saw the unending line of car headlights on what I later learned was the West Side Highway, I thought we had landed on a different planet.

I was hypnotized by the traffic on the highway and the lights from the skyscrapers.

Did anyone sleep in America? Were Americans "supermen"? We all stood at the railing all night, until the sun rose over Manhattan and a tugboat pushed us into a dock. An announcement on the loudspeaker asked us to gather our belongings and line up to disembark. Slowly the line of passengers moved down the gangplank to the dock.

I began to walk down the sloping ramp, hanging on to my one small valise. Several press photographers with large flash cameras snapped pictures of us that later appeared in the newspapers, because we were the first transport of orphaned children from war-torn Europe to arrive in the United States. People from the Hebrew Immigrant Aid Society (HIAS) stood on the dock and greeted us. Again I wondered what the unknown future had in store for me. It was December 20, 1946, the first day of my new life.